# DEATH

## AND

# MINISTRY

## Pastoral Care of the Dying and the Bereaved

J. Donald Bane

Austin H. Kutscher

Robert E. Neale

Robert B. Reeves, Jr.

EDITORS

*A Crossroad Book*

The Seabury Press     New York

The Seabury Press
815 Second Avenue
New York, N.Y. 10017

**Library of Congress Cataloging in Publication Data**

Main entry under title:

Death and ministry.

 "A Crossroad book."
 1. Death—Addresses, essays, lectures.
 2. Bereavement—Addresses, essays, lectures.
 3. Pastoral medicine—Addresses, essays, lectures.
I. Bane, J. Donald. [DNLM: 1. Death—Collected
works. 2. Grief—Collected works. 3. Psychology,
Pastoral—Collected works. BF789.D4 D283]
BV4330.D4          253.5          75-14134
ISBN 0-8164-0260-4

# Contents

# Foreword

Death has become popular. At least, talking and writing about death are popular. In recent years we have seen a flood of articles, books, television programs, and courses on death and dying. In all this material there are important themes which recur again and again:

—Death in our technological society often occurs in the midst of life-prolonging machinery rather than among familiar and caring hands and faces.

—Our funeral customs often seem to hide the reality of death under cosmetics, literally and figuratively.

—Health professionals, trained and dedicated to preserve life, often abandon dying patients emotionally because they represent defeat of their professional mission.

—Clergy, frequently called in "when all else has failed," sometimes offer conventional formulas that mask the expression of true feelings.

—Families, before or after a member dies, fail to communicate honestly out of a false notion of protecting one another from pain.

—All these factors increase the isolation of dying persons and their survivors, including the caring professionals.

Now that we know all of this, what can we do about it? The Foundation of Thanatology, through its symposia, research, articles, and books has helped focus public attention on questions about death and dying and has become a major source of helpful ideas about ways to improve the quality of life for all the participants in the final drama of life: the dying person, family, friends, the health care team, and clergy. Dr. Austin H. Kutscher is the founder and president of the Foundation of Thanatology. Together with the Rev. Robert B. Reeves, Jr., of Columbia Presbyterian Hospital in New York, and the Rev. Robert E. Neale of the Union Theological Seminary, he organized a symposium on "Ministry to the Dying and Bereaved" from which many of the papers included in this volume were selected.

This book is designed to help clergy and other professionals in their ministry to dying and bereaved persons. Each author is a member of one of the professions involved in the care of dying persons and their survivors: physicians, nurses, chaplains, parish clergy, social workers, psychiatrists, psychologists, and pastoral counselors. Some articles are addressed specifically to the clergy or another professional group, but most speak to human beings regardless of their professional roles. I believe that the most effective pastoral care for dying persons and their survivors occurs when there is a team of professionals who can communicate with each other about their feelings and attitudes and can appreciate each other's unique task. Therefore, one criterion for selecting articles was to promote such sharing among all members of the pastoral care team.

To minister effectively to dying and bereaved persons, a pastor needs to understand the psychological needs of a dying person and the emotional process of grief. He needs a theological stance that can integrate his religious tradition, his own experiences, and a view of the world that has intellectual integrity today. He needs to be aware of the ethical and legal questions that confront health professionals and families. He needs to be sensitive to unverbalized feelings as well as the meaning of words. There are articles in this book which speak to all those needs. But most important of all is the minister's willingness to experience and examine feelings and attitudes about his or her own death and the loss, real or potential, of his or her most cherished relationships. Without that, nothing else matters.

Ministry to the dying and the bereaved requires more than knowledge and skill; the professional's authenticity in working through his own feelings about death, particularly his own death, is indispensable. Persons of experience in all professional disciplines agree on this and say it in different ways in these articles. While I hope the book will provide valuable information and specific techniques for increasing professional effectiveness, its greatest value may be to spur the reader to examine his own feelings and attitudes. To this end I have begun the book with a section of personal stories which show how others have experienced the realities of mortality and bereavement. Each of us has knowledge and skills to contribute in a ministry to people facing those realities, but the awareness of our own humanness is the most important resource we have to help other humans be human to the end.

We are not, after all, the "living" ministering to the "dying." We are living persons, who will die, ministering to living persons who will die sooner. Sharing the last moments of one whose mortality is more tangible than our own can benefit both. The radical loneliness of the person who knows that he will soon die is ameliorated by the presence of other persons who are willing to risk coming closer to their own perishability. The care giver may also grow—may experience new life—in the encounter. Many persons who have recorded their feelings during that period of life called "dying" have told of a sense of freedom, a clarification of priorities, a release from pretense. The care giver, in sharing his or her humanness, may find such an experience sooner rather than later. "Once you have nothing, you can *be* anything. And that's a feeling of freedom." That is a feeling reported by the young poet Ted Rosenthal when he knew he would soon die of leukemia. He also said that dying is a lonely and tiresome business.

And that is another fact: death is a lonely business. Finally each of us will go to his or her death alone, no matter how intimately he or she has shared life up to that moment. Finally, no one else can help. As a pastoral counselor and psychotherapist, what I look for as a sign of personal growth is the degree to which a person becomes free from dependence on other people for good feelings. Growing up means learning to be alone—comfortable with oneself and self-sufficient. From such an autonomous position one can reach out and realize intimacy with other autonomous persons. When a person is in the last stages of dying, he may be dependent physically on other persons for life-sustaining ministrations, but he knows and they know that these ministrations are ultimately irrelevant. The dying person knows that he cannot depend on anyone to cure him or to save him. If he can, in fact, give up wishful dependencies, he turns to the core of his own being and to his connectedness with the ultimate ground of being that he may call God. He is alone, but if there are good companions around who understand the terrain and who are willing to share the trip without making or accepting unrealistic demands, he is not lonely.

Not all of us grow up, of course, and not all of us will be able to live with serenity as we approach death. We may be angry because the care givers cannot help; they cannot cure us or make us immortal. We may resent those who survive us. We may "rage, rage against the dying of the light." That is all right too. It is important for those of us who live longer to understand that rage, because if we can, we can still be companions for the end of another's journey, even one who will "not go gentle into that good night."

Being a survivor involves some of the same issues as facing one's own death—learning to be alone and responsible for one's own feelings. It is not someone else's job, no matter how close or important a person, to make one feel good about oneself. Grief that lingers on and on usually indicates a deficiency in emotional growth involving unrealistic claims on someone else. To grow is to learn to feel without avoiding the deep sorrow of irreplaceable loss, to integrate our experiences with persons we lose into our autonomous lives, and to be fully alive until we die.

That is what it is all about—life. This is a book more about life than about death. Once Christians saw life as a time of preparation for death. The writers of these articles see the honest facing of death as a preparation for life in this world, whether it be long or brief. As one author put it, "Death is not the enemy, procrastination is." One of the authors observes that paradoxically a person who lives life to the fullest accepts death most willingly; one who doesn't, fears death the most.

Any of us who elect to accompany other persons in the lonely business of dying or of bereavement, and who prepare for such journeys by facing our own deep feelings and by expanding our professional skills, may discover new depths in our lives; new priorities, new independence, new intimacies, new capacities for tears and sorrow and laughter and joy.

J. Donald Bane

# PART I

# *PERSONAL PERSPECTIVES*

*Just what happens when someone dies? What happens to the patient and what happens to the people around him? No one remains unaffected by the nearness of death; those who think they are untouched are simply not aware of a fundamental and important part of their humanity. The personal stories in this section are by persons from six different professions. They help us to see that the feelings we often deny are a valuable personal and professional resource.*

*A professor of religious studies tells who was helpful and who was not, and why, during the dying of a friend. A nurse describes the inward journey set off in her by her participation in the "last rites" administered by a medical and nursing team. A hospital chaplain describes the ministries to two dying patients and their impact on his own faith. A social worker tells of one of her terminal patients and the human and professional demands placed upon her by their relationship. A professional writer describes the bewilderment and destructiveness that can result when the strong emotions present during terminal illness are not understood and honestly met. Finally, a pastoral counselor shares his own experience of living with a diagnosis which carried with it the threat of death.*

*Such are the settings for ministry to the dying and the bereaved. These stories point up the needs of both patients and survivors, including family, friends, and professional care givers. They are illustrative both of effective ministry to the dying and bereaved and of its absence.*

1

# 1

# A Personal Odyssey: Experiencing The Human
## — PETER H. BEISHEIM

At 5:00 P.M. on Friday, September 28, 1973, Mary, a twenty-six-year-old relative, died of a cerebral hemorrhage. She had lapsed into a coma approximately two hours after giving birth to a baby girl on Monday, September 24.

Mary's age, a twenty-eight-year-old husband with two preschool daughters, the natural birth midst humor, a sense of camaraderie with the staff, and the joy of seeing and holding the new infant propelled the death from a natural human experience into the realm of the tragic. The following comments, observations and judgments are those of one who sat, slept, walked, and ate in the hospital for three of the five days.

The members of the hospital staff most disappointing in their aid to the family were the physicians and clergy. This could be because we only encountered the "specialist"—the neurosurgeon, gynecologist, and cardiologist—each only concerned with a specific medical problem, not really expected nor desiring to be involved with the family in the process of "letting go," of awaiting the inevitable.

On the other hand, the physicians were embarrassed in the presence of the survivors, partly due to the sense of helplessness and partly to the confrontation of raw human emotion. The cold, objective acknowledgment of truth, while desirable and necessary, can also shield the physician from the task of personally integrating death into his philosophy of life and thereby allowing him to be more attuned to the needs of the listener. There was no real concern with the reaction of the husband to truth by one doctor other than to write a prescription for Valium instead of investing some of himself to meet the needs of those intimately involved with his "patient."

A few hours before Mary's death, her husband, wondering why no one approached him for possible organ donation, decided to donate Mary's kidneys and corneas. The neurosurgeon responded with gladness and remarked that he had wished to request the organs but was

3

unable to approach the matter due to the tragic circumstances—
another sign of not really honestly confronting the reality of death
himself and not aiding the husband and others to confront the harsh
inevitability. How many potential organs are lost because death has
not been appropriated into one's understanding of life?

The clergy were likewise embarrassed by the situation and could
hardly wait to leave the presence of the family. The "religious clichés"
echoed a lack of a substantive theology of death which could come to
terms with the anger, despair, hostility, and frustration. Their embarrassment was emphasized by their apparent sense of futility in blessings
and anointing, indicating confusion between their sacramental functions
and counseling roles.

On the other hand, the nursing staff, cafeteria workers, janitors,
clerical staff, and other nonprofessional staff were absolutely beautiful,
expressing sorrow, empathy, and truth in a situation in which they
could have easily ignored us in fulfilling their duties. It became quite
obvious how much of the initial bereavement process ("letting go" of
dying) falls upon the other staff when neglected or avoided by the
physician and clergy.

The truism "The Truth shall make you free" applies in the process
of bereavement. By Wednesday, the most fatiguing and emotional of
the five days, we reached the turning point: the family accepted the
reality. The nurses' firm but compassionate "telling it like it is" was
the main ingredient in our turning from false hope to an acceptance of
the inevitable.

In reflection, many of our emotional expressions parallel the stages
or dramas indicated by Kübler-Ross and Nighswonger for the dying
person: denial, anger, even bargaining (promising to change one's
attitudes and actions in the family), depression (the inward silence
and nonverbal communication prior to the last stage), acceptance (finally accepting the death with a sense of relief). Often such conclusions arrived at in research dealing with terminal patients seem
remote, not touching our particular situation. Personal experience
now indicates otherwise.

The movement to acceptance is and can only be propelled by *truth*
and an understanding of the *whole* of life—an integration of all the human
events from birth to death.

# 2

# *A Crisis* – JUDITH BEST

It was just after 4:00 P.M. when I arrived on the floor. I hadn't worked the ward for some months so I quickly surveyed the floor. As I arrived back at the large ward, an elderly patient was being returned from X-ray on a stretcher. I walked over and assisted the nurse in transferring the woman to her bed. The patient was alert and responsive, though not talkative. She was an elderly black woman who looked old and very tired.

The patient was made comfortable, as comfortable as someone in her condition could be. She just lay there in the bed with the I.V. dripping. She was offered some water; cautiously she sipped, and thanked the nurse. Her eyes were closing as though sleep was arriving to impart its rest. Gently she turned her head, positioned her swollen hand which was carefully fitted with the I.V. tube, and shortly fell asleep.

Within minutes, the supper trays arrived, and my attention was diverted. Her family arrived; nothing seemed unusual. Though she did not eat to speak of, her family attempted to feed her. They gathered around her bed, the six of them, and just watched. Periodically she slept. Quietly they stood by.

Indeed they were quiet. They spoke little among themselves. Around them whorled the noise of the ward, but they were quiet as they stood and watched. It was going on 6:00 P.M. and the resident had just told them that her condition was such that she could have another heart attack at any time. (The odds were against her: she was old, had previously suffered two strokes, two infarctions, was a diabetic, and had recently suffered a so-called mild heart attack. Her urine output for the day was minimal. The I.V. dripped.)

Minutes after hearing the doctor's news, the family asked a nurse to come see if she noted something abnormal. The nurse in turn called for the resident. He arrived, listened to the patient's heart, observed, and he too now watched. Her breathing was very irregular. The curtain was drawn.

When the patient's urine had been tested for sugar at 4:30 P.M., it was noted to be negative. Could she be in hypoglycemic shock? I was

5

asked to check her pressure; applying the cuff, I could not get a reading. Her pulse was very irregular, and her skin was very cold and
clammy, but she was breathing. I was quickly asked to get the EKG
machine, then a syringe for arterial gases, then tubes for blood sugar,
then a cannula set, then a complete I.V. setup. Though there was an
open I.V., signs indicated an I.V. push, so another vein was opened.
The arterial puncture was done; the tube was thrust into ice and
rushed off for analysis. It was only to wait for the lab results on the
blood work before attempts would be made to equilibrate her with the
proper chemicals that would be thrust into her vein.

In the meantime, a second resident arrived, the EKG leads were
fastened in place, and the machine began its readings. Simultaneously, 50 percent dextrose was being pumped into the I.V. in the
hopes of arresting what might be hypoglycemic shock. The EKG was
grossly abnormal—no pattern I had ever seen in a book. Each lead was
tested, and each confirmed the abnormality. By now a third resident
had arrived with the patient's chart. It was quickly thrown open to a
previous EKG to check for signs of correlation. "No axis deviation,"
they said—her heart was bad to begin with. Throughout all the activity, the family waited, apart, beyond the drawn curtain.

The first resident now questioned whether she had shot a pulmonary
embolus; the second thought she was in cardiotonic shock; and the
third thought she had perforated what remained of her myocardium
with another infarction. They all watched; the dextrose had failed to
work. Her breathing became more irregular, and I inserted an airway.
The lab called back to confirm electrolyte imbalance; $NaHCO_3$ was
forced into her vein, and again no change. By this time, her blood
pressure was merely palpable. Her pupils were equal. The EKG was run
again, and still no positive clues. Only one thing was certain, she was
dying.

Suddenly, I came into contact with myself. Up to this point, the
whole hour had been very academic. I had been taught to read EKG
waves; I had been taught to understand the rationale of hypoglycemic
shock and digitoxin toxicity. Academically, I had assimilated well;
functionally, I performed. Emotions weren't called for up to this point,
but now I became frightened. It wasn't an academic game anymore, a
matter of medical minds outsmarting the intricate workings of this
woman's body. It was beyond that, it was a matter of time.

Again I tuned into the fact that the family members were still
gathered out in the hall. I recalled them standing there each time I ran
back and forth with another medical tool. Now we were to wait together, counting time.

My thoughts went back even further to the time my mother was
dying—to the time I, too, waited and watched behind a closed curtain. I
remembered that I had reached the point where I could no longer wait

and watch—that I had walked away, afraid and alone. I couldn't bear to be there for that transition from life to death. Now it was some other lady, but it was to be the same transition; soon, she would be "different."

Too much flashed back, and I began to repress; more significantly, I began to block. Now I was better disposed to know about these things medically, but, emotionally, was I any better prepared?

There was nothing more the doctors could do. The patient wasn't in a state of arrest that they could avert. She was still breathing. A respirator wouldn't help. They could go on reading their EKG machine, and it would still tell them the same thing: time.

The third resident was a woman. Our shared glance conveyed unspoken emotions. Quietly she said, "Four years of college, medical school, internship, residency, and still, all we can do is wait." There was to be no more frantic rushing, no more dramatic endeavors; all that was done. Frightened, I listened to the labored breathing and watched as life ebbed before my eyes, as once before, not so long ago.

The first resident asked me to "special" the patient. Academically, it was a compliment. Emotionally, it was a devastation. Had fate put me in this position to watch the transition that I had rejected three years ago? And her family, what were they to be told? Really, you don't have to be told about things like that; you somehow know.

The second resident felt that the family should be allowed to see the patient only after she had died. It would be soon. (By now, the bed site was cluttered with the remnants of the futile attempts to save her life.) He was gentle; he wanted to spare the family some pain—as though their pain hadn't already begun with the closing of the curtain.

The doctors talked. The third resident felt that the family should see the patient while she was still alive. She felt that the family should have the choice to be with her in the end. Again our eyes met, and I asked, "Clean her up?" The doctor's silent nod seemed to affirm something positive that still remained by way of life. Shortly, the doctors left, and I was alone with the dying woman—alone to resolve feelings of my own. I had my own guilt feelings about my mother's death, because I couldn't bring myself to stay with her when she died. Somehow I had hoped that if I weren't there, death wouldn't happen, but it did, and it was happening again. I looked at the woman. Was she really alive? Where was I?

Mechanically, I cleaned her up and changed the bedding. Another aide arrived and helped me wheel her into a semiprivate room. As we passed the family members, they stood immobile. Technically, I couldn't special this patient, but until a special duty nurse arrived, I was to stay with the patient—stay and resolve my thoughts of three years ago.

Mentally, I was present at my mother's deathbed. It was just after midnight, and I had just arrived from Troy. My mother was in a coma. Years had passed since we had lived together; I had chosen my life, my profession. We had maintained contact, but in that last year I had shared little with my mother. I was unhappy with my teaching and refused to discuss it with her when last I saw her conscious. At our last meeting, I had been cold and distant, and now, there by her bed, it was too late to tell her anything, to say that I was sorry or even to say that I loved her. Yet, even though she was unconscious, I had to tell her that I loved her.

I thought about this patient's family. I wondered why they weren't coming into the room. Were they as afraid as I was, then as well as now. I understood why they wouldn't—no, couldn't—come in. So I went out to them. I found the patient's son walking the hall. Tears were full in this grown man's eyes. Were my own tears showing? Gently, I put my hand on his shoulder and told him that if it was any consolation, she was still somewhat conscious, and could hear him if he spoke to her. He asked if I really meant that, and with all my heart I wanted to assure him that that was the truth, for I, too, wanted to believe for him. He turned and walked to her room.

Less than an hour later, I returned to the room. The resident arrived. The patient was still breathing as irregularly as she had been, but now with longer panic periods. The doctor asked for a flashlight and checked her pupils. I observed that they were equal and not reactive to light. Academically I blocked, for I failed to put the finishing touches on the sentence: Dead. I walked out of the room, refusing to make the connection. The resident approached the family and gave the news. Only then did I accept the condemnation—only when I heard the family weep.

The rest of the nursing staff was now in the hall, and as the weeping became less controlled, the nursing staff retreated. I stood there alone with the family, and I asked myself why? The patient's husband was wandering aimlessly down the hall. He was old and obviously disoriented by the news of loss. All I could do was assist him to a chair. My mind turned back to the body.

Lying in the room, the body was still fixed with the EKG leads, an I.V., and an airway. It seemed utterly unnecessary for these things to remain in position—for the family to see them as they saw her body. I asked the resident if they might be removed, and he consented. Mechanically, I attended to the above, and inserted the patient's false teeth. Somehow, I wanted the body to look "right" for the family. And then I realized that I wasn't afraid anymore. Yet, the whole event began to assume a surrealistic air. Why, I didn't know.

The family came, looked, cried, and left, and I understood. Now the body had to be prepared. I had never dreamed that my night would carry such an impact.

The RN arrived with the "death kit." Like a mummy, the body was wrapped. I focused on the distorted mouth and realized that soon it would set in that position, and that when this lady was lying in a coffin, it would look that way. I thought of her family, and I wondered how her mouth had looked when she was well and about. I wanted the family spared the sight of distortion. Suddenly, I found myself gently fixing the mouth in a natural looking position. Had someone done this to spare me when my mother died? Step by step, her body was bound with a ribbonlike material, and then a tag was tied to her toes.

Was this all life amounted to: a tag, a marking that said who she was? For a long time I stared at the tag. Just stared, not even thinking. The sheet was draped, and it was all over. Indeed it was all over. I had met death and resolved a very personal event of my life. I wasn't afraid anymore.

# 3

# The Impact of the Death of Patients on the Minister's (Chaplain's) Faith
## — JOHN M. HUMPHREYS

A brief comment should be made at the outset regarding one of the differences this chaplain sees between the role of the minister and the role of the chaplain that would have a bearing upon the impact of a patient's death upon him. Of necessity the time factor plays an important part inasmuch as the hospital chaplain probably has had no contact with the patient or his family prior to his admission to the hospital and probably will have little contact with the survivors after the death of the patient. On the other hand, the minister, who is pastor of a local congregation, has had considerable interaction and knowledge as it relates to both the patient and the family and will continue to do so following the patient's death. Generally speaking then, initially there is not as much emotional investment involved on the part of the chaplain as with a parish pastor, although it must be recognized that in a large parish with many families perhaps the pastor of that parish knows less about the family than does the chaplain in the institution where the terminal illness takes place.

In the two cases I present in this chapter, it is interesting to note that in one I functioned more as a parish pastor would, and in the second basically as the chaplain in a specialty hospital located in a large metropolitan area. It is not unfair to say that a chaplain's faith is affected by the death of every patient with whom he has had contact in terms of the refining, evaluating process that goes on with every experience of life. However, for the purpose of this chapter, the focus will be upon two instances that I recall whenever the subject of the dying patient is mentioned—two deaths that have had an impact upon this chaplain and his faith.

## Death as a Vital Part of Life

The impact of the patient's death upon the chaplain's faith is determined, in part, by the extensiveness and intensiveness of the relationship that has been established.

The patient was mid-fiftyish, female, a staff colleague in a large psychiatric hospital; over a period of six years she had served as a department chief to whom I reported and as coordinator for the regionalization of the institution—in all, a trusted, well-respected professional. She had been born into a religious family, but, in spite of her numerous efforts to identify with a particular faith group, she had not been able to find one that could command her commitment. Over the years of our relationship, she had shared some of her beliefs and doubts, especially in reference to my mainline Protestantism. When it was discovered that she had a terminal malignancy and had about six months to live, she asked me if I would be her pastor and share with her some of my beliefs about God and life as it extends beyond this life. Consequently, it became my habit to stop and visit with her for fifteen or twenty minutes each day on my way home. During the period that extended over the last months of her life, scripture and some published sermons of well-known clergymen were read and discussed. (She found St. Paul too heavy and depressing.) During one of these discussions, I made known my feeling about the damnable thing that was happening to her and noted the loss I and others in the hospital and community would suffer by her death. Her reply was spontaneous and profound when she said that she didn't look upon her impending death as damnable in that she felt fortunate to have the time to make her dying a part of her living. She went on to say that too few have this opportunity to close off their earthly life in a way that good-byes may be said and relationships terminated. The remaining months of her life were a beautiful demonstration of this philosophy lived out. Friends of years past and from all parts of the country would often make a special effort to visit briefly with her as their work would bring them into the Western part of the country. Each seemed to react in a similar way; coming to cheer her up, but finding instead that they were cheered and inspired by her honest facing of the situation and her willingness to discuss it without becoming morbid about it. Although the last week of her life was spent in a coma, she had fully utilized her remaining time and energy in such a way that a fitting end was brought to a productive and memorable life.

The impact of that experience is not measured so much in the death of the person but was and is felt more in the profound insight regarding death and life, which she not only verbalized but remarkably demonstrated during her last months. As a military chaplain for several years and a parish pastor for nine years, the experience with sudden death or long drawn-out terminal illnesses was not new to me, yet I had a vague discomfort and unspecified apprehension in talking with others about their impending death. Somehow, it just didn't seem to be right to talk about death even when it was recognized as being the inevitable outcome in a particular situation. The honesty and frankness with which my friend faced the inevitable, her ability to incorporate dying into her living, and to make this a growing experience by her willingness to talk about it, marked a turning point in whatever competence I possess in being able to minister to people in general and to dying patients in particular. Since that time, I have shared my colleague's outlook with others who are in a similar position. The value of this insight is measured not only by the ready acceptance of it by those with whom it has been shared, but by the obviousness of its truth in seeing the wholeness of both the fact of living and the fact of dying. It sets death not as an experience that intrudes uninvited from the outside into life, but as an experience that can be rich with meaning and an essential part of life itself. It encourages us to be actively engaged in living and feeling and expressing ourselves rather than passively allowing the dying part of our living to dominate us.

There is no doubt in my mind that an already good relationship was enriched and deepened during the last six months of my friend's life. The openness and freedom through which we shared our thoughts and feelings was at a deeper level than we had heretofore experienced. The acceptance of the other's view was based upon a genuine respect for the person and a valid expression of where the other stood at this particular time. Although the original request was for me as a chaplain to share my beliefs, it never seemed to become necessary or even important whether a specific religious formula was accepted or even agreed to. If God is love, and I believe He is, then the authentic search for Him is the kind of spiritual pilgrimage which God honors and accepts and which results, in my theological understanding, in a much broader concept of the nature of God and his relationship with us. Although my own growth in faith had been a rather steady movement away from a narrow sectarianism, this experience with my dying friend validated the correctness of that direction and the essential oneness of those who seek to know God and follow Him.

## Quality of Life

The other factors which I wish to illustrate by a case summary as having an impact upon the chaplain's own faith are the age of the patient and the intensity of the terminal pain. The death of children

either by accident or disease has always been difficult for me to understand and consequently to deal with both personally and professionally. Consequently, when as a parish pastor I was asked to conduct a
funeral service for a child or young person, there was a great expendi-
ture of emotional energy that often left me exhausted. The following
experience therefore has been a significant one in continuing to shape
and refine my faith and theological outlook.

A seven-year-old boy was admitted to pediatric service for unex-
plained tenderness around his liver area following a minor car colli-
sion in which he was thrown forward against the front seat. When
conservative treatment did not bring about any improvement, an exploratory procedure was done and a small tumor was removed. The
surgeon reported to the parents that although he felt he had been able
to get all the tumor, he wanted to follow the boy very closely over the
next six months. The tumor recurred and had metastasized when he
was admitted to the hospital again, with chemotherapy being the treatment of choice. As the chaplain, I had met the boy, his mother, and
maternal grandparents on his first admission and was visiting with
the parents when the surgeon reported to them the outcome of the
exploratory surgery. Although of a different faith from mine, I had
established a supportive relationship with the parents and a friendly
relationship with the patient, which included reading stories to him,
playing games, or just talking about his interests. The treatment
caused his hair to fall out, his abdomen became distended, and the
pain increased in intensity. I initiated a conversation with the parents
as to whether their son knew what was happening, and if he should
be told if he did not know. They said he didn't know and they preferred that he not be told, although the doctor told me later that the
boy had asked him directly and he told him that it was very serious.
During one of our daily, brief sessions when the pain was especially
intense, I offered him my hand to squeeze as a way to share some of
his pain. I told him what a brave boy I thought he was and that his
tears of pain were nothing to try and hide or be ashamed of. Rather
abruptly, as it seemed to me then, he said, "Chaplain, I love you."
The unexpectedness of his sharing what our relationship meant to him
and the depth of feeling expressed was almost more than I could
respond to, but I did manage to answer quite sincerely that I loved
him too and was sure God loved him. He died about a week later, and
in a letter of consolation to the family, I recounted the above conversation and how much it had meant to me to have known their son.

I feel the impact of this experience in a number of ways. Although
one would much prefer to see young children live long enough to taste
and savor all that life has to offer, mere length of life is no guarantee
of this. One need only think of Methuselah who lived nine hundred
years, which is about all we know of him, and Jesus Christ, who lived

thirty-three years and had a pivotal impact upon life. My young friend, it seemed to me, in his brief seven years had developed the capacity to establish a relationship with another person (the chaplain) that was meaningful and influential. He was aware that he had feelings and was able to express them and had a sense of identity. On one occasion when I came to visit, he asked the nurse, who was busying herself about his intravenous hookup, to leave so that he might talk privately. The visible demonstration that a remarkable quality of life is possible in one so young has affected in a positive way my ability to be a better pastor to children and their parents when death seems inevitable.

Another area of impact upon the faith of the chaplain has to do with the activity of God in the world. So often we hear people in a sincere attempt to console another use the phrase "It is God's will." Was it God's will that this young boy live for so short a time and die in a horrible and painful way . . . is this the way a God of love expresses himself? Does God choose to inflict suffering upon a child in order that a chaplain might become more understanding of life and improve his ability to be a pastor? An emphatic no is given to each of these questions. Rather, it makes more sense to me, and is far more consistent with the assertion that "God is love," to move in the direction of what might be called a natural theology. In brief, we recognize that we live in an imperfect world, inhabited by imperfect people, and thus we are subject to all kinds of diseases and difficulties which come to the believer as well as to the unbeliever. God does not choose to interfere with the effects of man's unique ability to exercise his free will; He takes neither the blame for those horrors which man brings upon himself and others by his sinfulness nor credit for noble and beneficial results which grow out of man's capacity for good. Thus, the believer is one who accepts the premise that the demonstrated intent of God in His relationship with us is love, and subsequently love is to mark our relationships with each other. We love because He first loved us. We are the means by which God is able to enter into the world and the lives of people, which is both sobering and challenging.

The death of this young boy raises again for me, as does every prolonged death, the issue of euthanasia. Once the diagnosis of terminal illness has been made and the outcome fairly predictable from past experience, both in terms of the kind of death that is involved and the probable time involved, why is it that we delude ourselves into thinking we are showing respect for life by allowing it to end so horribly and impersonally. This is not to point the finger at any particular group as being responsible, but to recognize that this is an issue which needs to be discussed much more openly than it has been. Ideally, the patient is the one to decide this, but we know from experience that by the time such a decision is needed, the patient is not capable of making it. This is especially true in the case of young children. I am aware that this approach raises problems while it seeks to solve them, and perhaps one of the difficulties is that the new problems present us with issues that we prefer not to have to face. For example, one of the immediate reactions when the suggestion is made that we need to rethink our traditional approach to terminal illness is, "So, you want to play god for the patient?" If there is any validity to the theology presented earlier that God relates to us out of a stance of love and that we are the instruments by which that love enters into human life and experience, then I must confess that I do want to play god and would fervently hope that all who are intimately connected with the care of the terminally ill, that is, the immediate family, the physician, the nurse, and the hospital administration, would see themselves as channels by which that love and concern gets expressed.

# 4

# *Vignette* – ZELDA FOSTER

I was assigned for a five-year period to the Hematology Service and was charged with the responsibility of being the social worker for scores of patients who were or would be dying. The enormity and totality of such a task was, if even comprehensible, overwhelming. What is the nature of the help needed and what is within the realm of social work skills became crucial and ever-present questions to be continually refined and deepened.

In my work, the needs of patients emerged first, and the beginning skill required was a capacity to be so open to the need and so attuned to it in its many forms and messages that my own universe of preception and safety could never again be the same. What came through was terror, loneliness, a sense of nightmare, a grasping of reality with a concomitant sense of unreality. Yes, strength and warmth and humor were there too. From the day of diagnosis to death, life became unalterably changed in vital and minute ways. The kinds of experiences and nature of experience took on qualities and colors which were irrevocably different. There was no turning back despite the wildest of dreams and hopes. Life was different, and each phase of the illness, each encounter and experience, would contain a cell of this. This then becomes the social worker's skill and contribution: to listen, to hear the worst, to go on a journey to the bottomless pit if needed, to laugh, to care, to believe and preserve the person's sense of being and identity. All true but too amorphous.

What became clearer was that the patient's struggle, though in part a lonely and inner one, had tremendous connection with other parts of my existence. He would live until the end in mutual and reciprocal relationships and constellation. He was part of a ward, a doctor-patient relationship, a family, an employment situation, and so on. There was no sphere in which he would not be called upon to perform, to make decisions, and to cope. There were life tasks inextricably bound up with the everyday of his world as it had now become and would continue to become until he died. Each engagement and set of relationships called out to him, and the nature of how he acted and what he needed to do was bound up in what was happening outside and inside himself. Thus, the job for the social worker became directed to that need to do, the struggle to cope with the pieces of his world, no matter how small. What were the binds, the obstacles, the dilemmas, the strains as he tried to go on. I learned that these patients needed help with so many steps, some tiny and some all encompassing. I learned too in the deepest part of my own existence that we needed to touch each other both in laughter and despair, but that we needed also to do the hard work that comes with the details of daily living and everyday problems. The social worker must be committed to the view that it is not the patient's job to do all the adjusting and dealing. The ward must change, the doctor-patient relationship must change, and the family must change. True, the patient will need help to make his needs and wishes clearer and more explicit, but the spheres in which he operates also need help and modification whenever they fail to address him as who he is and what he can be and do. This entire aspect needs to be spelled out, that is, the nature of help to ward, to doctor, to family. So we come to that part of the social worker's job—that of helping and mobilizing, not as an intermediary acting for a weak and impotent patient but as a professional capable of responding not only to the strain and dilemma, the needs and lacks, in the patient's immediate environment but also to the patient, his concerns, and his need to grow and move forward.

## The Setting

Our patients with few exceptions knew their diagnoses. I had been instrumental in promoting this. I learned that I could not control someone's life or death, pain or job, or the inevitability of their reality. I could give my heart, my own endurances, and my respect for their integrity, to which I responded openly, honestly, and directly. I gave up labeling people, deciding on their goals, trying to determine outcomes, and tried to maintain from beginning to end a vision that called for a faith in communication and a process of struggling for the living impact of a moment.

Perhaps a self-serving view, but I came away from this experience with the belief that social work should and could often provide the ongoing and continuing help that the patient needs as he enters and encounters all of the phases of illness and experience. I'll write about Doug first. Of the one hundred or more patients, so many were special to me. Doug was more special.

## The Beginning

He came to the hospital weak and with a weight loss. He still was a strikingly handsome, young, and vibrant black man. A plumber and sportsman, he was a man used to heavy work. The inactivity of being in the hospital and the sickness of many of the patients disturbed him. He hadn't anticipated all the tests and he quickly grew impatient for results. The diagnosis came and it was Hodgkins disease.

On the ward, we had been in a process of helping patients deal with the implication of the diagnosis. Each time, it was hard and frightening as we recognized the enormity of its meaning. The resident doctor told him, spelling out enough of the details for it to make a sharp impact. I saw him immediately after as he was experiencing his own shock, disbelief, fear, and anger. I stayed, helping him voice his feelings, curbing my wish to take away his pain, going over with him some of the problems of the present. The doctor and I sort of "followed" him around a lot for the first few days. Doug was perceptive and he told us to stop worrying. This helped us. One of the helping issues for the social worker is the ability to tolerate not only the patient's pain but the ambiguity that exists. There are no sure answers, and two sides of all feelings exist. It helped that the ward staff had grown and could reach out for one another. It was also good that the patients weren't excluded because of this bond and that deep bonds grew between patient and staff.

Doug went home and returned to work. Life went on at a slower pace. His energy decreased, and this was a constant sign and threat to him. His love for Cynthia and his two young boys sustained him. He came for treatment and for the next year continued to do much of what he had always done. He did however begin to incur debts and feel a continuing sense of tension and urgency.

I saw little of him during this period, since he was working and felt that he was managing. We stayed in touch, but he wasn't ready for more.

## The Middle

It may have been gradual but it felt like all of a sudden. He was back in the hospital. The job was over, the debts high, and he was feeling weak and at a low ebb. Cynthia became distraught, unable to bear his vulnerability and her own unmet dependency needs. She had a transitory breakdown and was hospitalized. The timing of social work help needs to be clarified. The family situation was entered at a point of deep crisis. How to move in sooner, how to begin to deal with the nature of their relationship, needs to be identified as the beginning point of the help offered to a family.

Doug remained in the hospital for a month. It was then that we moved deeply into the impact on him. His losses of status, independence, and sense of usefulness were overpowering. He had lost his apartment and grown dependent on relatives, and he struggled each day to try to look at what was happening, to figure out his next moves. The hospital itself was a constant irritation to him. He felt his constraints and regimentation, and many people on the staff acted as if the treatment being offered was to a passive recipient. Doug's vibrancy overrode the efforts to curb and define him. He struggled to engage, and we worked together to make his decisions fruitful for him. I never viewed him in terms of pathology or with a goal of personality changes. He was what he was, and his life struggle would need to be on his terms.

Doug finally went home. Cynthia was able to work, and life became a daily and seemingly endless battle with the disease process. Feelings of rage, hopelessness, and futility grew alongside the dull ache of knowing that it would never really be better. Cynthia had met a psychiatrist who became deeply concerned about her and she was growing.

## The End

We knew when he came in this time that it would be the last. Death was slow and took months. I saw him every day. He had a multitude of changing reactions. His drive for a mastery of control created bitter frustration for him. His pleasure in people and wild sense of humor offered some loving and hilarious moments. Able to see peoples' quirks, he became particularly adept at hitting at some core truths. This did offer him some sense of power and was a helpful expression of his increasingly aggressive feelings. It wasn't until he became totally bedridden that much of his day was colored by feelings of doom. He began to say that there was only unrelenting pain and suffering ahead and he wanted to die. He asked the doctor for help but was put off. Later in that week some of his fellow patients called me. They were a tightly knit group well in tune to each other. They were concerned that Doug was suicidal. He told me of his wish to die, his inability to tolerate the waiting, of his alienation from everyone around him. We wept together, but I could not help him to die or to want to live until the end. Later that night he made a feeble suicide attempt and was placed in psychiatry, and I intervened strongly to have him brought back to the ward where he did have some sense of connection and closeness. I felt that if the administration thought he needed protection then they should provide it on his ward. He was transferred to intensive care, but he continued to want to return to the ward. A minister who had visited him a great deal and whom Doug respected helped him to understand that his wish to kill himself arose from inability to tolerate the waiting and from the fact that death itself was outside his control. For the first time in his life he made a conscious decision to wait, to allow it to happen. His anguish lessened and there were some sad and funny moments. Other times he bitterly envisioned Cynthia going on living and marrying. There were times he couldn't bear to see her, knowing she'd go on and he would not. He and I grew even closer since I was a less charged object than his wife. Their separation from each was necessary, because of both their natures. A few days before the end he did say as I was leaving for the night, "You'll go on, you'll go home from work, have a Martini, have a good time, and you won't even remember who I was." His anger that I was leaving him, his feeling that life would go on for others and not for him, and his deep sense of alienation and isolation were surfacing as he coped with the final effort of saying good-bye to those he loved. I told him I would never forget him and I never will.

## Epilogue

This is one illustration of an intense social work contact throughout the course of a patient's disease and hospital experience. It is not enough to be related to the emotional component of dying. A sound and disciplined structure for providing such help must be as available as any other aspect of care. It needs to be available to the patient, family, and the staff on an ongoing basis.

The demands which this situation makes on everyone involved is so total and consuming that one becomes deeply intertwined with day-to-day needs and concerns, that must be attended to and made a legitimate, continual, and essential part of the hospital structure and service.

Also, in retrospect, I have developed a strong conviction that the hospital needs to provide individual and group service to families prior to and following the death of the patient. The group service would essentially offer mutual help as each relative experiences the multitude of processes which are part of loss and grief.

It is my continued belief that relationships with patients who have been "protected" from knowing about their disease are handicapped and limited. The quality of the relationship becomes permeated by the evasion, by a sense of control over the patient, and by unconscious messages. An inability to work on real issues becomes apparent, and as the conspiracy develops, the social worker, patient, other staff, and family are caught in an inextricable network of lies and manipulations.

# 5

# To Write About Death, We Must Contemplate Our Own Death
## — CIMA STAR

"It's as though John hated me all those years and was just pretend-ing to be happy. I was no help to him at all in the end. He couldn't stand the sight of me! Or of Rosanne."

Janet Jensen's husband died last year, after a long struggle with cancer. Theirs had been an exceptional marriage. For over thirty years they worked as partners in their own business, which they loved. On weekends and vacations they skied, they danced, they traveled, they laughed together. Their daughter married, and the young couple evolved from admiring, even adoring, children, into a rare state of friendship with their parents. It was an almost storybook kind of life, but a very real one to the Jensens.

Only today, to Janet, it seems all a lie. No one expects a man who knows he has cancer to be happy. But John's unhappiness turned to rage. He refused to see his daughter. He tolerated Janet only for the bare minimum of care. He died, not in peace, but wrenched by bitter-ness, consumed with rage.

Because of the torment of those last years, Janet is bewildered and wracked by guilt. "What did I do wrong?" she asks. She has never cried for John. She remains numb; unable to grieve, unable to accept or understand. As a result, she feels incapable of moving on to build a new kind of life.

This case (only the names have been changed) is all too typical of what can happen in today's affluent, urban society.

Fifty years ago, we were more aware of death. From infancy, we saw our mothers, aunts, cousins, and strangers in the streets dressed in mourning from time to time; we watched, silent and solemn, as fu-neral corteges passed in the road. Old people died at home, surrounded by family, comforted by clergymen and family doctors.

Medical science has extended our life-span. Urbanization, job mobil-ity, greater education, and affluence have spawned the nuclear family,

21

who often live far away from grandparents and other relatives. We have drifted away from religions which speak of death, religions which teach that life on earth is mere preparation for a better world.

Today, it is easy to reach middle age without ever having witnessed the death of someone close.

Ignorance is the result. Having never known any death at all, we are totally unprepared to face our own death or that of our loved ones. When it strikes, it can be cruel.

In the case of the Jensens, it was especially cruel. From the beginning of John's illness to the end, nearly every emotional aspect of his impending death was handled badly. He was never told the truth. On the few occasions when he asked, his imminent death was vehemently denied by his wife and his physician. In fact, his doctor never actually told Janet that her husband was dying, although he ultimately implied it, saying "there really isn't much more we can do, you know."

John was an outward-directed, action-oriented, gregarious man, not given to introspection or reflection. He had never been exposed to death, and so he had never thought about it. This was no new business problem to tackle, nor a ski jump to be mastered. This was the ultimate, inevitable reality, and when John sensed the truth, he was overcome by terror.

Janet, who had a similar personality, understood nothing of what he was going through, of anticipatory grief. She could only shrink back in horror at what she perceived as a total rejection of their lives together.

The Jensens' physicians and nurses were all engaged in technology, in lifesaving endeavors. Perhaps these medical professionals were overworked and had no time for their patient's emotional problems; perhaps they were involved in their own denial of death. In retrospect, it is hard to say.

No social worker or other therapist was ever called in to the case, even near the end when John's doctor began to suspect that his illness had somehow "overcome" him emotionally.

Possibly a minister might have been able to help. Both Janet and John had grown up in strict Baptist homes in the Midwest, but they had long since left their Church and considered themselves, more or less vaguely, agnostics.

This kind of tragedy, of well-educated, affluent people suddenly confronted by the one thing about which they are in total ignorance, appears to be increasing.

History is not likely to reverse itself. We will not return to an era of extended families and shorter life-spans. So we must find other ways of learning to understand and accept death, dying, grief, and bereavement. That, of course, is what thanatology is all about. We have a responsibility to bring this new specialty to the attention of the public.

Yet to write about death is to wonder about our own death, and the death of our loved ones. It is to grow anxious and sometimes depressed. It can exacerbate whatever latent hypochondriacal tendencies we have and prompt us to spend money on visits to doctors to ascertain that we are, after all, perfectly healthy.

More surprising, to write of thanatology can mean facing a certain amount of censure from colleagues, editors, friends, and potential interviewees. "What a gruesome subject," is a not infrequent remark. "We all have to die sometime, but do we have to talk about it?"

But continued exposure to thoughts of death and bereavement leads to a more rational approach. We begin to accept the fact of our own mortality, something which most psychoanalysts will agree is a rare enough state of mental health.

Socrates said, "To fear death is nothing other than to think oneself wise when one is not; for it is to think one knows what one does not know. No man knows whether death may not even turn out to be the greatest of blessings for a human being; and yet people fear it as if they knew for certain that it is the greatest of evils."

Those words are as true now as they were in ancient Greece. Hopefully, over the centuries, we have learned that we fear only that which we do not understand. While we live, we must learn to try to understand death, or at least its approach, for until we do, we cannot fully understand life.

# 6

# Response to the Threat of Death, Immediate and/or Postponed
## — CARROLL A. WISE

"I think it is my duty to inform you that your condition can kill you at any time, but on the other hand, you might live another thirty years."

These words were spoken to a patient by a cardiovascular surgeon after he had performed an angiogram and made a diagnosis of a 25 percent occlusion in the artery in the neck.

Let us be clear at the beginning that I was the patient. What follows is my understanding of my own responses insofar as I can grasp them. This is the first time that I have attempted to reveal the meaning of my condition in this manner, though I have spoken to two groups of clergy and physicians about my experience in the hospital.

It is ten years since that event took place, so I have had ten out of the possible thirty predicted. I was in my late fifties at that time, and I was beginning to feel some of the early indications of the aging process. During these ten years I have been aware of the close relationship between these two conditions, and the difficulty in making complete separation. They both lead to the same end. I have also been aware that my condition is shared by numerous others, many of whom are not aware of it.

The knowledge imparted to me by the physician had a sort of double impact. There was the immediate impact of the verdict. For several days it occupied my mind rather intensely. Then as I got back into my usual routines it receded, but it is never far from awareness. One of the symptoms of this condition is the tendency to black out if I move too quickly from a relaxed position to a standing or active position. Blackouts may also occur if I look upward too quickly at an airplane, or a bird, or a book on the top shelf. They will occur more easily and frequently if I am overly tired or if I am in poor general physical condition. These blackouts, or little deaths, are the other part of the double impact. They come as occasional warning from my organism, as the ringing of a bell somewhere down a corridor of uncertain

24

length. About a year and a half ago, under conditions of extreme tiredness due to a local infection that had not yet been detected, I blacked out in a situation where I sustained superficial head injuries and, of course, severe fright.

As though warnings from within my own organism are not sufficient, I also receive many warnings from family, physicians, and friends. These all converge at one point, the advice to take it easy. I understand the anxiety and concern in these people, and I appreciate it. But changing the patterns of a lifetime is not an easy proposition. In addition, the emotional adjustments accompanying retirement complicate the picture. I believe I have developed a good sense of what they are as distinguished from the other condition, and yet these experiences are certainly intertwined. To "take it easy" is a two-edged sword. Activities beyond a certain level of exertion are dangerous. On the other hand, insufficient activity of the appropriate kind results in a poor general physical condition which I believe is equally harmful.

At times I have found myself comparing my experience with that of a criminal who hears the judge pronounce the sentence of death. There is one common factor: guilt. A person wonders what he has done to bring this condition upon himself. A person with a sense of the wholeness of his being cannot easily dismiss responsibility for what happens in part of his organism. There is also a great difference. In the case of the criminal the imposition of death is by an external authority. In situations like mine the patient struggles, either against or with processes in his own organism, and these processes are physiological, psychological, and spiritual. My religious background, my theological training, and my experience as a hospital chaplain, a parish pastor, and a pastoral counselor, have all brought me face to face with the issues of life and death in others, and often very painfully so. Out of this background, my personal experience made me fully aware of the Biblical insights into the struggle between life and death. This awareness includes elements of that struggle which are beyond the control of the individual and in which he is, like it or not, completely dependent. It also includes elements where he has some autonomy and decision. The Biblical record also speaks of the final victory of life over death, a faith which has brought responses of intrigue, mystification, distortion, denial, and acceptance. I believe it was the same experience that Freud was trying to formulate in his concepts of Thanatos and Eros as instincts.

Persons who share in this kind of experience of course face all the anxiety of death that a cancer patient might face. The words of the physician, and I believe he was right in telling me what he did, came as a threat to the self. My narcissism, or sense of omnipotence or desire for power, was reduced. My autonomy was limited, and I was forced to seek a clear definition of those areas and the extent to which I retained autonomy. The threat, accompanied by indefinite and possible lengthy postponement, meant that I was thrown into a state of constant bereavement for myself. I am dying, but not yet. I am being called upon to give up myself, but not yet. So I have the experience of mourning for a loss that is coming but has not arrived. This underscores another Biblical insight, that no man knows the day or the hour. The basic uncertainty of life is intensified in patients like myself. Fortunate are those who have a sustaining faith at such a time.

Let me move now to a discussion of the psychological reactions which I have experienced, and here I shall follow the concepts outlined by Dr. Kübler-Ross in describing the emotional stages and coping mechanisms of dying patients—denial, anger, depression, and acceptance.[1] Dr. Kübler-Ross is discussing more acute experiences of death and dying, rather than the immediate-postponed threat. However, in my experience these processes are not stages in the sense that they follow each other. They are responses which fluctuate from time to time, depending, I believe, on the level of energy my ego has to work with.

Denial was clearly part of my response. I wanted to tell the doctor he was wrong. And I found denial in other people. I saw quickly that there were few who could face my condition with equanimity. We live in a culture which wants to deny the profound reality of death, and we all share in this. Yet we go on inflicting death on ourselves and on others.

Denial, like any ego defense, is not all bad, as many believe. It is a necessary response when the ego feels too weak to cope with some reality. It becomes unhealthy if allowed to become chronic, rigid, and impenetrable. Under these conditions it continually blinds one to reality that needs to be reckoned with. There is a difference between intellectual or verbal denial and the denial of action; or better perhaps, between easy verbal acceptance and the denial of action. To overcome actions which are essentially denials, intellectual insight must be deepened into emotional insight and acceptance, and the will must be brought into play to modify responses of a lifetime which are no longer appropriate. There is a depth of struggle involved here through which inner resources are released and denial turns into faith and hope. Not that such a patient should receive preachments in this regard. Preachments of faith and hope usually come from anxious persons. People who have faced some painful and destructive experience in themselves and have emerged with a sense of a creative reality they can trust are the best medicine for the denying patient. In this immediate-postponed kind of threat the patient must not only accept his condition, but he is called upon to find a new way of life, particularly of the inner life, which meets the terms imposed by the condition. This requires that he find some creative realities within himself. He faces the task of preparing to live in the future even though he has been told on good authority that he might die tomorrow.

The second stage in the scheme of Dr. Kübler-Ross is anger. The real point of anger is that the patient wants to destroy the enemy. But who is the enemy? It is an unseen object within himself which is found only by intricate medical examination. It is something he cannot get at to destroy. To be sure there is a possibility of an operation, but excellent men in the cardiovascular field decline to operate until the occlusion is at least 50 per cent, because of the high risk involved. Blocked in direct expression toward the real enemy, the tendency is either to turn it in on oneself or direct it outward toward others. The futility of either of these soon becomes apparent. They change nothing constructively, and they may be destructive of human relationships at a time when close, warm relationships are needed. They are regressive responses which weaken the sense of ego mastery and foster increased need for regression. The answer is to turn aggressiveness into the service of life, into the mastery of some aspect of the real world, into creative work within the limits of strength or into the mastery of an artistic technique. The issue is whether the patient is responding with healthy anger or with neurotic hostility.

Depression is the counterpart of attacking something outside oneself. In this condition depression grows out of a sense of loss accompanied by introjected anger. The little daily reminders of loss, real and possible, are almost a constant invitation to depression. Gradually, however, one may learn to master these, by warding off well-meant warnings from others or by seeking as realistic an evaluation of his own internal physical and emotional status as possible. At this point the threat of separation may be experienced as a factor. One of the most poignant wishes I have experienced is to live long enough to see my five grandchildren grown up. I want to know them as adults. But this is not realistic, though it is remotely possible. The answer to this seems to be in the present enjoyment of these children, and let the future take care of itself. It is difficult to feel depressed in the midst of such youthful bundles of energy. The threat of loss and separation, however, is not something which is worked through once and for all. It is a recurring struggle that calls for the mastery of anxiety.

The final stage according to Dr. Kübler-Ross is that of acceptance. Keep in mind that she is dealing with the experience of imminent death. There are frequent comments in the literature to the effect that shortly after acceptance the patient dies peacefully. Sometimes acceptance is equated with resignation.

In what I have been calling the threat of the immediate yet postponed fatal condition, resignation could lead to quick deterioration. Yet there is a sense in which the possibility of one's death needs to be accepted and provided for within one's deeper attitudes and feelings. But in this condition life itself is not to be disdained. Indeed it becomes the more precious, not in the sense of something to cling to anxiously, but to be used, enjoyed, and fulfilled. In those moments when one slips back into an attitude of denial or rejection of the threat, the little deaths that may occur serve to bring back a sense of realism. Acceptance of the condition, though it means changing the patterns of a lifetime, is essential. But this calls for a re-evaluation of one's values and a new orientation to life rather than resignation to death.

This brings us to a consideration of sources of strength in facing the threat of death, immediate yet postponed. The first source of strength is in the patient himself. This is the major source of strength in the face of any threat. The threat, when it comes, is likely to bring some regressive responses as we have noted above. Whether these responses become pathological or whether they are turned into creative uses depends on whether they are used in the service of the ego, that is, of mastery, or permitted to become a chronic condition. It is the difference between permanent retreat and retreat in order to recoup one's powers and move forward on new lines. This, I believe, depends to a large part on the level of ego maturity already achieved. Erikson's[2] understanding of ego development, particularly in the last two stages, was very helpful to me in understanding my own responses and in discovering areas for movement. In short, the threat should not be allowed to curb one's need to nurture others, nor to destroy one's inner integrity. One's own inner fortress must remain strong.

Let no one think that this is a solitary pursuit. The closeness, appreciation, and warmth of family and friends cannot be discounted, even though most of the time the conversation is on other subjects. The response of persons who come to me for personal help, knowing nothing of my condition, who permit me to help them in some way, is another source of strength. Assuming the direction of a new pastoral counseling center when I retired from my teaching position has some minus factors in terms of fatigue but many positive factors in terms of continued professional activity. Relationships with professional friends, especially several who are able to express their concern in positive ways, have been of great value. All of this adds up to the strength which comes from relationships of closeness, warmth, and understanding from other persons. This gives support which cannot be measured.

A second source of strength is a new appreciation of living things found in nature. Much more meaningful to me have become the words of William Cullen Bryant:

> To him who in the love of nature holds communion with her
> visible forms
> She speaks a various language.[3]

This is a resource learned in youth, not overly cultivated in busy maturity, but now returning with new meaning. There is a fuller sense of appreciation and identification, of concern with form, line, and color, but also with the mystery of it all. This sense of mystery, I should add, extends to human life as well. With all of our vaunted scientific knowledge, a knowledge of mechanism, how little have we pierced the mystery of life itself in the sense of why.

With this new sense of appreciation of living things there has also come a new sense of the superficiality and meaninglessness of much in modern life. Wordsworth wrote:

The world is too much with us; late and soon,
Getting and spending we lay waste our powers;
Little we see in nature which is ours.[4]

In a sense he is correct, but I would change the emphasis and say that we are too much with the world. Things and activities have become a way of escape from our most precious but often feared possession, our inner selves. I can understand how some persons, under the threat of loss of life, would turn even more intensely to things and activities. But this is a rejection of the self and its profound sources of strength. Things and activities are important, but only as they serve the nurture of the self. This is a hard lesson for modern men to learn. To apply this test gives the self an altogether different perspective, as it puts the emphasis on quality and meaning rather than quantity.

Still another source of strength, and this clearly from within, is the increased potential for creative work. This is clearly an internal change within me. Over the years I have done some creative writing, but it has been hard. Today, both writing and speaking in groups have become much easier. There is more freedom, ideas flow, and movement takes place. I do not work under internal stress and pressure as I once did.

I can account for this change in part by altered attitudes. Achievement as measured by others is no longer a great concern for me. I have achieved in that sense and found it wanting. Relationships based on achievement quickly vanish when the product is no longer desired. Likewise the evaluation which others place on my work has diminished greatly in importance to me. My own sense of satisfaction in doing it and my own personal evaluation of it are far more important. The writing of this paper, for example, has not been drudgery. It has been an experience of joy mingled with sadness. My concern is not what others think of it. My concern is to put myself on paper as honestly as possible. What is there to fear except fear itself; and on such a universal human theme, what is there to hide? I experience this new freedom, not as a defensive maneuver against the threat of death, but as the release of deep life processes.

One expression of this creative impulse is a deep interest in the art of photography. Judged by artistic standards, my work at best is mediocre. But that is not the point. The point is that it gives the opportunity for creative self-expression. It picks up on other sources of strength. I love to photograph people, particularly revealing facial expressions, but I often refrain from this because I have a sense of the inherent privacy of every person. However, my grandchildren are prolific subjects. Nature offers a multitude of subjects such as the tiny flower eking out its isolated existence in a barren sand dune, or a stunted and gnarled oak that shows evidence of years of struggle with the elements and its continued insistence on life, or a beautiful sunset overlooking a lake, or a fog-bathed shoreline where one sees only as in a glass, darkly, or many other such subjects. It is not the physical representation of such objects that absorbs me, although this is important. It is the inner, symbolic meaning that I want to catch, that is, its meaning to me. Sometimes others find a meaning also and that tells me that I have done something to nurture their inner spirit. But if they don't, I am not disturbed. My concern is to express something of my own inner self as fully as possible. What the viewer brings to the subject is half of the communication process, and I cannot control that. I would, however, recommend to any who face this immediate-but-postponed fatal condition that they consider some form of art as a means of creative self-expression.

Before discussing religion as a resource, let me add a word of interpretation of what has already been said. How do we account for the increased freedom to live in the face of the threat of death. Some would call it compensation or perhaps overcompensation. Others might interpret it in terms of some kind of stimulus-response theory which makes the patient a mechanism rather than a human being; others could move along the lines of some kind of an unconscious process which reduces the human being to a sort of automaton rather than an autonomous self. These I would reject as inadequate theories.

Along with many others in the healing professions, I have long been impressed with the tremendous curative powers within every living organism. I understand man as a living organism which has many dimensions, which to some extent can be separated for special attention, but in whom there is a fundamental drive toward integration or wholeness. In this process of integration the emotional and spiritual attitudes and wishes play as important a part as do physiological processes, and at times, a more important part. The threat of death or illness is not only a threat to the body. It is also a threat to the self or spirit, and these spiritual dimensions are powerful factors in the curative process. I therefore understand what I have experienced as a threat followed by an attempt to cure. But the physiological condition has become so structuralized that it cannot be reversed by internal means. It can only be removed by the surgeon's scalpel. Therefore, as far as my organism is concerned, the healing has to be directed to other dimensions, to the self or spirit, and this is what I have been describing. My physical condition is in the hands of the surgeon, and I have implicit confidence in him. But my total condition, my wholeness, is in my own hands. This is the healing of the spirit, and it is a constant process of becoming inwardly whole even though my outward man is decaying. It also requires finding avenues for the expression of that wholeness as a means of preserving and promoting it.

I now turn to the religious dimension of my experience. This has already been briefly discussed and I shall try not to repeat. On the creative side, this experience has brought to me a new appreciation of the profound inwardness of religious faith. This is difficult to describe in a way that is meaningful to many today. It deals with the deep intangibles of life and can be expressed only in symbolic language which is largely foreign to the modern temper. Again, reaching into my past, I found that this threat of death brought a flowering of spiritual processes of which I had been only dimly aware. I would describe this in part as a deepened sense of trust, not in the sense that anxiety is removed, but rather that it is taken up into faith and there neutralized or mastered. This is a kind of experience no man can give to another, in spite of the feverish efforts of some pastors to do so. A man meets his God, whoever or whatever his God is, only in the deep recesses of his own soul and there he makes his peace or continues his rebellion. This experience is in part the recognition of those relationships in life on which I am absolutely dependent, those on which I am only partially dependent, and those where I have a measure of autonomy and responsibility. Each person must find this recognition for himself and he must express it in what is for him adequate symbolic form, as well as in direct action in all of his human relationships.

This new emphasis on the inwardness of faith has brought a sense of the superficiality and meaninglessness of much modern religion. So much that takes place in our churches is either a ritualistic attempt to deal with real issues rather than an open facing of them, or it is grounded in a kind of intellectualization which avoids the real significance of the verbal symbols, or it is a reaction against internal anxiety by trying to change something "out there," in other words, externalization. This is why so many of us have sought to redeem the ancient religious practice of confession by moving into pastoral psychotherapy, where we are trained to deal with inner realities, the essence of religious faith.

I have already spoken of the value of a deeply internalized knowledge of the Bible. The Bible is a book of life. It squarely faces the issue of death and proclaims that death is swallowed up in victory. This may sound like nonsense, and it will sound that way if we take this as a superficial kind of descriptive talk rather than the symbolic expression of inner experience. It is easy to get hung up on the symbols of faith and lose the life of faith itself. The Bible needs to be absorbed as a living document which speaks realistically of life and death and of all the struggles that ensue between birth and death.

Also important is the influence of my years of experience as a hospital chaplain and a parish pastor. The pastoral concern with death is quite different from that of the physician. The pastor seeks to assist people to find a return to wholeness in the face of the acute separation of bereavement. He often stands at the open grave or spends hours with a bereaved family. There are many questions, but no answers. The answers are found only in inner healing, in the curative process, in becoming whole in a new way. He can only assist in this process, but this is a tremendous responsibility for which he may be only poorly prepared. When the threat of death comes to the pastor himself, he faces all his own strengths and weaknesses. Not that he can cure himself; no man can do this, though it is often expected of the pastor. But certainly any real ministry he has brought to others should stand him in good stead now. I have felt this to be true and am grateful for it. It is one of the compensations of the ministry.

A final word about religious experience and the creative process. Here we need to make some distinctions. Self-expression, or the undisciplined outlet of impulses, may have some benefit to the individual, but this is not creativity. Neither is productivity, which stresses quantity, with quality taking a secondary place. Productivity may be accompanied by very little joy. This does not discount the curative value of work.

Creativity combines self-expression with work but adds other dimensions. Creativity produces something which has more than a utility value to others. The utilitarian value of art may be very low, but the aesthetic, communicative, and spiritual values are high. In true creativity the impulses of the individual are disciplined by elements of universality. Line, form, color, and other characteristics are universal qualities. Even more, those areas in which religion is primarily concerned with creativity, the areas of human relationships, are grounded on universal qualities. Who can deny the universality of love?

The inwardly religious person is aware that he does not produce his own creativity just as he cannot heal himself. His own inner potential is released only in and through relationships, with himself, with others, and with his God. For this reason the Christian faith has always interpreted creativity as the action of the Holy Spirit, or the spirit of God, on the human spirit. There is even more mystery here than there is in the modern notion of unconscious mental processes. Modern man resists the idea that there are processes within him, controlling him to some extent, of which he is unaware. The writers of many books of the Bible knew these processes; they understood them not only as private phenomena, but also as a power that had universal and cosmic dimensions. This power was the Holy Spirit acting on, yet never reacting to, the spirit of man or the inner self. The goal of such activity is not productivity of things but the fulfillment of the self.

Many issues involved in this interpretation are beyond the scope of this paper. But for the person facing the condition we are discussing, the focal issues are what I call the disciplines of inwardness. These are not a schizophrenic turning in on oneself in fantasy. They are rather an attempt to become aware of one's deepest feelings, thoughts, and strivings in relationship to universal qualities of a similar nature in other persons, and to move toward a comprehension of oneself on a level of personhood which transcends the threatening physical condition. Periods of meditation, thought, introspection, of facing the issues as they emerge, of prayer—not in the sense of superficial petition but rather of discovering and bringing reality to bear on one's deepest wishes—are among the creative disciplines. These should not be formalized; this kills them. The process of spontaneous emergence on the basis of what therapists call free association is much more effective and helpful. One's deepest insights come in strange and unexpected moments and situations, and they require an openness and readiness to deal with them when they arise, not to push them back. The discovery of a sustaining truth is one of the creative experiences of life and cannot be produced by will. "The wind blows where it wills, and you hear the sound of it, but you do not know whence it comes or whither it goes; so it is with every one who is born of the Spirit" (John 3:8).

The reader may become aware of the lack of any discussion of immortality. In the first place, I accept the New Testament concept of eternal life, not immortality, as a quality of life in the present which is worthy of being eternal. In the second place, I am too absorbed with the excitement of living today to be concerned with something in the future about which I know nothing and could only fantasize. On the other hand, I am very much intrigued by Robert Jay Lifton's[5] concept of the drive toward immortality being central in persons. I believe this needs fuller thought and exploration, and I can understand why it has not seemed to have gained wide acceptance.

In this chapter I have tried to distinguish what I call the threat of immediate yet postponed death from the acute threat of death as in a cancer patient. I have dealt with some of the issues involved in terms of certain psychological understandings of reaction to possible death. I have tried to outline some of the sustaining resources which I have experienced. In the face of this kind of threat, resignation is not the answer. The answer is in a kind of creative experience which brings a wholeness which in turn takes the anxiety of death up into itself and transforms it into a source of strength. To me, this is essentially a religious experience, which one hopes will be found by the patient but never artificially produced by any technique. I have tried to speak out of my intensely private experiences to what I believe are universal experiences, and I have experienced a renewed sense of wholeness in the endeavor. I am grateful for the opportunity now, even though for a long time I was very reluctant to embark on this project.

## Notes

1. Elisabeth Kübler-Ross, *On Death and Dying* (New York: The Macmillan Company, 1969). [Dr. Kübler-Ross includes "bargaining" as a third stage (Chapter V). Editor's note.]

2. Erik Erikson, *Childhood and Society*, 2d ed. (New York: W. W. Norton & Company, Inc. 1963).

3. William Cullen Bryant, "Thanatopsis."

4. William Wordsworth, "Ode."

5. Robert Jay Lifton, *Boundaries: Psychological Man in Revolution* (New York: Random House, Inc., 1970).

# PART II

# *MINISTRY TO THE DYING*

*Knowledge, attitude, skill, and awareness of self are elements in effective ministry to dying persons. The chapters in this section explore these elements.*

*In Chapter 7 the late Carl Nighswonger describes the drama of a person's final pilgrimage and how a minister can learn to participate helpfully in that drama. Knowing what emotional events to expect, in both patients and care givers, is the essential first step.*

*A professor of nursing, through interviews with hospital chaplains, examines in Chapter 8 the effects of attitude in caring for the whole person who has been labeled a "hopeless case." "The Waiting Vulture Syndrome" (Chapter 9) describes professional intervention that is helpful to family and patient when death is inevitable.*

*Clergy sometimes misuse the "tools of their trade"— prayers, blessings, sacraments, theology—to put distance between themselves and persons who are dying. Sensitively used, these "tools" can be instruments of healing, enabling persons to live their last days with a sense of wholeness and meaning. In "Prayer and the Dying Patient" (Chapter 10), a medical-center chaplain suggests a way to use prayer to meet the needs of patients. In Chapter 11, David H. C. Read relates some of the concepts of God he has heard from dying persons in his experience as a pastor, and he tells of the importance of understanding these concepts for effective communication between minister and patient. A professor of psychiatry then points the way toward integrating theological insight with the personalities and unique belief systems of patients (Chapter 12).*

*The last chapter in this section discusses the pain of dying, prescribing significant relationships as the most important therapy. The author, a psychologist, also describes a hospice— a total environment designed to provide maximum opportunity for such relationships. This approach to care for the terminally ill is receiving wide attention.*

*The ability to use knowledge about the emotional process of dying, to share a realistic yet hopeful attitude, to employ helpfully the peculiar contributions of religion all depend on the minister's self-awareness. Ultimately, the minister, like the health care professionals, cannot do anything. Once the minister has accepted this, he or she is free to be with patients, sharing their common humanness as children of God. That remains the greatest resource in ministering to the dying.*

# 7
# Ministry to the Dying as a Learning Encounter
## — CARL A. NIGHSWONGER

It is the intent of this chapter to examine the dramas of death as the context in which one ministers to the dying, and to explore the dynamics of this encounter as a learning experience for the theological student or clergyman. The data for this presentation comes from reflection on the experiences of almost one hundred theological students, pastors, and chaplains, who have participated in a Death and Dying project as part of their Clinical Pastoral Education program, and of almost four hundred terminally, or fatally, ill patients who have consented to be our "teachers" during the five years that the program has been in existence.

Space will not allow dealing with many of the important aspects of death and dying, such as the cultural factors which condition our attitudes and responses to death, the basic assumptions one must make about dying, the vital signs of the family of the dying patient, the importance of synchronizing the *anticipatory* grief of the family with the preparatory grief of the patient, and the crucial importance of interdisciplinary cooperation. Such concerns have been discussed in other presentations, and are mentioned here only to acknowledge their importance for a fuller grasp of the dynamics of death and dying in the current American culture.

Lest we begin on different wavelengths, let us take a moment to define our terms, as they have been spelled out in Webster's Dictionary. By *ministry* is meant the specific act of ministering, of doing things needful, or helpful, which is a subjective experience involving both person and role in a concrete pastoral relationship. *Learning* refers specifically to the acquisition of skills and knowledge by study and instruction. *Encounter* refers to the experience of coming face to face with another, sometimes in conflict. *Drama* refers to a series of events having dramatic unity and interest, usually vivid and moving.

Thus we are talking about the very real human experiences of walking through the Valley of the Shadow with another, of sharing the last chapter in his personal pilgrimage, and of reflecting on the meaning of those experiences as they affect our understanding of ourselves and of our pastoral roles as ministers. For the vast majority of students, this adventure with the dying patient has come to be the paradigmatic model for the student's own reflection and growth, personally and professionally, and most often has been indicated as the highlight of his clinical experience.

As our teachers, the patients have helped us to understand the *unique* and *dynamic* nature of dying as it is experienced through a series of dramas which lead to the fulfillment of one's pilgrimage in either peace or forlornness. Briefly, these dramas are:

   I. The Drama of Shock: Denial vs. Panic.
  II. The Drama of Emotion: Catharsis vs. Depression.
 III. The Drama of Negotiation: Bargaining vs. Selling Out.
  IV. The Drama of Cognition: Realistic Hope vs. Despair.
   V. The Drama of Commitment: Acceptance vs. Resignation.
  VI. The Drama of Completion: Fulfillment vs. Forlornness.

## Drama of Shock

This drama begins with the reception of news that stuns and over-whelms one. To be told that one has a fatal or terminal disease is usually such an experience. *Denial* is the emotional shock absorber that allows us to pretend that we did not hear that which we cannot emotionally accept. It is a psychic anesthetic to an otherwise unbear-able reality. Such a "not me" response to the news of one's diagnosis may be a healthy and normal response to shock. It allows one time to muster his inner forces to cope with a situation which would other-wise overwhelm him.

Prolonged denial, however, indicates a person's inability to deal with the drama and may well prevent him from ever seeking further treatment for his condition. Partial denial, which is an intellectual acknowledgment, without an emotional acceptance, can also be help-ful, but it tends to compartmentalize the person's feelings so that they remain unexpressed and the conflicts unresolved.

*Panic* is the alternative response in this first drama. Rarely is it found to be constructive. All structure and reality checks become lost, and the person resorts to impulsive, uncontrolled, and unrealistic be-havior. Fright, alarm, and terror may make the situation so fluid that the person sees no way out except to escape reality through magic, self-destruction, or psychosis. We have seen examples of each in our patients.

The student's ministry may assist or inhibit the patient's dramatic response to shock. On occasion, the student panics and flees the patient, employing many defenses to justify or evade his own fears and alarm. For many, it becomes their first real encounter with death, and the only way they can cope is to withdraw from the relationship.

More often, however, the student shares in the patient's own denial system, and often without realizing it, reinforces the patient's need to pretend that it really isn't true. If the student continues to deny the reality after the patient has begun to move through the drama and to drop the denial, the patient often recognizes the student's need, takes his cue from the student, and continues to pretend in the presence of the student.

Through supervision and group reflection the student is enabled to learn from this encounter. Many times he discovers that he has identified with the patient, and he, too, has not come to grips with the meaning of death in his own life. At other times, the "baggage" of his own past unresolved grief surfaces and he is enabled to work through the death of a parent or friend in the drama of his own pilgrimage.

Frequently, the student is confronted with his own role expectations. He experiences the helplessness that there is *nothing* he can *do* to keep the patient from dying. He finds his words are empty, his expectations unrealistic, and he begins the painful process of discovering what it means *to be* with another at such a time.

## Drama of Emotion

Usually the drama of shock is short-lived, and reality sets in, bringing with it the second drama of emotion. If panic can be averted, or as the denial slowly gives way to reality, there is usually the flood of emotion which either finds expression in *catharsis,* or is turned inward against the self in *depression.*

Catharsis is the open expression of one's feeling. Usually there is a flood of anger as the person asks, "Why me!" with the flavor of the unfairness of it all. The anger may be directed at oneself, a loved one, a doctor, or God. Often the student finds the anger directed at him as a representative of God.

All too often, the patient is not allowed to experience the catharsis so essential to the resolution of the conflict of this drama. *External* controls may be applied by family, friends, staff, and even the student, which do not sanction the expression of negative feelings. As one patient said, "When I get down in the dumps, people come in and try to cheer me up, and if there is anything I do not need, it is cheering up when I am feeling blue!" Many of us are more comfortable if the patient is nice, pleasant, and cooperative, and we may unwittingly prevent him from letting his true emotions come out.

But many persons also have strong *internal* controls against the expression of negative feelings. It is wrong for them to be angry; it is un-Christian; it is unloving; and, therefore, they dare not express their anger at family, staff, or God. In either case, whenever the feelings are swallowed rather than expressed, the anger is turned inward, the realistic guilt and shame achieve neurotic proportions, and the drama stops in depression.

We have found a variety of student responses in their encounter with the drama of intense emotion. Those who have never challenged God themselves tend to defend God to the patient, which results in further external controls on the patient, or an intensification of the patient's own shame and guilt, or in alienating the patient in the pastoral relationship.

Often the student withdraws emotionally from the relationship and intellectualizes with the patient. Many sermons are offered as substitutes for an honest sharing of oneself with another in a sensitive listening relationship. The student who feels he must *do* something takes the question of "why me" as an intellectual inquiry, rather than as an expression of existential anguish, and offers the best of his theological conceptualization.

Students who identify with the patient often discover themselves in the same drama and intensify the patient's emotions with the *r* own feelings of frustration and anger.

Fortunately, the student encouraged to reflect on the situation before him recognizes the dynamics operating within himself as well as the patient, and he is enabled to reexamine his own feelings of selfhood and pastoral concern. In those instances in which the student is able and willing to risk his own finitude and humanity, the patient is enabled to move through the drama more rapidly and creatively.

## Drama of Negotiation

The intensity of guilt and shame in depression often leads the patient to resolve the conflict of the third drama of *selling out* instead of living through the negotiations of bargaining. The badness and unworthiness, which he feels, convinces him that he is getting what he deserves. Or the alienation from others which he experiences in his depressive withdrawal becomes so intense that he concludes, "What's the use?" In either case, the drama ends in spiritual bankruptcy.

In our experience, it is not uncommon that the student discovers his own spiritual bankruptcy. He finds his own responses not only inadequate for the patient, but for his own life as well. Often it is at this point that the student really becomes involved in a spiritual pilgrimage and his theological inquiry takes on new dimensions of depth and intensity.

One hopes, however, that the dying patient is enabled to move from the "not me!" into the *bargaining* of "maybe not me." The drama becomes one of attempting to negotiate a deal. Perhaps it is with the doctors, that if he cooperates fully, the staff may make an extra effort, and a new drug or treatment will be found which will cure him. Or the negotiation may be with God, sometimes with the aid of the student, in the hope that God can be persuaded to intervene in the disease process on behalf of the patient.

The danger in bargaining, however, is that the student often gets caught in the game, and reinforces the negotiations rather than remaining a sensitive and understanding listener as the patient struggles with the hope that there may yet be a way out. One needs to remember that such negotiations are very human and very normal and may indeed help the patient in his readiness for the next drama.

## Drama of Cognition

Rarely does the patient negotiate for long, however. The progress of the illness, treatment procedures, etc., tend to remind the patient that it is in reality happening to him. As he becomes increasingly cognizant of his condition, he faces the dramatic struggle of the *meaning* of it all. The question of "why me" is less an expression of emotion than of a serious concern to make some sense out of death and dying. The alternatives in the drama are *realistic hope* or *despair*.

If left alone, the patient who experienced spiritual bankruptcy from selling out is left with little choice but despair. The awareness that he is dying simply confirms the feeling that there is no meaning and no hope. Such despair may be expressed as stoic bitterness or it may manifest further symptoms of depression with dimensions of gloom and hopelessness. (The deeper theological diversions of despair's emptiness and meaninglessness may erroneously be equated with or mistaken for the psychological dynamics of depression.)

On the other hand, the patient may be helped to experience a realistic hope in the future of his pilgrimage by discovering some sense of meaning and purpose which offers the possibility of personal fulfillment in his own death.

Often such hope is difficult for us to grasp. We tend to associate hope with getting well, or a cure. But for the person who has come to this point in his pilgrimage, hope becomes much more realistic.

Such hope reflects the focus of concern of the patient at this moment. If he is primarily concerned with the meaning of death, he may be concerned with the future, as with the patient who, having been rejected for the dialysis program after both kidneys had failed, questioned what hope there was in the possibility of being "accepted in the next garden when she had been rejected in this garden."

Later, having resolved this conflict, the same patient expressed the hope that there "would be a warm hand to hold hers as it grew colder and colder." Often such concerns for when and how death will occur become the central focus. It may be the hope that one's dying is not prolonged; that one will not linger on as a vegetable; or that there will not be a great deal of pain; or that it will not become a financial burden to the family after the insurance coverage has ended.

The student encounters a new dimension to his ministry at this point. He becomes acutely aware of the patient's need to find meaning and purpose in his death, as well as the assurance that he will not be alone or rejected, either now, or in the future, or both.

Such questions reflect two realms of meaning. In the *realm of specificity* the patient may be seeking answers very definite and specific to questions regarding the progress of his illness, treatment procedures, family needs, economic concerns, etc.

But the patient may also be asking questions which cannot be answered so specifically and factually. The questions of "why me," "why now," "what is its meaning," as well as, "what is the meaning of life," "what is there in the future," "is there an afterlife," etc.— these questions can be answered only in the *realm of destiny*, as one seeks the assurance of *ultimate meaning* and *ultimate purpose*.

From our experience, the patient in despair is rarely helped unless he can go back and relive the earlier dramas of emotion and negotiation more constructively. But the patient who is still seeking and searching can be helped to find a *relevant life perspective* through which he can reassess his pilgrimage, past, present, and future, and can come to a new awareness of himself and of his destiny. The success of this venture becomes the foundation for the drama which follows.

## Drama of Commitment

It is sometimes difficult to distinguish when realistic hope moves into *acceptance* just as it is often difficult to recognize when despair has reached commitment in *resignation*.

Essentially, the shift is experienced as movement from intellectual assent to emotional response. The hope is affirmed in the confidence and the assurance that meaning will be experienced, just as resignation is the emotional confirmation of the ultimate sense of despair.

Resignation is the inevitable result of a pilgrimage that spiritually ended in the third drama; having sold out, and in despair, one resigns himself to the inevitable, meaningless end of existence. He finds himself in "the sickness unto death."

But one may also say "yes, it is I" as an affirmation. The drama may lead one to the point where he is able, with the "courage to be," to affirm death as the natural fulfillment of life and the completion of its meaning and purpose.

The challenge for the student in this encounter is to become an agent of change in that he enables the patient to experience an *internalized trust* in the goodness of life, its meaning and purpose, and its ultimate fulfillment in death. The student encounters the need to distinguish between *extrinsic faith,* which functions essentially as a defense mechanism, protecting one from reality, and the *intrinsic faith* which allows one to affirm reality. He concerns himself with the transforming task of ministry as he seeks to remove remaining barriers of bitterness, unresolved grief, previous hurts, etc. which stand in the way of the person making such a faith commitment. He seeks to help the dying patient experience a congruence between what he *believes* about life and death and what he *feels* about living and, now, dying.

## Drama of Completion

One final drama remains for our consideration. As death approaches as an inevitable reality, the patient completes his pilgrimage with either a sense of fulfillment or *forlornness.*

The *forlornness* is often viewed as withdrawal and depression. It is the completion of resignation. Abandoned, forsaken, and despairing, the patient forlornly welcomes death as an end to the living hell which remains. Each pain, each moment of suffering, is endured and tolerated but not ignored.

Few of us, much less the student, share in these moments of forlornness. Our experience suggests we have much earlier parted company with these patients and, whether out of frustration, bewilderment, or fear, we have contributed to their aloneness.

In contrast, the dramatic experience of *fulfillment* has often enriched the lives of each of us, particularly, perhaps, the students. As a learning encounter, they have discovered the mutuality of ministry. As they have shared in the lives of patients who experienced the peace, tranquillity, and dignity of fulfillment in death, they have not only learned something about ministry, but they have grasped something about the drama of life itself!

# 8

# *Another Look at the Hopeless Case* – JOSEPH R. PROULX

Emphasis in the health care setting is largely focused on the technical: a cure, the relief of pain, a medical treatment, a surgical procedure. With such emphasis on objective elements it is no wonder then that the whole area of communications within the setting may be characterized by an impersonal content and a bureaucratic network or structure. In addition, most of these communications may be identified by their labeling or stereotyping functions. The term "hopeless case" as usually used in the institutional setting is an excellent example of such categorization.

Too often the terminal patient is exposed to communication which implicitly *and* explicitly says: "There is no hope." Examples might consist of dwindling verbal interactions between staff and patient; the patient may be moved so that he is physically isolated and human contact becomes virtually impossible; acquaintances and/or helpers may cease their visits and rounds to the dying person. Unfortunately the literature abounds with descriptions of such behavior, and more tragically, this depreciatory and dehumanizing form of communication is evident to us who occasionally work at the bedside.

Ultimately it would appear that the idea of hopelessness is but a part—and the wrong part, so to speak—of medicine's timeless struggle with death. If aspects of cure and recovery are no longer possible, the patient is abandoned as a case beyond help, and the technology, energies, and communications of the health team are turned to other patients who may be "saved" or spared from the ignominious fate of death or prolonged disability. But what happens to the human factor —the person—that lurks under the guise of the patient?

LeShan, in his work with critically ill cancer patients, has demonstrated that the personal elements of the individual may be successfully explored despite the medical prognosis of the case.[1]

Help is really needed in terms of how to live, not how to die. It might seem it is a strange and wrong time (when the patient is severely ill) to tackle the problems of how to make the most of one's being. This is far from the truth. It is only by going as quickly as possible to the real problems of the patient's life, to the questions of his existence that he has been unable to answer in a satisfactory way, that the will to live may be awakened and mobilized.[2]

This is not meant to imply that LeShan is interested in prolonging life; rather, he is concerned about how one is to live regardless of the time span allowed. The main problem is not the fear of death, but the fear of life itself.[3]

## Defining the "Hopeless Case"

In attempting to get some empirical data related to this problem of the "hopeless case," interviews were conducted with a small number of full-time hospital chaplains who were serving in state and general hospitals located in four Middle Atlantic states. Specifically, the communication obtained dealt with responses to the question: "How do you define the hopeless case?" In general, the chaplains expressed opinions similar to LeShan's, namely, that the focus of any kind of communication with the terminally ill should be on the total person rather than on a categorical, medical case.

Reports from the chaplains and commentary on the interview materials appear below. Subsequent quoted material, unless otherwise indicated, denotes the chaplains' remarks.

One respondent returned the question: "Hopeless for what? The assumption is based on the data, the material the patient has to work with." This person suggested that the chaplain's investment of time and energy would bring new data and new material to the patient, and thus new avenues of hope would be created.

Another redirected answer was: "Who defines it [the hopeless case] as such? the physician? the nurse? the family?" Here the chaplain indicated that the physician's role was directed toward a cure and that the members of the medical profession would be uncomfortable with anything less. Nurses, as partners of physicians in the struggle against death and disease, are also cure-oriented. As the chaplain said: they [nurses] are too often task-oriented, and do not invest themselves fully in a relationship with, say, a terminal patient."

Other respondents stated more simply: "I never had anyone that has relinquished all hope. People are always hoping for something, even if it is an end to their agony." And from another clergyman: "I never found a patient who has relinquished all hopes. Hoping for a peaceful death is a redefinition of hope, but it is still hope." And then the ultimate generalization: "No one is a hopeless case."

Two important criteria in moving away from the static and bureaucratic definition of "hopeless" seemed to rest in the areas of communication and faith in self. "As long as the patient is conscious and capable of some kind of interpersonal interaction (verbal or nonverbal), there is no such thing as a hopeless case. Rather, it is a matter of scaling down hope to the concrete specifics that seem appropriate to that person at that time."

Whenever a person loses confidence in himself, a tendency toward hopelessness may arise. As two similar responses revealed: "The hopeless case is the person who has given up on himself, who apparently has no regard for himself any longer, who apparently has no trust in life as a validity for him. He becomes darkly despairing." And "A person who has given up on himself has accepted the fact that he is helpless."

A religious theme was recognizable in the answers of some of the respondents. One stated: "If the chaplain does not give up, then it is expected that the patient will not give up hope either. Never give up hope from a religious standpoint." Another indicated: "Eternal hope is a sustaining thing for some types of patients." And lastly, a truly hopeless case was seen as a person who is "completely untouchable," who may be completely without hope. In dealing with this latter type of person the limitations of the human spirit were pointed out, and a reliance on divine intervention was suggested: "God loves them [hopeless patients] and can reach way beyond what I can reach . . . God can do what I can't do, or others can do what I can't do."

Even if it is granted that the "hopeless case" is a rarity, there still remain a vast number of hospitalized individuals who have difficulty in finding and expres. ng hope while immersed in the captive situation. This is particularly so in terms of the terminal patient. It is a critical juncture in the relationship between professional and patient when the former tries to ignite the spark of hope in the latter. This effort is made all the more difficult by the fact that the helping person might himself at times be subject to feelings of hopelessness. Nonetheless, the prerequisite to a beneficial interaction is a hopeful attitude on the part of the helping professional. The professional must always be on guard against succumbing to the possibilities of hopelessness in himself and in the situation.

## Communicating with the Dying Patient

How may communication be undertaken with those that seem to have fallen victim to despair? A majority of the chaplains who were interviewed indicated that being with the patient in despair is the first step in attempting to reorient bleak feelings toward a more hopeful outlook. The importance of a human relationship was stressed in the following question: "Who is left to listen to and communicate with the patient who is not getting better and who will not be getting better?"

Two other chaplains assessed the despairing patient's condition as one of isolation and alienation. They spoke of the ever-present anxiety on the part of the professional in terms of the necessity to "give hope" by rushing into the patient's room with Bible in hand, offering a hurried prayer, and hastily retreating. This mode of action is neither realistic nor helpful, and points to the unpleasant fact that few people will listen to or be with people in despair. At times, particularly when there is nothing physical to do for the patient, just being with him, hearing his despair, and if indicated, "sharing our own hopelessness" can be most beneficial.

The person in despair must be dealt with in nonverbal terms before verbal mechanisms may be employed. Work with this type of patient is initially silent and it is an attempt to fathom "how total the darkness of despair must be." It is giving the patient "a sense of my attempting to fathom it (despair) with him, and a sense of my being there with him. It is regard for him in spite of his despair, if not because of it."

Another chaplain saw work with the person who apparently has relinquished all hope as dealing with a mental spark:

> If we are dealing with a spark at least . . . if the person has not died mentally. . . . But, if there is a spark of life to him, mentally, to work with, then I could not call him hopeless. I can't give him hope, I can't give him my spark, which is what we all try to do. . . . The much more courageous thing to do is to trust that the person has something that will keep him alive, and I can do my best by abandoning (almost) what is my hope and really getting close enough to him as a person, to appreciate what it is that is his spark of life, and to reinforce that in his life.

Just as a sense of hopelessness may be transmitted, fortunately a more munificent attitude, hope, can also be communicated. It would seem that what the terminal patient needs is someone to be with him. This is a first step in building meaningful communication which implies: "We care. . . ." Conversation is not necessary at this point. What is important is the *presence* of a caring person, be it physician, nurse, chaplain, or what have you. The dying patient's feelings of loneliness are shared and his isolation is mitigated by the presence of the professional. The very nearness of the other suggests to the patient that someone cares. From this basic assumption the patient takes hope. The dying person is no longer at the mercy of his own ineffective attempts at overcoming the trial. "The person acknowledges his own limited abilities for escaping the situation of captivity. At the same time he places his confidence in another person and his powers. There is an exchange that occurs. The person gives or shares his need with another and at the same time receives an assurance of the possibility of change."[4]

After the initial step of actual presence has been established, the helping person may want to respond to cues coming from the patient and engage him in conversation. For verbal interactions to be most meaningful they should be focused on the patient's perceptions of the captive situation, and his expectations and hopes in relation to coping with or overcoming this state. In effect, this means that the professional person is a listener; he does not propose goals for the patient but, instead, allows the dying person to formulate his own hopes and plans within reason. The professional may then offer appropriate commentary on these hopes.

Hoping—like hopelessness—is a process which has a contagious aura about it. A hopeful attitude on the part of one person might instill the same in another.[5] The helping person comes to the terminal patient with hopes for him; although these hopes are tacit, they constitute what may be called *a hopeful attitude*, and the patient responds to this positive force by hoping himself. Hope is transmitted from one person to another.

The whole idea of hope as a communicated endeavor may best be summed up in Marcel's phrase: "I hope in thee for us."[6] The crux of the hoping process is an interpersonal relationship between the professional person and the dying patient. The latter is caught in the captive situation and hopes for someone to be with him and to share his feelings. By stepping into the situation, the professional affords a caring, communicating presence, which kindles the spark of hope and extinguishes once and for all the notion of the "hopeless case."

## Notes

1. L. L. LeShan, "Some Observations on the Problem of Mobilizing the Patient's Will to Live," *Psychosomatic Aspects of Neoplastic Disease*; eds. D. M. Kissen and L. L. LeShan (London: Pitman Medical Publishing Co., 1964), pp. 109–120.

2. Ibid., p. 111.

3. Ibid.

4. Noble Lynch Butler, "A Theory of Hope Based upon Gabriel Marcel with Implications for the Psychiatrist and the Minister" (Ph.D. diss., Boston University, 1962), p. 175.

5. Ibid.

6. Gabriel Marcel, *Homo Viator: Introduction to a Metaphysic of Hope* (New York: Harper & Row, Publishers, Inc., Harper Torchbooks, 1962), p. 60.

# 9

# The Waiting Vulture Syndrome*
## — GLEN W. DAVIDSON

The Waiting Vulture Syndrome sometimes appears when relatives and staff have processed their initial sense of loss after realizing that a patient will die, but before the patient's demise. The physical symptoms of the Waiting Vulture Syndrome are: drooped head, shoulders falling forward, and general exhaustion. The emotional symptoms are: affect, somewhat despondent and a general sense of "there's nothing more we can do." Sometimes there is evidence of guilt: "We're ready too soon." Relatives and staff who are afflicted with the Waiting Vulture Syndrome appear startled by how quickly they have accepted the reality of a patient's dying and have accommodated themselves to their anticipated loss. Therapeutic intervention is needed in order to restore the patient's sense of dignity and relatives' and staff's sense of propriety.

One of the goals of thanatology is to help us learn how to help patients, relatives, and health care staff members learn how to accommodate themselves to the reality of dying and to utilize their resources of the grieving processes in order to cope with their loss. Appearance of the Waiting Vulture Syndrome is a sign of both success and failure of our efforts. It is the sign of success because it indicates that those afflicted have begun to process their sense of loss and have converted "anticipatory grief" into "real grief." It is a sign of failure because it exposes those afflicted to the sense that they have precipitously accommodated themselves to a loss which "feels real," and therefore leads one to assume that "there is no more relationship possible with my loved one," but which has yet to be culminated by the expiration of the loved one. Feelings of helplessness, namely, "there's nothing more we can do," are coupled with feelings of guilt, such as, "we're ready too soon."

*Glen W. Davidson's "The Waiting Vulture Syndrome" has been included in this volume by permission of Columbia University Press from their book, *Bereavement: Its Psychosocial Aspects,* edited by Schoenberg, Gerber, Wiener, Kutscher, Peretz, and Carr, copyright © 1975 Columbia University Press.

# Case Study

Typical of the conditions when the Waiting Vulture Syndrome appears occurred during the care of Betty, a forty-three-year-old mother of two. Betty was readmitted to the hospital with advanced cancer of the colon. Exploratory surgery found that her colon was totally blocked and that her cancer was rapidly and widely metastasizing. The patient, like her family, had come into the hospital with the full expectation that whatever it was that was now wrong could be corrected again by some medical procedure. Two previous admissions, with surgery, had relieved her of cancer symptoms.

The patient was quiet, articulate, and fully in command of her senses. At no time from the point of admission to the hospital until she died was she without the presence of at least one member of her family. To the casual observer, to most of the staff, and to many of her relatives, she had a very strong ego. She played a very strong role in family affairs. With her husband, however, she had a dependent personality and endured his alcoholism and promiscuity with countless rhythms of martyred feelings, forgiveness, and reconciliation.

When Betty was told that she was inoperable, she responded to the physician with the rhetorical question, "Then that means that this will be my last hospitalization, won't it?" The physician was direct but not blunt in confirming her suspicion. The patient went into shock for a brief period of time, but after a similarly brief period of catharsis, set herself to the immediate task of getting her affairs in order.

Several of the in-laws responded to her initial efforts to get her affairs in order by running errands, collecting legal papers, and making telephone calls for her. Her husband fled from the hospital upon receiving the physician's diagnosis and was found the following day in a tavern. Her children went into almost immediate shock and had difficulty functioning for more than forty-eight hours.

Both physicians and nurses sensed that Betty would deteriorate quickly. They conveyed this to the family. They responded in positive and therapeutic ways to both the patient's and family's needs. Their behavior could be summed up in the words of the head nurse, who said, "I believe we are doing everything possible to make them comfortable."

On the second day after diagnosis, most of the family came out of their shock and spent their time crying or going through catharsis in other ways. They would not grieve in front of the patient and took turns being in the patient's room when they were in command of their emotions. The male members of the family had begun to concern themselves with three questions by the end of that day: (1) Are we doing all that can be done to help her suffering? (2) How much more time is there? and (3) Is it all right to begin making "final arrange-

ments?" To the first question, several of the hospital's staff gave sympathetic encouragement by suggesting things the family could do to
help. To the second question, the physicians and staff were noncom-
mittal as to the precise time that death could be expected, but noted
that Betty's physical condition continued to deteriorate rapidly. To the
third question, the staff encouraged them to "make arrangements" as
rapidly as they felt competent.

On the third day after diagnosis, the patient began a siege of vomiting, and the staff expected the patient to expire at any time. The
patient's mind remained oriented but focused on the single concern of
how to be comfortable. Between bouts of nausea, the patient from
time to time concerned herself with healing ruptures in family affairs
and would call estranged members of the family together at bedside.
By the end of the fourth day, the patient seemed ready to die and
informed me, "I think all of my business is finished now." The family
had, by and large, expressed their grief less frequently and for shorter
periods of time. They had completed legal, financial, and funeral arrangements. As for the physicians, they called several times during
the day to see if she was still alive.

On the fifth day, the patient revived dramatically. She had ceased
vomiting and was mentally so alert that she reported on the emotional
and physical conditions of all her family with the same kind of detail
she shared about herself. She was so bright in spirits she was telling
all who would listen, "I think I'll be going home again."

The relatives were physically and emotionally drained by the fifth
day. They stood in the hallway and in the patient's room manifesting
the physical characteristics of waiting vultures. And they became increasingly angry; first with the patient, then with the staff, and finally
with themselves. They expressed their hostilities toward the patient
by avoiding eye contact with her, by not responding verbally to her
comments and questions, and by long absences from her room. As
one of her brothers blurted out "If she's going to die, why doesn't she
go ahead and die? If she's going to live, what are we all standing
around here for?" Then he quickly controlled himself and said, "I
don't really mean that. I want her to live, but not if she's going to be
eaten up with cancer some more." The family also expressed feelings
about how the staff had misled them into thinking Betty was going to
die. The staff had even encouraged them to make final arrangements.
Now what would people think of them? What would Betty think of
them if she were ever to find out? What were they to think of themselves? They felt guilty and angry with themselves for precipitously
acting out their sense of loss when they were told that the patient
was dying.

Many of the hospital staff were very uncomfortable with the turn of
events. They had expected the patient to continue going through the

"stages all terminally ill patients are supposed to do," as the nurses put it. "Now she's out of sync!" They were embarrassed by the patient's failure to conform to preconceived ideas of terminal illness and by the relatives' hostility. "We've thought we were really doing everything we were supposed to."

By the end of that day, the patient felt estranged, and said so. "It's as though I've become some sort of pariah. I'm being treated like I'm an object, changed from a person into a thing by my cancer." The relatives seemed unable to respond. "What more can we do, we've done everything we know how to do!" Thinking they could best support the relatives by agreeing, the staff assured them they *had* done everything they could do.

## Therapeutic Intervention

The Waiting Vulture Syndrome was broken by therapeutic intervention in three ways: (1) The patient was encouraged to release most of her relatives from staying continously at the hospital in order to get a night's sleep. Two of the closest relatives would stay with her through the night. (2) The relatives were encouraged to consider that there were several things that would be needed from them so long as the patient lived—affection and assurance that she wouldn't be abandoned. They were encouraged to hold her hand, massage her legs and arms, brush her hair. (3) Relatives and staff were encouraged, in very small groups, to articulate their frustrations. Members of both the family and the health-care staff seemed relieved by discovering that neither side was holding quite the expectations of the other that was assumed.

When the patient died on the eighth day after diagnosis, she died with a sense of ease. Several times during her final hour, she thanked those around her for their presence. She had remained concious until about fifteen minutes before her death. The relatives and staff seemed genuine in their self-assessment: "We *did* do everything we could."

# 10

# Prayer and the Dying Patient: Intimacy without Exposure
## — DANIEL C. DeARMENT

Many dying patients feel isolated most of the time; all dying and extremely sick people feel isolated and even alienated some of the time. The content of *some* of this isolation is an absence of relationships of intimacy—relationships in which the patient feels another person as warm, close, safe to touch and hold, available for sharing negative feelings without destroying the relationship, and capable of experiencing mystery and transcendence. Some patients who experience this kind of isolation do so because they fear intimacy. Some patients, though able to relate intimately, are kept from doing so by external factors—for instance, the "others" cannot tolerate intimacy now, the environment is too public, etc. Intimacy is more desirable than isolation for all persons who have achieved this life-task of adulthood.

The assumptions above are the basis of a conviction which has grown as I work (and see students work) with sick and dying persons: Shared prayers between the patient and a religious figure are often a way to intimacy without exposure which allows the patient to feel less isolated. By "religious figure" I mean a person whose role is defined in such a way that "offering prayers" is an accepted and nonthreatening aspect of his visit. It must be more then simply a devout or religiously inclined person.

It is commonly accepted that the experience of sickness threatens the ego, and that the experience of dying presents a kind of ultimate fear of loss of self. The dying patient himself avoids, and is asked by others (doctors, spouses, friends, lovers) to avoid situations which call for self-abandon—situations like close affiliations, orgasms, close friendships, physical combat. Erik Erikson, whose concept of ego-loss I am using here, says: "The avoidance of such experiences because of a fear of ego-loss may lead to a deep sense of isolation and consequent self-absorption."[1] It has been my experience that dying patients do indeed feel a profound sense of isolation and self-absorption and that simple and direct prayers seem somehow to make the patient feel less isolated, more in touch with me and with God. I began to reflect on these experiences and observed that very often the content of the prayers spoke of fears, hopes, regrets, and particular people and experiences which either could not be shared before as we spoke eye-to-eye or were eductive of feelings which had not been expressed before.

Two patients, whom I will call Mr. Brown and Mrs. Green, illustrate these reactions.

## Responses of Dying Patients to Prayer

Mr. Brown is a fifty-year-old, blue-collar worker. He is a Presbyterian elder and active in his church. He knows he has cancer but deals with this largely in terms of "I really think that they have 'got it all' this time—I'm going to be fine." But at another level he frequently says, "What are you going to do? All you can do is pray." He deflects any suggestion that he feels lonely, unjustly treated, or angry, although he says things like: "I've always worked hard, and been a good father and husband and yet you see some of these bums, these violent types—nothing ever happens to them." And, "She and the kids used to come to see me every day, but they are busy; she has to go to work and they have their social life. I can understand that. . . . Now, I don't mean that I feel lonely, or that they *should* come more often, but . . . well . . . Say, did you hear the Phillies won today?"

I mostly small-talk and then the following takes place.

CHAPLAIN:  "Mr. Brown, I would like to say a prayer with you."
MR. B.:    "Yes, I wish you would." (He reaches out his hand.)
CHAPLAIN:  (Taking his hand firmly, I note that Mr. B closes his eyes immediately.)
           "O Lord of Life, we know you are with us, even when it *seems* you are far away. This, thy servant, Mr. Brown, is sick—he is sometimes afraid and sometimes he feels alone. You know his needs better than any man—touch his life, help him to feel your warmth and tenderness, your presence, in his working and sleeping, in good days and bad. In Christ's name—Amen."
MR. B.:    (Squeezing my hand very tightly and holding on—looking me right in the eye.) "Thank you, Chaplain. Thank you. Please come back again."

Here in the prayer Mr. Brown felt in touch, close and accepted, while all my skill and compassion in the earlier contact was resisted as Mr. Brown experienced any attempt to come close to him as a threat to his ego, which was afraid to risk intimacy and would settle for isolation.

Mrs. Green, on the other hand, illustrates another type of reaction. She is a thirty-five-year-old housewife, with Hodgkin's disease. Like Mr. Brown, she knows how sick she is and also tends to avoid this reality in all her relationships, especially with her husband, who has spoken of her "coldness" and "aloofness" as "what this disease has done to her." Likewise, as the chaplain, I am treated with great respect and distance. She changes the subject, averts her eyes, and both physically and symbolically pulls away whenever I move to discuss her husband, although she describes her husband as "wonderful" and the marriage as "ideal."

The following exchange took place, after I had been seeing her for about a week every day. The patient is Catholic; I am a Protestant chaplain.

CHAPLAIN:     "Mrs. Green, I know you are a Catholic, but would you mind if I said a prayer with you—now?"

MRS. GREEN:   (Pausing to think, and then responding without reservation.) "Why, not at all. I think that would be nice."

CHAPLAIN:     (Slowly and thoughtfully, as I am individualizing the prayer.) "Lord God, Father of us all, we are needy people, and we are often lonely and confused. Mrs. Green is trying very hard to get well, and everyone is working to help her; be with them, her doctors and her nurses. Be with her husband, for he too needs your comfort and your presence. (Pause.) Grant your presence to us all— through the here and now of this prayer, through the Sacraments of the Church, and through mysteries which we cannot understand. In the name of the Father, Son, and Holy Spirit. Amen."

I had heard Mrs. Green sob when I mentioned her husband in the prayer and had paused to consider where to go next. I moved into more general area, gave time for her to gain composure, and then ended the prayer.

MRS. GREEN:   (Her eyes were still filled with tears, she looked embarrassed.) "I guess I got sort of carried away."

CHAPLAIN:     "And now some tears are a cause for embarrassment. . . ."

MRS. GREEN:   "Yes. . . ." (Pause.) "I mean, well. . . ."

CHAPLAIN:     (Sensing that she is about to close up again,—I come in quickly.) "Mrs. Green, I can see that you are upset and struggling within yourself. I guess something I said in my prayer touched something pretty deep and important to you. You don't need to go into it with me, but you don't need to run away from it either. I believe that God can reach into our lives and touch us and help us.

Sometime you may wish to speak more of this, but now just let your tears be—let them be."

MRS. GREEN: "Thank you. I really can't talk about it now, and I appreciate your understanding that. But I guess you know that sometimes a good cry does wonders for a lady and . . . well (She begins to fill up again, then collects herself.) . . . well, that's how I feel. I've had a cry, and I feel better."

CHAPLAIN: "Sure, I know what you mean." (There is a long pause, with some pretty powerful non verbal communication going on.) "Well, I'll be going now. It has been a real special kind of a talk—real special. Thank you."

Here the chaplain's prayer triggered a wave of feelings, in which the patient was aware that she needed her husband, loved him very much, and had shut him out. She could not verbalize all this, but she could briefly experience the intimacy of her relationship in the prayer. Thereafter she struggled to close that off, and yet the presence of the chaplain allowed her to risk just a little bit more. If I had pushed to have it verbalized, she would probably have retreated. As it was she moved briefly from an intimate feeling of relationship with God and her husband, into a fleeting moment with me as the chaplain. That moment was sensed by both of us and represented for her a genuine ego-risk in intimacy and hence a genuine ego-feeding incident.

## Appropriate Use of Prayer

Incidents like the two described above have led me to see that prayer with a dying and/or extremely sick person is a way of allowing the patient to experience a feeling of intimacy, while minimizing the risk of further isolation and fear of ego-loss. Before discussing why I think this so, and what some of the particulars of all this are, I want to look at the dangers involved in my thesis and its application.

Most obviously at stake is the question of whether or not the chaplain will misuse the offering of prayer as a way of violating the patient's defenses, making him or her feel that the office of the ministry and the power of God have stripped away what conventional good manners, changes of subject, and other defenses could effectively keep covered. It is perhaps a further verification of my position that we all know the potential danger here. Prayers have great power. To the believer, this power is in terms of some style of conventional piety; to the non believer, there is probably a vestige of mysticism, awe, or even fear surrounding this phenomenon. But let it be clearly said that the timing, the content, the length, and the follow-up of each prayer is perhaps *more* important than the analysis of other parts of the conversation.

Because of the exposing power of the words and postures of prayer, the chaplain/pastor would do well not to have any "canned" prayers which he thinks apply to *all* situations. Stated prayers, and parts of stated prayers, can be used, but consider well their content! For it is not our intent here to allow the use of prayer to strip the patient of defenses, but to offer him a feeling of intimacy, while at the same time allowing the defense, or the distance, if you will, of the prayerful moment.

A second potential pitfall in all this is that the *chaplain* who is threatened by intimacy (or by the fact of death and dying, or anything which precludes a more human and open relationship between himself and the patient) will use the device of prayer as a means of avoiding the patient. Thus he must raise against his use of prayer the same hard questions which he raises regarding all elements of his conversation: namely, why did I say that, and what was I feeling at the time? And if he finds that prayer keeps cropping up at a point where the patient seems ready to speak face to face, then *mea culpa*! Better to change the subject, or even leave, than *use* prayer as a way of avoidance. (One frequent sign of this problem is the tendency to use prayer as a way of departure, of getting away from the patient and his feelings.) A further test of a dynamic and thoroughly legitimate use of prayer at the bedside is the willingness to stay and respond to the feelings and words of the patient which the prayer has touched.

## Prayers and Intimacy

I see two related factors which underlie my position. The first has to do with body language and the posture of prayer. The second is the interplay between man-to-man relationships and man-to-God relationships.

It is quite natural to think about shared prayer in terms of the "posture of prayer," for the art of prayer is almost always connected with some body movements and postures. These are not universal, but in my hospital ministry they have seemed appropriate in 95 percent of all bedside prayer led by a chaplain and joined by a patient.

The eyes are either averted down or up or (most often) closed, by both the religious figure and the patient. There is a reaching out and touching, usually hand-to-hand between the two. This reaching can be initiated by either party, but when it is initiated by the chaplain, the patient almost always responds with acceptance. Even when the reaching and touching is not effected, there is usually a movement closer to the patient, a step or a bowed head. There is ready recognition by hospital personnel of the special nature of this body language —witness the nurse or doctor who comes upon patient and chaplain in prayer, recognizing the posture and offering instant silence or withdrawal, even when the doctor or nurse is not a frequent participant in such formalized prayers.

What all of this seems to mean is that in the posture of prayer we reach out and touch another person, achieving both intimate contact and social distance. The eyes, the organ of greatest intimacy other than our sexual organs, are averted from each other during the prayer. Again, the language is saying, "I am in touch with you but we will not allow our eyes to meet as this would be too threatening and diverting from the purpose at hand: being in touch with God!" But after the "amen," there is usually some eye contact and hand squeezing which says, "See, I am me, a person; and you are you; we have returned from our brief journey inward."

The body language is closely related to the relationships which are "believed" to be present. Intimacy involves some relationship. One can hardly feel intimate alone. Buber spoke of an "I-Thou" relationship with a tree, and certainly many have felt intimacy with a place, a ring, a book, and all the associations these things raised. But in prayer the "object" of intimate relationship is tacitly agreed to be God (however He may be defined) for *both* the patient and the pastor. We look toward Him together, and meanwhile some words are spoken which describe in interpenetrating language the intimate relationships of men (We pray for the members of Mrs. Brown's family, who are concerned about her) and the intimate relationship of God and man. Interestingly, sometimes the patient, who does not himself feel a close personal intimacy with God, can and does in a vicarious way believe that the "man of God" feels intimate with His God, and therefore the patient senses intimacy which is more than person-to-person.

By now the thesis regarding prayer and intimacy is presented in several different ways. There is paradox here: A way of intimacy with social distance, a suggestion that we can move away from isolation and help another to do so without risk. How can that be? There is danger here that prayer, a transcendent moment for believers, will be psychological at best, and that patients will be manipulated and hurt at worst. But nevertheless I would hold with my position that: Shared prayers between the patient and a religious figure are often a way of intimacy without exposure, which allows the patient to feel less isolated.

## Notes

1. Erik H. Erikson, *Childhood and Society*, 2d ed. (New York: W. W. Norton & Company, Inc., 1963), p. 264.

# 11

## *Dying Patient's Concept Of God*
## — DAVID H. C. READ

This chapter is based on some observations about how the terminally ill think about God, rather than being a theory as to how they *ought* to think about God. I am drawing on experiences as a parish minister, an army chaplain, and a university pastor. I shall try to be accurate in my memories and realistic in my evaluations.

Any theological thinking about death must be existential. In fact, thanatology could be a clue to realistic theological thinking on any subject since the immediate prospect of quitting the life we know calls into question the religious convictions held since childhood. Thus a discussion of this kind must be thoroughly personal and shaped more by actual experience than by theological proclivity.

The nearest approach to the situation of the terminally ill that I have personally experienced was undoubtedly shortly before I was taken prisoner by the Germans in World War II. At that moment I was convinced that I had just a few minutes more to live. Reviewing my thoughts of that time, I recall a sense of disappointment amounting to agony at having to leave behind a life which I was very much enjoying, but also a dominant sense of the presence of a God in whom I could trust for whatever was to come. This was articulated in my mind by a verse of scripture, "My God shall supply all your needs according to his riches in glory, by Christ Jesus," but it would, I think, have been there without such words having come into my mind. I remember feeling that all kinds of beliefs were falling away as unimportant as I struggled through to the only reality that seemed to matter.

This experience leads me to suppose that in the mind of a terminally ill patient a similar process of concentration and condensation goes on. Dr. Johnson remarked concerning a condemned criminal: "Depend upon it, Sir, when a man knows he is to be hanged in a fortnight it concentrates his mind wonderfully." This kind of concentration in the case of soldiers facing death ranges from the desperate demand for some assurance about the future to the flippant remark of a British officer to me after a service before battle: "I always think, Padre, that a spot of religion is a good thing in a tight corner."

For those in a "tight corner" and those who are terminally ill, the question of God arises as anything but a theoretical discussion. It is obviously closely linked with the immediate question as to whether the experience of death is in any way a prelude to another kind of life. Here again the question cannot be abstracted from previous training and religious experience. I am not at all convinced that "there are no atheists in foxholes," I think it unlikely that Russians who died by the thousands on the battlefields were enabled to shed their atheistic training at the prospect of sudden death. But this, of course, is something that one can never know.

## Patient's Religious Background

It is, I believe, a fairly common experience for those facing death to be thrown back into an infantile situation with its dependence on the security of mother love. For those for whom this has been associated with early religious beliefs, it is probable that when dying they conceive of God as being the "everlasting arms" in whom such security and peace may be found. It does seem as though such memories play a stronger part at such a moment than do any subsequent formulations of religious belief.

It is extremely difficult to explain the relationship between the religion professed by an individual and the strength of his confidence in God on the approach of death. It can by no means be stated that the so-called religious person inevitably approaches death with a calm and confidence that is not observable in the irreligious. On the contrary, it would seem certain religious temperaments react with considerable fear and distress at such a time while a certain stoicism seems to give the irreligious a readiness to meet the end. A remark made to me perhaps illustrates this. An elderly woman said, "I have no faith at all, and yet I am not in the least frightened of dying." On the other hand, I have known many people who were considered extremely devout to be enormously troubled in mind and conscience at the approach of death.

A good deal of this must depend on the quality of previous thinking about God and an understanding of the inner meaning of faith. I have known many for whom the approach of death seemed simply to be an aspect of knowing more fully the Father-God in whom they had believed. One such person said to me shortly before his death: "I don't know why people make such a fuss. This is going to be the most exciting adventure of all." On the other hand, those whose relationships to their God have always been haunted by vague doubts and scruples are apt to find these mounting when the hour of death approaches. I have known them to ask desperately if certain acts of charity they have performed would count for them as they reached the other side. Here the pastor comes up against the difficulty of inducing a new conception of God at this stage, and I must admit that it has always proved hard to inject an idea of the grace and mercy of God—especially when this part of the Christian gospel had undoubtedly been heard many times without apparent effect.

## Conceptions of God

This leads me to consider the ingrained attitudes of so many people, whatever their religious beliefs, concerning the nature of their relationship to God. Both those who have been regularly exposed to the Christian gospel and those who have no connection with organized religion often seem to share a conception of God in which their "claims" upon him seem to dominate their minds. They seem to perceive God as the one responsible for bringing them to this point of crisis and death, and they are inclined both to justify themselves and to register their complaint at the harsh treatment they have received. Mingled with this is often the powerful idea that what they are enduring is some kind of punishment inflicted upon them by God. One of the most common remarks revealing this attitude is: "What have I done to deserve all this?" Such a remark may come from someone who has been a devout church member and feels badly rewarded for his long service. It may also come from someone whose thoughts about God have been infrequent and clear: He has been a shadowy, menacing figure in the background.

What seems certain, at least to a preacher, is the comparative failure of the Church to convey the conception of God that lies behind the doctrine of "Justification by Faith." It seems as though, in spite of hearing innumerable sermons on the grace of God and receiving the sacrament of Holy Communion in which it is made evident that "Nothing in my hand I bring, simply to thy cross I cling," average churchgoers often fail to grasp this central theme of the gospel. They are not content to be prodigal sons utterly dependent on the Father's mercy and bounty but see themselves rather as elder brothers with some claim on the Father for their years of service. Although pious literature abounds in stories of deathbed repentance and conversion—"Between the stirrup and the ground, he mercy sought and mercy found" —it has not been my experience that this happens often. Those with the "elder brother" complex seldom become prodigals at the last minute. Those who approach death with the greatest confidence seem to be the ones who have been sustained by what is expressed in the opening of the Heidelberg Catechism: "What is your only comfort in life and death?" "That I belong, body and soul, in life and in death, not to myself but to my faithful savior, Jesus Christ. . . ." With the lack of strong catechetical instruction today and the prevailing ignorance of the Biblical teaching on grace, one must expect fewer to face the end with this kind of confidence and hope. Yet it would seem from the thoughts expressed by the terminally ill that many are groping after such a concept of God and recognize it when it is expressed to them in prayer or scripture reading.

It is my experience that the impersonal and highly philosophical concepts of God that have been promulgated in many quarters have little relevance at this point of crisis; at least I have never heard expressed any sort of confidence in being absorbed into a "stream of being," or being confronted with "one's ultimate concern." (To be fair, I should note that the Tillichian concept of "accepting that one is accepted" is a powerful thought at such a time.) In my experience the dying person's concept of God is normally highly personal, and it is to the most personal type of address in prayer that he clings.

## Communication between Minister and Patient

One is conscious at the deathbed of the overpowering desire for utter sincerity in all that is said or prayed. The dying who share their pastor's belief want to hear it expressed again, while those who have been without any deep religious conviction often seem to be reaching out for genuine assurance and communicated faith.

This raises the question of how their concept of God is reflected in the words of one who is attempting to minister to them. I have at times been conscious of a look of disappointment if the content of my prayer seemed too conventional or falsely optimistic. While, conversely, there seemed to be gratitude whenever, in however a stumbling way, the facts were faced and a faith confessed. It may be that through the words of another a vague sense of the presence of an understanding and merciful God is being given focus and reality.

The late Cardinal Cushing related that when he asked the victim of an accident whether he believed in "one God, Father, Son, and Holy Ghost," he received the reply, "Here I am dying, and he's asking me riddles." This anecdote indicates the necessity for concentration and understanding as one offers a reflection of God. But, on the other hand, for a devout Catholic there would undoubtedly be comfort in the repetition of the familiar words. This links up with what I have said about the echoes of childhood teachings and worship that are aroused in the terminal days.

These notes about the concept of God in terminally ill patients should not close without reference to another factor that is disturbing for many. The Churches have been inclined to convey to their flocks that faith in God will be especially real and vivid at times of mortal danger. Perhaps we have not warned sufficiently against the spiritual repercussions of weakness and pain. While some mortally ill patients have confided to me their sense of God's presence, others have been distressed by the fact that the things they thought they most surely believed were somehow becoming distant and difficult. There is undoubtedly some need for some religious education to the effect that physical weakness may temporarily cloud the sense of God's presence. Therefore, in my view, the reality of God's grace should be stressed even at times when weakness and suffering have temporarily obscured one's apprehension of it.

These reflections indicate the need for franker discussion of this topic *before* the period of terminal illness is reached. It is encouraging to note that the trend is now away from covering up the fact of death and toward allowing frank and full discussion of all its implications, both for the believer and the unbeliever.

# 12

## The Psychological Function Of Religion To The Dying Patient
— EDGAR DRAPER

Postmortem accounts of dying are exceedingly "rare"—in fact are unknown. Even Houdini's iron will could not batter down the pearly gates, and his report of the "other side" never came. But even if an account of the death and dying experience were possible (it no doubt would make interesting reading), we would be forced, nevertheless, to take it with a grain of salt. Why? Because the reporter would be giving us his interpretation, which would have to be as unique as his interpretation of life, adding only description of the final capstone to the life uniqueness that is Everyman's now.

Although there are reports of the experience of being "born again," the real beginning of life or the actual birth experience are equally unreported. Thus, all we have in the way of reports about human experience are highly individualized interpretations of events or idiosyncratic observations that pertain to the period between infancy and death. In addition, there are those more broadly shared interpretations of life that we call philosophy or theology.

No one person's autobiography or his genetic inheritance is like anyone else's. Although various interpretations of life may have common appeal, expressed either through various philosophies or religions, we have shown that one's personal philosophy of life or personal religion is as unique as he is. It is a reflection of his birthright, raising, personality, unique experiences, and his current life situation.

This chapter will attempt to elucidate the uniqueness of the dying man's philosophy or religion, to treat briefly those unique qualities about dying that "square" or even "cube" the individual's uniqueness in the dying situation, to search out stable or nonunique aspects in facing death or dying, and finally to discuss principles in management of the dying patient as they relate to his personal religion or life philosophy.

64

As far back as 1960, I became involved in researching the psychological meaning of religion to patients, preceded by a lifelong interest in what religion meant to me as an individual. A group of psychiatric and medical colleagues with equal curiosity found in some pilot studies that there was a very close relationship between the current personal belief system of an individual and his cross-sectional or diagnostic psychiatric assessment. Although it ought not be surprising to learn that one's belief system is related to one's life experiences, none of us anticipated just how close that relationship actually proved to be. The hypothesis which evolved was as follows: If indeed personal religious convictions are not handed down from on high, nor derived primarily from formal religious training, but are the outcome of life experiences including early developmental experiences, then these beliefs are the "natural choice" of the particular character personality. They are influenced by the current life stage or situation. By learning the details of a man's religious or philosophical ideas, we should be able to make correct diagnostic conclusions about him, including his character structure, his psychological symptoms, his genetic or developmental attainment (degree of maturity), and his current psychological stresses or conflicts.

To test this hypothesis, we studied fifty random cases chosen from the inpatient and outpatient services of the department of psychiatry at the University of Chicago. A medical student, untrained psychiatrically, saw these fifty patients in what we called a "religious interview." He secured a religious history and asked a set of thirteen "religious" questions of a projective nature. This material only, gathered in thirty-five to forty-five minutes, without benefit of clinical or observational data about the patient (even without the knowledge of whether the patient was an inpatient or outpatient), was then presented to the other members of the team, all of whom were trained psychiatrically in similar orientations. We then committed ourselves to setting down independently our clinical diagnoses (symptom and character), genetic (developmental) diagnosis, and speculatively our psychodynamic formulations, including what current life struggles brought the patient for help. We then compared our diagnostic conclusions with those of the department-of-psychiatry staff who obtained the usual clinical data from histories, observations, and psychological testing. Of the fifty cases, the research team missed the clinical diagnosis in only two, giving us 92 percent correct diagnostic conclusions about the patients we never saw and about whom we knew only their personal religious beliefs, attitudes, or religious history. Our intent was not to create one more new diagnostic projective test using religion as the avenue, but rather to test the hypothesis above.

We spent little time formulating the questions which others have since improved on, and which we changed in the situation to suit patients (e.g., asking Catholic patients, "Who is your favorite saint and why?" rather than "favorite Bible character?"). To give an idea of their evocative quality geared to get individualized answers vis-à-vis "orthodox ones," the questions are listed below, and a case illustration follows.

## Projective Religious Questions

1. What is your earliest memory of a religious experience or belief?
2. What is your favorite Bible story? Why?
3. What is your favorite Bible verse? Why?
4. Who is your favorite Bible character? Why?
5. What does prayer mean to you? If you pray, what do you pray about?
6. a. What does religion mean to you?
   b. How does God function in your personal life?
7. a. In what way is God meaningful to other people besides yourself?
   b. How is God meaningful to your father or mother?
8. What religious idea or concept is most important to you now?
9. What is the most religious act one can perform?
10. What do you consider the greatest sin one could commit?
11. What do you think of evil in the world?
12. What are your ideas of an afterlife?
13. If God could grant you any three wishes, what would they be?

## Case Illustration

A nineteen-year-old Pentecostal woman attended "church picnics every week." She stated that her mother felt strongly that "by faith we will be healed," and that her mother had seen others healed at religious meetings. She remembered being inspired by a pastor at age four and age eleven in church. Her favorite Bible story was "Exodus—when Jesus (sic) came and took all the people away from Egypt and led them out to the land of milk and honey." Her favorite Bible character was "Jesus—who fed the multitudes." She felt God's function was to answer prayers. She found that faith and communion ("you know, the bread and the wine") are the most important religious ideas. She looked forward to going to heaven, which is "not the same as here." Her favorite Bible verse was, "I will lift up my eyes unto the Lord, my help cometh from the Lord."

Comment: The team's diagnostic impression was chronic depression of an anaclitic variety [i.e., infantile dependency—Ed.]. From the material, this young lady was assessed as immature and emotionally deprived. The powerful wishes to be fed and cared for, and the orientation around mother and God as givers of food and support, were viewed as a consolation fantasy resulting from unfulfilled dependency wishes. The lack of conflict over the wishes to be taken care of, together with the depressed, fatalistic outlook, pointed to a severe, long-standing depression. The hint in the wish to be healed led to the conclusion that she might be struggling with serious physical illness. The helplessness, the use of religion for nourishment, and the wish for a more blissful state indicated social withdrawal, with probable suicidal fantasies. The material indicated magical thinking, severe regression, blind obedience, and an archaic superego. Distortions in her religious ideation indicated the interchangeability of the rescuing party, for example, Jesus, instead of Moses, reflecting her object vagueness [i.e., immature emotional relationships with other persons—Ed.].

Clinically, she was revealed to be the last of fourteen children in a deprived family. She had pulmonary tuberculosis and grand mal seizures, and had recently been released after a prolonged hospitalization in a sanatorium. Her discharge had led to depression, irritable demands, and suicidal ruminations. She used fantasy solutions to reality problems, and had been withdrawn, depressed, and dependent all her life.

# Results of Study of Belief Systems

The result of the study was summarized as follows:

We do not think that the contribution of this study is the construction of one more potentially useful projective test. . . . What we do consider significant, however, is that a patient's religious and philosophical views present as useful an avenue for psychiatric diagnosis as any other personal facet of his life. The rich resource that religious material offers dynamically qualifies it as another royal road to the unconscious. . . . Formal religious teachings were invariably individually interpreted and stamped by the mark of the person. Since each formal religious group offers myriads of activity or beliefs, patients chose those elements having current signal importance. . . . Finally, our study conveys that in the diagnostic realm, religious and philosophical views need not be considered automatically sick or healthy, nor avoided, nor overrespected as too personal, nor ignored as irrelevant. They need not be categorized as expressions of one compartment of the mind, such as the superego, nor reduced to pat formulae, such as "God is the projection of the infantile prototype of the father." Rather, it would appear that the religious and philosophical convictions of patients offer an intimately private and uniquely personal communication, worthy as any other, not only of respect, but also of diagnostic curiosity.

Given the finding that for these fifty randomly chosen patients, whom we could assess accurately (from "religious" data alone) as to their character makeup, symptoms, degree of maturity, and often their current life stresses, one could raise the question of the *relevance* of the study to dying patients in two forms: "What do these findings have to do with dying patients?" And even though randomly chosen with a wide variety of formal religious preferences (Buddhist, Jewish, Catholic, Protestant, atheist), "these patients aren't 'normal'—acknowledge their psychological difficulty in coming for help—so isn't the study limited to psychiatric patients?"

To acknowledge the second objection first, this study has been replicated by using nonpsychiatric general-hospital patients and divinity students and continues to be a means of evaluating physicians applying for psychiatric residency. With these people who are not psychiatric patients, the ability to make clinical diagnoses and to evaluate personality strengths and weaknesses, character makeup, maturity, and current life conflicts by learning their personal life philosophy and belief systems is equally possible.

As for the first objection, we can note that question 12 pertains directly to the afterlife and the stimulus of death and dying. As noted in the case cited, this girl's concept of the afterlife is unique to her, but completely consonant and complimentary to the rest of her answers. She describes the afterlife as "not the same as here," namely, without suffering or need. More important than her idiosyncratic and personalized responses to this question, or the other forty-nine patients' responses to this question, is the consonance of the answer with the *rest* of the person and her other responses. That is, although dying is a unique experience, it comes in the context and at the finale of a life already "set in its ways."

Although beliefs do change with life experiences and developmental influences, belief systems arise from what we are like as human beings. Beliefs do not simply disappear with news of death's nearness. We found, for example, that immature individuals have immature belief systems (e.g., magical or omnipotent or suckling religious expectations). A paranoid person had persecutory or grandiose beliefs; obsessive-compulsive characters were attracted by the orderly aspects of their formal religion; hysterics by the affective-expressive elements; etc. Thus, even with the threat of death at hand, we do not expect, nor do we see, the usual dying patient resort to a "foxhole" of religious or attitudinal retreat. The dying patient typically faces that ultimate crisis as he has the less ultimate ones, living out his same character patterns, strengths, and weaknesses and holding the belief systems of that particular stage of his life whether child, adolescent, or aged in years.

## Case Histories

Two examples may serve to illustrate. I was asked if I would serve as the psychiatrist and psychotherapist for a dying member of our medical staff in another city. This young man, afflicted with cancer, had lived a professional and personal life of coolness, was seldom seen to smile, and offered a surly exterior prior to the known onset of his cancer. Apparently his wife and the nursing staff, rather than the patient, initiated the request for help. Because I had not worked directly with him and because my clinical skills were respected, I was asked if I would "see him through." His dying days were, as I experienced them with him, much like his precancerous days, only with accentuation. His surly, morose attitudes moved to galling bitterness, his taking-from-others to a persistent demandingness, his mildly expressed distrust to suspiciousness and distrust, his pessimism to abject hopelessness. As far as his belief system went, he said, "If there were a God, I'd curse him." He died in physical and mental anguish, largely untempered by meaningful relationships to people.

In contrast, I had the privilege of knowing and working with Professor Paul Tillich while at the University of Chicago, setting up and moderating an extended seminar with him and our department of psychiatry's staff. It became apparent in these meetings that his zeal about concepts of ontological anxiety as the "primary anxiety of man" was no longer evident. He was not defensive about it, nor, if you will, anxious about it. He was even willing to consider the idea that ontological anxiety might be an expression of usual human anxiety of which one could see its extreme in a patient with a cardiac neurosis (a state of near constant irrational fear of sudden death). He was proud of his contributions to theology, but now was philosophical about them. It was no surprise to hear, then, after he had his coronary (eventually fatal) that he told his intern, "I feel my work is complete and I'm ready." He also carried his humor and self-perceptiveness into the dying process. He told this same intern a day or two before he died, "I dreamed last night that I was back in World War I as a chaplain. There were young men dying all around me. You don't suppose my psychoanalytic friends would have an interpretation for me, do you?" In a sense, he was "ready" before his coronary, satisfied with a full and contributive life and a sense of mission achieved. He gave evidence of having grieved, having given up old friends, including favorite ideas, to leave behind.

Although both of these men consciously faced their numbered days, how they faced Exit was completely consistent with their personalities, their interpersonal investments, and general life-styles.

More classically, Macbeth, knowing his end was near, complained, "I have liv'd long enough: my way of life has fallen into the sear, the yellow leaf, and that which should accompany old age, as honor, love, obedience, troops of friends, I must not look to have; but in their stead, curses, not loud, but deep: mouth-honor, breath, which the poor heart would feign deny, and dare not" (act V, scene III). Completely consistent with his ambitious, competitive, and murderous motives, he shouted in his final duel, "Lay on Macduff, and damn'd be him who first cries, 'hold, enough' "(act V, scene VIII).

We take for granted that the continuity and constancy of a man's character, life-style, etc. will play its role in dying. But the uniqueness of that person is paradoxically sustained and added to by the uniqueness of the dying process itself. The young man had a malignancy, Tillich a coronary. It took the former one and a half years to die, the latter one and a half weeks. One death was a painfully protracted, stormy ordeal, the other a quiet, but equally permanent, fade. We also falsely assume that no one wants to die, but 27,000 suicides per year, not to mention anhedonic [i.e., chronically unable to experience pleasure—Ed.] and depressed but not suicidal patients, tell us otherwise. We know, too, there are dying patients, not depressed, who yearn to "cross the bar." Furthermore, Elisabeth Kübler-Ross' stages of dying are not to be taken too fixedly, either in their order or universality (by her own comments). Finally, the age of the patient and his relationships to family and to friends all contribute to a grand compilation of data for diagnosis.

## Grief Process

Having burdened you with complexity, let me offer a bit of hope and stable constancy toward understanding these patients in their situations. I have already mentioned that patients' particular unique, unorthodox beliefs will often offer an avenue to understanding a very complex person in his perhaps most complex challenge. In addition, in the dying patient there is a process whose quality and degree of presence or absence is a North Star for assessment and management. That process is the grief process. I owe to two teachers and colleagues, Heinz Kohut and C. Knight Aldrich the platform ideas for building this extension. Dr. Kohut saw ideal grieving in the loss of a loved one as recapturing every possible meaningful memory trace, deflating it of affective investment, and acknowledging with pain the loss of that particularized recall of the dead one, that is, burying forever by "working through" the totality of that person's impact on one's life. Dr. Aldrich recognized that the dying patient might grieve for himself. *Combine* these ideas and one sees the monumental grieving task of the dying patient. From his standpoint, he has not only to grieve a loved one or himself (a giant task all by itself), he is challenged to grieve the entire composite of all who are or were dear to him, unless that work has already been partially done, (e.g., an aged person who has lost all friends or relatives, his work, etc. in preceding years). Further he must grieve his ideas, achievements, activities, symbols, future aims, everything; everything is headed down the drain.

I personally believe two additional things about grief: (1) It is a sign of psychological strength and health expressed in multiple ways and not by tears alone; (2) To reach a stage of "acceptance," grief is an absolute necessity. Psychological withdrawal at the end of grief work is not to be misconstrued as pathological, even though it may hurt relatives who wish the dying man were like his "old communicative self." Psychological withdrawal, *after* evidence of grief work, is the prologue to final withdrawal for those fortunate and strong enough to have worked through life's final challenge. The dying person not only gives up his future, and his own life now, but his past as well.

Thus, complex as the dying individual and his situation is, we expect that both his current belief system (personal philosophy or personal religious credos) and his "grief reading" will tell us about him diagnostically to give a firm handle to confident management. (It must be said, here, that his religious beliefs are *one* avenue to understanding him among many avenues. Also, his religious ideas about dying or afterlife are only one facet of his total "beliefs" and therefore not to be overvalued or taken out of context).

## Helping the Dying Patient

The implications for management from out study and these observations regarding grief are:

1. Grieving must be facilitated in the patient as well as family and recognized when it is occurring. For example, a man whose "masculine" image is so firm that tears cannot be shed, even alone, may nevertheless grieve vicariously through those around him. "Doctor, you know this is awfully tough on my wife and the boys." Such a man may do his grief work by displacement.

2. One's own fearful reactions to death or to past losses must not, if at all possible, be imposed on the patient or his family. We had to bodily remove from the hospital one such person. A scavenger "evangelist," seeking converts, got hold of a list of patients on "critical." He sought to peddle his personal brand of religion to

each. If pat methods are the doctor's or pastor's routine, it is not likely he knows or has taken into account what the patient's needs are. A wise pastor once told me he had to ask a colleague to help him with the dying, death, and burial of a parishioner that occurred one week after his own wife's death.

3. A diagnostic curiosity about the status of the dying person and his family is as necessary as assessment of his symptoms. Although we may have personal rituals or borrowed ones from religion, the dying person's "unorthodoxy" should not be a target for imposition of our "orthodoxy," including last rites or after life concepts. The ministering physician or pastor ought to be a facilitator of communication and grieving to the dying patient and his family. The patient may not think his future will be a mansion in his Father's house.

4. The patient's religious language is a royal road to understanding him and his reactions. Therefore, if he uses or requests religious language or customs, these should not serve as confirmation of our own biases or invitation to our own religious brand of belief or custom. For example, insistence on an afterlife may afford opportunity to promote the grieving process. E. Stanley Jones, a famous Indian missionary, told with pride his mother's injunction to use only white in her funeral to symbolize her victory over death. Although he identified with her courageous affirmation, he clearly was enjoined by her not to grieve.

The emphasis of this chapter is on the use of religion as a diagnostic tool to the dying patient. Once an assessment has been made and the patient clearly calls on the bulwark of religion, the pastor takes on a clearly therapeutic role. Available to him at that point is the use of an entire religious armamentarium that is best suited to this particular person and his family.

## Suggested Readings

Draper, E., "Religion as an Intrapsychic Experience," *Cincinnati Journal of Medicine* 50 (1969): 111–119.

Draper, E., et. al. "On the Diagnostic Value of Religious Ideation," *Archives of General Psychiatry* 13 (September 1965): 202–207.

# 13

## Communication and Pain —
## — KENNETH A. CHANDLER

A greater understanding of enduring pain is of major concern. Our efforts are directed toward the goal of more effective modification, amelioration, and perhaps the elimination of such experiencing. Yet how do we really define pain? Sometimes specific physical damage can be identified with pain as its sequela; yet there is also pain when there is an absence of such a physical locus. As Szasz has pointed out, the many meanings of the term attest to its ubiquitousness.[1] It is not surprising that a review of the research literature shows studies ranging from biochemistry and microscopic anatomy to philosophy, all concerned with enhancing an understanding of pain. It sometimes appears that the more we learn about it the more enigmatic it becomes. Pain has served as the cornerstone of philosophies, the potent driving force of human endeavor, and from one vantage point is the price man pays for his existence. Primary concerns are the psychopharmacological approaches to enduring pain and an enhancement of our efficacy in dealing with it

### Definition of Pain

A review of the neurology of pain does indeed provide much detailed information concerning structures—peripheral neural fibers involved in its transmission;[2] conduction to the thalamus via the lateral spinothalamic tract; as well as identification of thalamic nuclei (parafasicular and intralaminar) found to be critical in the surgical relief of pain.[3] Such findings are important in clarifying the neuroanatomy of pain and assist in the conceptualization of sites for pharmacological action. Yet paradoxes concerning the experiencing of pain, such as congenital sensitivity,[4] phantom pain,[5] and hypnotic[6] and placebo effects,[7] while not challenging the representation of pain at the higher cortical levels, do indeed point up the multiplicity of factors involved in the experiencing of pain. Melzak and Wall,[8] in the presentation of a "gate" theory of pain, make clear their concern for the role of prior experiences, affects, and attention as they may influence the gate-control system. That early experiences do indeed affect response to pain is demonstrated when puppies raised in isolation from infancy and protected from usual pain situations were found to be defective in the perception of tissue damage.[9] Similarly, it is clear that in human infants there seems to be a developmental difference in "withdrawal" to painful stimuli as opposed to the later development of expressive response. Observation of a child who is banging his head to the point of losing conciousness arouses puzzlement relative to what appears to be a lack of response to pain at the moment, for when such a child is tested he is revealed to respond adequately to pinpricks and other irritants. Similarly, self-mutilation in early childhood is not always accompanied by a clear demonstration that there are deficits in sensory processes.

It would appear, then, that a large segment of what is meant when pain is described is the variety of responses made by the patient to his discomfort, and that such responses reflect the developmental history of the individual. In this sense, then, pain is *not* "a hurt that we feel," as Sternbach[10] put it, but rather "a *feeling* that we hurt"; it is thus the result of the differentiation of feeling over the course of the individual's experiencing. From such differentiation emerge the cognitive structures (symbols) employed in the description of pain. Certainly Ostenasek's statement, "When the fear of pain is abolished, the perception of pain is not intolerable,"[11] is more readily understood from this vantage point. Sternbach appears to reverse his initial position as revealed in his later statement, "When anxiety (affect) is decreased, pain responses (physiological, overt) are also diminished."[12] Perhaps the epitome of this view was expressed by Cicely Saunders in her description of pain as "an attitude."[13]

## Communicating with Patients in Pain

Leriche counseled that "it is only by listening . . . that one can discover the individual in the disease";[14] it occurs to the author that if we listen to those experiencing pain, we may well learn how to contribute more effectively to their enduring pain. Saunder's patient who said, "The pain was all around me . . . and then I came here and you *listened* . . . the pain seemed to go just by talking,"[15] seems to be a case in point.

Often those writing about the dying cite the role that feelings of abandonment and loneliness play in exacerbating feelings of hopelessness and futility. Those involved in the treatment of such patients have shared that feeling of helplessness, when there seems to be no place to turn to alleviate the suffering. Indeed, "We are never quite so alone as when we are in pain."[16] It does not appear to be just accidental that those dying and facing death, as well as those enduring pain, report feelings of being abandoned, separated from others upon whom they were emotionally dependent, for in the enormity of painful feeling, the differentiation of self becomes eroded, and all that is left is to lie in stupor. Yet it is indeed striking to note the response of such patients when approached in a manner that has less to do with specific alleviation of specific pain and more to do with establishing an empathic relationship.[17] If feelings of abandonment and loneliness are the hallmarks of those dying and those enduring pain, it would follow, then, that treatment procedures that take these feelings into account would be more effective in ameliorating the suffering. The emphasis then lies here in providing the patient with a relationship that has as its focus the development of an emotional bond as opposed to one that is insight-oriented. As one patient replied when asked what he looked for most in those who looked after him, "Well, for someone to look as if they are trying to understand me. . . . I'm hard to understand."[18] In such a goal-limited therapy, Coleman states that the patient "wishes to feel understood, but is content to have it remain emotional rather than an intellectual experience."[19] It would seem then that the treatment of patients enduring pain must not only provide for assistance in the specific alleviation of discomfort through medication where appropriate, but also provide an enduring relationship within which the patient's experiences of his pain and himself in pain can serve to restore his image of self.

## A Place to Live Till the End

The author has visited a number of institutions both in this country and England where care was provided for patients suffering from later stages of cancer and for whom no further active treatment was deemed possible by other centers. Some comment is warranted concerning the importance of the establishment of a particular milieu within which no patient feels lost or feels neglected; where the patient, within the limits possible, may be more active in his own treatment. St. Christopher's Hospice, England, under the directorship of Dr. Cicely Saunders is an example of such a warm, supportive milieu. What is most striking there is the fact that the patients seem relaxed, serene, and cheerful, even though at various stages in their terminal illnesses. The time made available by staff members for their patients (perhaps it is the quality of the interaction rather than physical time per se) is most impressive. The author talked with these patients, and seldom was there more than a brief mention of their discomfort. The staff does indeed convey Saunders' view that "personal, caring contact is the most important comfort we can give."[20] Janis[21] is supportive of the importance of reducing anxiety in its relationship to stress. Certainly,

a good deal of effort is directed toward the management of pain phar-
macologically within the context of listening to the patient for clues in
order to achieve a balance between clarity of consciousness and a
reduction of pain.

Rather than care becoming chronic, the continuing care by the staff
contributes in no small way to the patient's desire to continue living
to the end.[22] Decisions about whether to be up and about or at bed
rest are often jointly determined with the patient; often the amount of
medication is similarly arrived at. Much in the way of discussion with
the doctor occurs, and families are an integral part of the patient-staff
effort. It was notable, during the author's visit, that a nursery for staff
children engaged many patients as they sat overlooking the play area.
A student attempting to describe the atmosphere of St. Christopher's
described it as being cheerful with an atmosphere more like that of a
homecoming. The author was impressed by how important it is to
ensure that in dealing with those enduring pain, an environment be
maintained where (1) the person is not lost in being a patient, and (2)
confidence and hope is obvious by its presence in the day-to-day
continuance of caring. When patient care is hurried, the patient's
sense of dignity and feeling of personal worth are decreased.

Frank has stated that perhaps the most critical factors of the therapeutic situation that heighten a patient's positive expectancies are
those that "convey the therapist's concern and competence."[23] Saunders[24] expresses a similar opinion when she writes that for her the
most important factor of all is the sort of atmosphere of welcome and
confidence engendered by the staff. Hinton[25] felt that in such a setting the subjective effects of drugs were enhanced. It strikes this
author that what both of these people are talking about is the importance of being with the patient. This is most succinctly presented in
a note from a patient after a particularly meaningful experience that
said, "To be, is to be with . . . that is to be."[26] Yet how to be free
to be with? In the midst of distress and in the presence of anguish
how does one intervene? How does one reach through the agony
of pain to build a bridge for a meaningful experience? These are indeed the questions to be concerned with and it is clear that there is
no single approach to such distress, rather engagements at a variety of levels with these questions guiding their direction.

## Helping Patients Live with Pain

Often, requests to see such patients come when others involved in
their treatment have come to the end of *their* resources; when they
themselves need to be reached in terms of their own feelings of helplessness. It is not uncommon to find that at this point meaningful
communication with the suffering patient has decreased to where the

patient has become virtually isolated from those around him.[27] The patient's own feelings of hopelessness have been reinforced by the withdrawal of those charged with his care. It would seem that if one can make a situation that appears to be serious and desperate no longer desperate and much less serious, then one moves in the direction of enhancing feelings of self-mastery.[28] Coleman,[29] in speaking of "particularly frustrating and unyielding therapeutic problems," suggests that special forms of intervention may serve in such a situation. His approach is one that suggests that humor in the form of warm banter may be a most significant form of affectionate interchange. The attitude within which banter is employed for him has a "highly personal, mothering implication,"[30] promoting the patient's feelings of being accepted, cared for, and loved. It fulfills his criteria of a therapeutic relationship that says, "I support you, I care about you. . . . I am strong enough to stand against your pressures, I keep you within bounds."[31] In this sense, then, the therapist echoes the patient's complaint with amiable exaggeration . . . with a "touch of friendly chaffing which turns the crown of thorns into the corn of clowns."[32] Once the overwhelming aspects of suffering have been penetrated, the patient found behind the veil of pain, then the continuing presence of the therapist becomes effective in the empathic sharing (and blunting) of terror and fright.[33] The use of banter in such intervention may occur at both verbal and nonverbal levels. Illustrations of such an approach are presented below.

A fifty-two-year-old mother with husband and family available was admitted to a continuing care hospital after major surgical procedures could no longer be effective in the care of her terminal cancer. She had been told by her physician that she had only weeks to live. The reason for her referral was that she had (1) stopped eating, refusing the milk shakes, etc., (2) stopped talking, turning away from nursing staff and family, and (3) appeared depressed! In reviewing her personal history, it was clearly evident that she had been a strong, active, and independent woman who indeed had directed her course of life; here it appeared as though she had become convinced she could no longer play any role in what was happening to her. It was interesting to note that earlier she had indicated her desire for last rites and visits from her family; under the present circumstances these had been most difficult and had been suspended. According to the most recent medical statement, she was not confused and was of clear mind. The author approached her at bedside with the statement that he was there to see her. The patient stared, then began to turn her head away. At this point, the following verbal interchange took place:

THERAPIST: I understand you've stopped eating.
PATIENT: (No response except what appeared to be an increase in her visual attending.)

THERAPIST:   You know, if you don't eat, you're going to die.
PATIENT:     (With a broad smile.) Well, that's the strangest thing
             anyone has ever told me.
THERAPIST:   Yes, that's what I'm here to talk with you about.

The ludicrous statement that she would die if she didn't eat, in the presence of her situation, enabled her to smile for the first time about something. A good thirty-five minutes was spent talking about her feelings of loneliness and pain and about some of the things she wanted to do before she died. This patient was visited by the author three times in the following week during which she began to eat and asked for and saw her priest as well as her family. The day before she died she was still engaged in sharing with him the things she wanted to do.

A second example illustrates the use of nonverbal banter as a means of intervention in stress. The patient was a fifty-eight-year-old married male whose stroke had left him partially paralyzed and bedbound. The referral was a request to assist in controlling this patient's continual crying. It was clear that the staff members were coming close to being unable to tolerate this man's distress as his crying seemed to continue without interruption. The physician in charge was reluctant to sedate more heavily and did feel the prognosis for limited recovery was good. Until his stroke, this patient had been viewed as the rock of Gibraltar to his family and in his community; now he could only cry! Seeing the patient in a private room, the author introduced himself, whereupon the patient burst into what seemed to be overwhelming, uncontrollable crying. The author sat for a few moments, then handed him a large Turkish bath towel; the patient suddenly stopped crying, started to laugh intermixed with tears, and asked, "What's this for, doc?" The author's comment that it looked as though he needed something that big to handle his flood of tears seemed to evoke further smiling and his discussing how it felt to be helpless, etc. When the patient left the room, he took the towel with him. Over a period of several weeks there were other meetings; he made jokes about the towel and began to become more interested in moving to a wheelchair and showed concern for the physical therapy program. He left the hospital to live with his family, but the week before leaving, he wheeled into the author's office, handed back the towel, and said, "I don't think I need this any more."

Saunders[34] has suggested that if pain and suffering are shared, they need not be desperate or even too solemn; joking to her is not at all inappropriate at times. To laugh at oneself, to take distance, to find oneself again, to experience the emergence of feelings of mastery may be the effect of humor.[35] In the use of banter, as illustrated here, it is felt that we may be of assistance in helping the patient clarify his ambivalence in reaching out for help; accept dependency needs without stifling his self-esteem. If we are to enhance the endurance of pain, we must provide means by which the patient may live in its presence.

## Notes

1. T. Szasz, "Language and Pain," in *American Handbook of Psychiatry*, ed. S. Arieti (New York: Basic Books, Inc., Publishers, 1959).

2. G. H. Bishop, "Anatomical, Physiological, and Psychological Factors in Sensation of Pain," in *Progress in Neurobiology*, vol. V, *Neural Physiopathology*, ed. R. G. Grennel (New York: Paul B. Hoeber, Inc., 1962). And H. Pieron, "Nervous Pathways of Cutaneous Pains," *Science* 129 (1959): 1547.

3. F. R. Ervin and V. H. Mark, "Stereotactic Thalamotomy in the Human. II. Physiological Observations on the Human Thalamus," *Archives of Neurology* 3 (1960): 368. See also V. H. Mark, F. R. Ervin, and P. I. Yakovlev, "The Treatment of Pain by Stereotaxic Methods," *Confinia Neurologica* 22 (1962): 238.

4. G. A. McMurray, "Experimental Study of a Case of Insensitivity to Pain," *Archives of Neurology and Psychiatry* 64 (1950): 650.

5. M. L. Simmel, "On Phantom Limbs," *Archives of Neurology and Psychiatry* 75 (1956): 637. "The Conditions of Occurence of Phantom Limbs," *Proceedings of the American Philosophical Society* 102 (1958): 492.

6. T. X. Barber, "Toward a Theory of Pain: Relief of Chronic Pain by Prefrontal Leucotomy, Opiates, Placebos, and Hypnosis," *Psychological Bulletin* 56 (1959): 430.

7. L. Lasagna, F. Mosteller, J. von Felsinger, and H. K. Beecher, "A Study of the Placebo Response," *American Journal of Medicine* 16 (1954): 770.

8. R. Melzack and P. D. Wall, "Pain Mechanisms: A New Theory," *Science* 150 (1965): 971.

9. R. Melzack and T. H. Scott, "The Effects of Early Experience on the Response to Pain," *Journal of Comparative and Physiological Psychology* 50 (1957): 155.

10. R. A. Sternbach, *Pain: A Psychophysical Analysis* (New York: Academic Press, Inc., 1968).

11. F. J. Ostenasek, "Prefrontal Lobotomy for the Relief of Intractable Pain," *Johns Hopkins Hospital Bulletin* 83 (1968): 229.

12. Sternbach, *Pain*.

13. C. Saunders, Lecture presented at Yale University Medical School, New Haven, Conn., October 1970.

14. R. Leriche, *The Surgery of Pain*, ed. and trans. A. Young (Baltimore: The Williams & Wilkins Company, 1939).

15. C. Saunders, "The Moment of Truth," in *Death and Dying,* ed. L. Pearson (Cleveland, Ohio: Case Western Reserve University Press, 1969).

16. Sternbach, *Pain.*

17. D. Cappon, "The Dying," *Psychiatric Quarterly* 33 (1959): 466; K. A. Chandler, "Three Processes of Dying and Their Behavioral Effects," *Journal of Consulting Psychology* 29 (1965): 296; L. LeShan, "Psychotherapy and the Dying Patient," in *Death and Dying,* ed. L. Pearson (Cleveland, Ohio: Case Western Reserve University Press, 1969); C. Saunders, "The Care of the Dying," *Guy's Hospital Gazette* 80 (1966): 136; Saunders, "Moment of Truth"; and Weisman

18. Saunders, "Moment of Truth."

19. J. V. Coleman, "Banter as Psychotherapeutic Intervention," *American Journal of Psychoanalysis* 22 (1962): 69.

20. Saunders, "Moment of Truth."

21. I. L. Janis, Psychological Stress (New York: John Wiley & Sons, Inc., 1958).

22. K. A. Chandler, "Continuing and Discontinuing Care" (Paper presented at the International Conference of Social Science and Medicine, Aberdeen, Scotland, 1970).

23. J. Frank, "The Influence of Patients' and Therapists' Expectations on the Outcome of Psychotherapy," *British Journal of Medical Psychology* 41 (1968): 349.

24. C. Saunders, "The Need for Institutional Care for the Patient with Advanced Cancer," *Anniversary Volume, Cancer Institute,* Madras, 1964.

25. Hinton

26. Chandler, "Continuing and Discontinuing Care."

27. A. Verwoerdt, "Communication with the Fatally Ill," *Journal of the Southern Medical Association* 57 (1964): 787.

28. Coleman, "Banter as Psychotherapeutic Intervention."

29. Ibid.

30. Ibid.

31. J. V. Coleman, "Aims and Conduct of Psychotherapy," *Archives of General Psychiatry* 18 (1968): 1.

32. Coleman, "Banter as Psychotherapeutic Intervention."

33. Chandler, "Three Precesses of Dying and Their Behavioral Effects."

34. Saunders, "Need for Institutional Care for Patient with Advanced Cancer."

35. S. Freud, "Humor," Vol. XXI, The Standard Edition (London: The Hogarth Press, Ltd., 1927).

# PART III

# *MINISTRY TO THE BEREAVED*

*More than any other group, clergy have opportunities to minister to persons in bereavement. Even families having little or no connection with a faith group will frequently welcome a minister's help with funeral and burial arrangements. At such times sensitive ministers can help with much more than the funeral; they can facilitate the first stages of the grief process. The essential skills required of the minister, intervening in the lives of bereaved congregants or strangers, are the willingness and the ability to listen and to encourage the expression of feelings, no matter how painful. Important, if often neglected, opportunities for ministry continue beyond the burial. It is appropriate for the minister to take the initiative to follow up with bereaved families and friends in the weeks, months, and even years following a funeral.*

*When he knows what emotional events to expect in bereavement and what helps a person complete the process of grief, the pastor will be more at ease in his own role as well as more responsive to the changing needs of the bereaved. Chapter 14 describes the elements in healthy grief and suggests that they are part of optimum personal development for everyone. In the following chapter this theme is expanded, and bereavement is described as a normal developmental stage, with differentiations between normal and pathological mourning.*

*It is essential to complete the grief process, because left incomplete, it will inhibit an individual's personal growth and may cause pathological reactions in future times of stress. The apparent return to "normal" of a distressed survivor does not always indicate that the necessary "grief work" has been done. The incompleted task can be unconsciously transformed* into a myriad of other forms of distress from physical illness to unhappy personal relationships. In Chapter 16 a pastoral counselor explores the significance of grief work in family life, illustrating how unresolved grief can be a source of family and marital conflict many years after an experience of loss. He underscores the importance of therapeutic mourning in the prevention of some forms of family stress.

The clergyman's faith community and professional role are important resources for his ministry to the bereaved as illustrated in Chapters 17, 18, and 19 by a parish priest, a rabbi, and a hospital chaplain.

In Chapter 20 a pediatrician writes of the special dimensions of bereavement when children die and when young children lose parents.

The grief following divorce, which parallels the emotional process following death, has been given far less than its share of sympathetic attention. The final chapter in this section tries to rectify that inequity.

To love is to risk loss. Learning not just to cope with loss, but to experience it fully is a task for all of us. To assist that growth through pain and sorrow is what a ministry to the bereaved is all about.

# 14

## The Cup of Mithridates
## — WILLIAM L. NUTE, JR.

For myself, bereavement is more to be feared than death.

It would be pointless to attempt a logical defense of this assertion or to claim that it is true of everyone or will always be true of me. It is simply a rooted feeling, persisting through a long period of time and much reflection.

Death is final and a certainty; its permanence and certainty give a sense of security. Bereavement goes on having to be endured.

And since bereavement, being repeatable, is even more common than death, and must be survived, it is worth asking how people can better survive it. It is my suggestion that doing some of the work of grief in advance can help.

Lindemann[1] has indebted us all with his classical description of grief. He has spoken of the five signs of acute grief and also the three elements in the successful work of grief. These are emancipation from bondage to the deceased, readjustment to the environment from which the deceased is missing, and the formation of new relationships.

He then goes on to mention two obstacles to this work, which must be overcome. These are avoidance of the distress of grief and avoidance of the expression of true feeling. It would seem to me helpful, therefore, to rephrase these two in a positive form and add them to the characteristics of successful grief work.

That is to say, before he can begin to achieve an emancipation from the deceased, a readjustment to a bereaved environment, and the formation of new relationships, the bereaved has to face the fact of bereavement. Things are different. It's a new ball game. And it hurts. Indeed, as Volkart[2] has pointed out, role conflict may be a source of suffering and guilt which is especially distressing because of the extra inhibitions—over and above the inhibitions which our culture, or some subcultures, place upon the expression of feeling—which may be placed upon its acknowledgment, even to one's self. That is, whereas heavy social pressure undergirds the assumption that the bereaved has suffered loss, we shrink from recognition, at least openly, that the bereaved may have gained freedom from some very heavy burdens and is to be congratulated.

One has to face the pain. Failure or refusal to do this renders the other steps impossible. This is what is implied in referring to the *work* of grief: It *is* work; it has to be worked on; it is not an automatic process to which the bereaved can passively submit and let it happen.

And secondly, grief has to be permitted. But this permission is a positive act of letting go the tears, the sobs, the self-pity, the acknowledgment of weakness (insofar as any departure from stoic repression is defined as weakness). Just as one must directly face the pain, one must face the tears, one must look at oneself and say, I weep, I am someone who must weep, and does. Failure to do this is a denial of one's humanity, a rejection of a part of one's self, a self-mutilation, a semisuicide.

All this may labor the obvious, but I think it worth the effort to state these two conditions explicitly and in a positive sense rather than simply in terms of obstacles to be overcome.

## Anticipatory Grief Work

Reflection on my own experience has confirmed an impression that bereavement may be lived through best when some of the work of grief can be done, or rather begun, before bereavement has in fact occurred as a specific objective event. I remember facing, in anticipation, the loneliness, the loss of meaning to life, the question whether in fact life would be worth living, whether its normal strains would be endurable in the absence of the support which would no longer be there. The work of grief found its completion the more easily because of this preparation.

Yet in referring to the *objective*, specific event of bereavement I have intended to allude to a possible danger: one of the elements in grief work is emancipation from the deceased. Can this liberation be achieved, or even initiated, without by that very fact engendering some degree of *subjective* and premature death of the dying person? Kastenbaum[3] has discussed the phenomenon of "psychological death." Must anticipatory grief work put such an emotional distance between the dying person and the potentially bereaved as to deprive the dying of his own rights to support? Can the potentially bereaved person protect himself and enhance his own chances of surviving the still future event without generating a subjective process which injures the dying person? Obviously if this took place, it would not only be an injustice and injury to the dying, but by the same token a potential source of serious guilt feelings in the survivor. It would be as though one had saved one's self from drowning by climbing on the shoulders of someone else now dead.

In answer to this question it may be helpful to distinguish between acceptance and resignation. This is consistent with the emphasis in the foregoing on the *active* nature of grief work.

An attitude of resignation would be one in which, essentially, the bereaved says, "This bereavement is something which is happening *to* me, I can do nothing about it but let it happen." He dissociates himself from the event and from the experience. He is passive with respect to it. He admits of no mitigating aspects of it, expects none, seeks none.

An attitude of acceptance, on the other hand, would be one in which the bereaved person would say, "This bereavement is an event which I was or am powerless to prevent as an event, yet the influence upon me of this event is something which I *can* affect, the bereavement as experience is something in which I can take an active, even if not dominant, role. This experience, though it hurts me, can also enhance my life."

This alternative is crucial for the effect of anticipatory grief work upon the dying and upon the relationship between the dying and the prospectively bereaved. For if the process of emancipation, of readjustment, and of forming new relationships is one of affirmation, creation, and enhancement of potential, all without rejection of dying, it must surely provide a source from which strength may flow from the surviving person to the dying—strength, be it stressed, not for an unrealistic struggle to live but to accept death.

It should be underlined that in the description of grief work the concept of emancipation from bondage does not imply rejection. This is why emancipation becomes compatible both with the need of the dying not to be abandoned prematurely and of the survivor to be free of the guilt of having robbed the dying.

## Grief Following Bereavement

Is it justified to speak of anticipatory grief work as though it were a variation of the work of grief which follows bereavement? Are we really talking about the same process in variant forms or about two different processes which should not be confused by the use of similar terminology?

The answer to this will depend upon whether the same or similar processes take place with the same or similar outcomes. I believe that there is not an identity but a similarity and that we are justified in regarding these two experiences as variants of the same thing.

Certainly anticipation of an event which has not yet occurred but is expected to occur is different from recollection of an event which is already in the irrevocable past. (One thing, incidentally, about my own death which distinguishes it from all other future events concerning me is that it partakes of the same irrevocable certainty as all past events.) Anticipation of an (undesired) event must always include an element of fear; it is impossible to fear what has already happened and can never happen again. So this at least is one major difference.

Nor do I mean to suggest that all the work of grief can be done and completed before the actual death of the dying. Rather, a start can be made on this work, when death can be foreseen, before the finality of death has dealt a weakening and dispiriting blow. What cannot be completed, at most can only partially be begun, is readjustment to the environment from which the deceased is missing, so long as that person in fact is not missing. Indeed, in the period before death, the dying is likely (where death is anticipated) to be the most dominant element in the survivor's environment. One can prepare for that adjustment, but one cannot in other than an intellectual sense more than begin to accomplish it.

## Further Applications of Anticipatory Grief

If the foregoing suggestions are persuasive, it follows that the helping professions, or for that matter helping individuals, can deliberately direct their efforts toward encouraging and facilitating anticipatory grief when circumstances permit, that is, depending on the relationship.

But it follows further, from the observation made earlier that bereavement is a burden which nearly everyone must face and from the obvious fact that not all bereavement can be foreseen, that something like anticipatory grief work may well be an appropriate task for all of us. There is something to be said for Mithridates in Housman's poem:

> There was a king reigned in the East:
> There, when kings will sit to feast,
> They get their fill before they think
> With poisoned meat and poisoned drink.
> He gathered all that springs to birth
> From the many-venomed earth;
> First a little, thence to more,
> He sampled all her killing store;
> And easy, smiling, seasoned sound,
> Sate the king when healths went round.
> They put arsenic in his meat
> And stared aghast to watch him eat;

They poured strychnine in his cup
And shook to see him drink it up:
They shook, they stared as white's their shirt:
Them it was their poison hurt.
—I tell the tale that I heard told.
Mithridates, he died old.[4]

Let us now take another look at the elements of the work of grief. To Lindemann's three elements I have presumed to suggest the addition of three more:

1. Facing the pain
2. Permitting emotional expression
3. Emancipation from bondage to the other
4. Readjustment to altered environment
5. Formation of new relationships
6. Acceptance

As one looks at this list, what happens if one eliminates all reference to death and dying? One has a list of processes, attitudes, or habits which are life-enhancing in any case, quite apart from bereavement. It may be advisable to put the work of grief into the context not of something necessary for some people and under special circumstances but as part of the mainstream of good mental hygiene.

## Notes

1. Erich Lindemann, "Symptomatology and Management of Acute Grief," *American Journal of Psychiatry* 101 (1944): 141–148.

2. Edmund H. Volkart, "Bereavement and Mental Health," in *Explorations in Social Psychiatry* (New York: Basic Books Inc., Publishers, 1957), pp. 381–404.

3. Robert Kastenbaum, "Psychological Death," in *Death and Dying*, ed. Leonard Pearson. (Cleveland, Ohio: Case Western Reserve University Press, 1969).

4. A. E. Housman, *A Shropshire Lad* (1896).

# 15

## Bereavement, an Opportunity for Emotional Growth

## — HARRY S. OLIN and GRACE B. OLIN

Mourning, the emotional response of an individual to the loss of a significant personal relationship, has been viewed traditionally as either a normal process or as a nidus for a pathological reaction. Freud[1] described the normal grief "work" of mourning, in which loving investments to the lost object were painfully detached. The pathological state of melancholia or clinical depression occurred when the "shadow of the [lost] object fell upon the ego. . . ."

Although the literature on normal bereavement and clinical depression is voluminous, bereavement as a normal developmental stage of adult life has not received much attention. Even Erickson's eighth stage of man, "Ego Integrity vs. Despair,"[2] does not emphasize bereavement as a means to gain a perspective on life in which there can be a "comradeship with the ordering ways of distant times and different pursuits. . . ." Mourning would seem to be one of the tasks of this age and stage, or even of an earlier one. Beginning in the third decade and continuing into the next several decades of a person's life, most adults suffer the loss of one or both parents. Rochlin[3] demonstrated that the experience of loss served as "engines of change" in activating restitutive processes. What Rochlin pointed out for losses in general this chapter attempts to elaborate specifically for bereavement.

Development is a process of maturation. The purpose of this chapter is to describe the potential emotional development of the adult, son or daughter, who loved a parent and mourns his loss. The areas of adult emotional development are manifold, but for our purpose the development of two attitudes have been selected: the attitudes toward *death* and *responsibility*. The earlier, more primitive, childish attitudes are compared with the more mature, adult attitudes. It is our belief that bereavement can be a powerful force enhancing maturation.

Obviously, all loss and bereavement do not contain the potential for

growth. Loss of one or both parents at an early age can have catastrophic consequences as tragically evidenced by young children who
have experienced early and prolonged emotional deprivation. Again,
our interest is the adult who loses a parent or parent substitute, and
then enters into a period of bereavement.

# Death

Although Freud stressed the difficulty in giving up anything and
that we cannot fully believe in our own death,[4] there is nonetheless a
clear difference between a child's notion of death and that of a mature
adult. The child's experience with death is obviously limited as is his
perspective of life. Death is unreal for the child. Despite the intensity
of life-death games in which selected toys of other child players "die,"
death is, for him, reversible, and a "dead" toy soldier or animal is
used actively in play moments later. Even the death of a loved pet
poignantly described in *Junior Miss*[5] may be forgotten as quickly as the
tears dry on the young girl's cheeks as she rushes to new activities.
Related to the child's notion of death is his notion of mortality. His
belief is seriously flawed, because he feels that his life will stretch on
endlessly and that he can fulfill all of his ambitions, if not immediately
then at some time in the hazy inexhaustible future.

The adult brings many of his childlike notions of death, with varying degrees of modification, with him into his adult life and his
"adult" unconscious. However, the reality of aging and actually experiencing the death of a parent begins to alter ideas of unreal, reversible
death. Elliott Jacques,[6] a thirty-six-year-old analysand, eloquently expressed this developmental change. "Up till now" he said, "life has
seemed an endless upward slope, with nothing but the distant hori-
zon in view. Now suddenly I seem to have reached the crest of the
hill, and there stretching ahead is the downward slope with the end
of the road in sight—far enough away it's true—but there is death
observably present at the end."

The inevitability of personal death becomes clearer during bereavement as illustrated in another example. A forty-year-old lawyer's father, whom he had loved deeply, died. The son revisited the gravesite
three months after the funeral, and felt with fresh awareness that he,
too, in time would die. His life-span was viewed in a perspective
never before seen so clearly. The living presence of the father had
protected the son from immediate realization of his own future death.
When the father died, the son's view of his own grave was unob-
structed. This experience helped to define his life and made it more
precious. The love for his wife, children, and surviving mother deepened at that moment. Diminished were the inflated and unrealistic
hopes he had held for his children, that they would accomplish what

had eluded him. Rather he saw them as individuals with their own transient lives to lead. The certainty of future death freed him from needing to accomplish everything. He felt instead a sense of relief at limiting himself to what he wanted and what was possible.

The original relationships of the young child are largely in his family. A favorable normal growth sign of latency occurs when the child searches for outside relationships, and his horizons widen as the number of persons significant in his life increases. When as an adult, he mourns the loss of a person important to him, especially a parent, he is presented with an opportunity to have "a relationship with a dead person."[7] By accepting this opportunity, that is, by relating now to the living and the dead, he has realized his potential for developing relationships. He has matured through his bereavement. Semrad[8] has characterized the mind as a house with many rooms. Significant persons live in this house, in their own rooms, as it were. When one of these persons dies, the individual has the option of closing the door and never again entering or of leaving the door ajar. If he chooses the latter, then he is free to wander about in his house feeling the appropriate sadness when in the dead person's room. To be able to wander freely in one's "house" is a step toward increased maturation.

One form of pathological bereavement occurs when the mourner identifies in whole or part with the deceased in order to keep the relationship intact and thus avoid the full emotional impact of his loss. In contrast, the normal survivor identifies with the dead and at the same time feels his loss. His identification serves as a reminder that life is a natural process with a beginning, middle, and end. His ending is more clearly visualized and thus his view of life becomes more realistic and complete; his mature relationships include the living and the dead.

## Responsibility

Who is accountable for the individual's life? The child repeatedly disowns responsibility for himself, while others are blamed for unhappy events befalling him. At times, his brave words or boisterous demands may seem responsible, but the child is not accountable to himself in the same way that an adult is. In answer to the question of who is running the individuals' life, the individual can either accept or avoid his responsibility. The transition from having little awareness and then the acceptance of owning up to the responsibility of directing one's life is a gradual process.

Bereavement can enhance this process. For example, an eighteen-year-old girl became aware of the gravity of her father's illness which made working and supporting his family no longer possible. In order to remain in college, as she and her family wished, she applied for and received scholarships, and in addition, worked after school. She surprised herself at her capability and self-sufficiency. When her father became bedridden, he entered a newspaper contest in the hope he would win a prize to supplement the shrunken family income. His daughter, unbeknown to her father, pleaded with the newspaper puzzle editor to publish her father's name as a winner and offered to supply the prize money from her own savings. The editor refused, though he understood the daughter's effort to bolster her ill father's self-esteem. He died when she was twenty. Some years later in reflecting on her action, she realized she had changed places with her parent by caring for him. She became the adult and he the child. Secondly, she realized that she had become her own parent by caring for herself. Her maturing in self-sufficiency developed from her father's terminal illness and death.

## Conclusions

Although it is difficult for children and adults to conceive of their own death, and the wish for immortality may be universal, there are distinct differences between how children and adults think and feel about death. For the mourning adult, a process of maturation can take place in which more realistic attitudes are acquired. What this chapter emphasizes is the potential developmental features in the state of bereavement which go beyond the immediate adjustment to a personal loss.

## Notes

1. Sigmund Freud, "Mourning and Melancholia," in Collected Papers, vol. 4, (London: The Hogarth Press, Ltd., 1924–1950), pp. 152–170.

2. Erik H. Erikson, Childhood and Society, 2d ed. (New York: W. W. Norton & Company, Inc., 1963), Chap. 7, p. 266.

3. Gregory Rochlin, Grief and Discontents: The Forces of Change (Boston: Little, Brown and Company, 1965), Chap. 4, pp. 121–164; Chap. 5, pp. 165–223.

4. Sigmund Freud, "The Relation of the Poet to Day Dreaming," in Collected Papers, vol. 4, (London: The Hogarth Press, Ltd., 1924–1950), pp. 172–183.

5. Sally Benson, Junior Miss (Garden City, N.Y.: Doubleday & Company, Inc., 1941), Chap. 2, pp. 27–44.

6. Elliott Jacques, "Death and the Mid Life Crisis," International Journal of Psychoanalysis 46 (1965): 502–514.

7. Avery D. Weisman, Personal communication (1970).

8. Elvin V. Semrad, Personal communication (1968).

# 16

# Mourning, Family Dynamics, and Pastoral Care
## — RICHARD G. BRUEHL

Traditionally, following an individual approach to personality rather than an interpersonal one, studies of grief processes in both the psychological and pastoral literature have focused on the person as a self-contained unit and have tended to ignore the larger ramifications of "grief work" in family life. While much of value has come from the individual approach, best exemplified in psychoanalytically oriented studies, workers in the various helping fields have become increasingly interested in broader relational concerns and implications of individual reactions to loss.

For pastors, who, according to various studies,[1] are confronted most often with family and marital problems, a trend toward studying interpersonal as well as intrapersonal grief processes would be especially beneficial. In the author's clinical experience, he has been increasingly impressed with the presence of long-range "fallout" from unresolved grief processes which lead more or less directly to marital and family conflict. Repeatedly one finds persons coming for marital and family pastoral counseling who are experiencing difficulty in working through affectively either a specific loss of relationship or an environmental event which has called forth previously unresolved mourning (e.g., as a child begins to draw away from the family circle). We have been persuaded that the behavioral and emotional impact of loss cannot be viewed solely as an individual phenomenon but must be seen also in the context of relationships of significance.

In this chapter the author explores the problem of the role of loss and mourning in marital and family conflict, offering a theoretical basis for viewing the problem, case examples which illustrate it, and some conclusions on the implications of this knowledge for pastoral care and counseling.

## Theoretical Background

As a shorthand way of introducing some important theoretical considerations involved in the problem of the relation of mourning to marital and family dynamics, several hypotheses are offered:

1. The seemingly universal feelings associated with grief (separation anxiety, hostility, and guilt) will, in one way or another, be expressed.[2] Though specific ways of dealing with these irrational feelings may vary from culture to culture, they (the feelings) must have their day. In our culture the major choices for expression seem to be "working through" (often in the context of a positive relationship to religious ritual and symbol), physical-symptom formation (e.g., many of the classical psychosomatic illnesses), and "acting out" of feelings and defenses in relationships.

2. With regard to the last alternative for dealing with feeling derivative of mourning (acting out), family and marital relationships, because of their intensity and significance, offer a primary arena for working out one's feelings regarding recent or old losses.

3. Marital and family conflict, often presented to the clergyman, may mask unresolved mourning processes in one or more family members.

4. Recognition by the clergyman of the pervasive role of mourning processes in human relationships provides him with a useful key in making significant preventive and ameliorative interventions in family and marital conflicts which root in difficulties in affective mourning.

David Switzer has identified the source of the reaction pattern sometimes ambiguously described as "grief" as separation anxiety.[3] Perhaps the single most devastating threat to human existence, reminiscent of the earliest traumatic experience of infancy, separation anxiety translates into the fear of the dissolution of the self in relationship.[4] If separation anxiety is the fundamental affect stimulated by the loss of significant relationship, the feelings of hostility and guilt follow closely behind at a more superficial level, appearing as defensive reactions whose functions are to try, at all cost, to ward off the anxiety of self-loss. Hostility and guilt seem to be the most pervasive affects which may contribute to the acting out of grief in interpersonal relationships.

In addition to these general psychodynamic formulations, there is some evidence that affective mourning plays a significant role in marital and family conflict as well as in human life in general. Paul and Grasser[5] found in a study of fifty families of schizophrenics and twenty-five families of hospitalized psychoneurotic patients that the common element in the families of these patients despite varying ethnic origins, religious affiliations, and socioeconomic status, was the "variable patterns of maladjustive responses to object loss."[6] The authors further state:

> Although the original losses may have occured as much as 50 years ago the response to them exercised a lingering effect on the present. Such loses were usually suffered by one or the other parent often before the birth of the patient. Affects and attitudes toward the lost person remained essentially unchanged and recent losses evoked similar reaction patterns. The current style of family life appeared permeated with varying degrees of denial or "warding off" of losses and disappointments. Major changes in family homeostasis, such as those which might result in separation or independence of its members, were resisted.[7]

In these families dominated by fixations upon past losses the "refusal to mourn"[8] created a disruptive family situation and resulted in symptomatic behavior in one or more family members.

As a therapy for the families of their patients, Grasser and Paul introduced the technique of "operational mourning," a directed inquiry into the losses and mourning reactions of the family members, especially the parents. Though these investigators experienced formidable resistance in the families of schizophrenics, therapeutically induced mourning was by and large successful in breaking relational impasses and in fostering more healthy familial patterns and thus the healing of the "identified patient."

Paul[9] has also focused on the important role of shared mourning in the conjoint marital therapy context. He describes emotional responses to losses by death and desertion as "critical factors" in the etiology of marital impasses. Further, he feels the ability to share affectively previously encapsulated responses to loss is a primary factor in increasing empathy between the couple and in breaking up "symbiotic fixity" in role relationships.

Hilgard, Newman, and Frish[10] sampled both hospitalized psychiatric patients and a large population of "normals" to determine the traumatic effect of the loss of a parent upon children. Their results indicate that the degree of trauma to the child upon the death of one parent is related to the "separation tolerance" of the pre-loss family. "Separation tolerance," a somewhat global term, points to the ability of the surviving parent to grieve effectively and to avoid undue dependency upon the children in working out his mourning. In short, although the authors do not state this directly, it seems justifiable to conclude that parental loss will in large measure be traumatic to the child to the degree that mourning is not completed successfully by the remaining parent.

In an interesting case study from the standpoint of the relationship between grief and family conflict, Sherman[11] recorded the details of the case of a young middle-class man, Mr. B., who sought help for a variety of phobic responses and debilitating anxiety about his work. As it turned out, his wife had recently been having an extramarital affair, which was the immediate occasion for his anxiety attacks. Sherman asked himself the all-important question "Why at this time?" His further study of the case revealed that Mrs. B.'s "acting out" occurred shortly after her mother's death. Mrs. B., Sherman tells us, had been overly involved emotionally in a "close relationship with a morally rigid, essentially impersonal mother." Though identified significantly with her father's "sportiness," Mrs. B "played dead" through adolescence and married a man whose personality was quite similar to her mother's. Mrs. B. had for eight years, in return for her husband's assistance in helping her maintain control of her impulsivity, shored up her husband's defenses against anxiety. When Mrs. B.'s mother died, she reacted by refusing to maintain the complementarity of the marital relationship and came alive to her own needs. She experienced her reaction to loss as liberation from mother's domination and, we seem justified in assuming, began expressing long-repressed anger toward her mother. In this case again the symptom of mourning in reaction to Mrs. B.'s mother's death marked the beginning of a severe family crisis focusing on the interface between Mrs. B.'s internal developmental struggles and her relation to her husband and family.

These data together with our clinical experience indicate that many times when the pastoral counselor is presented with a marital or family problem he will do well to take seriously the possible relationship between incomplete mourning resulting from loss as a component of the conflict. The question "Why at this time?" is nearly always a fruitful one and not infrequently leads one more or less directly to a loss (real or perceived) of a significant person.

## Clinical Investigation

It would appear profitable at this point to explore by way of clinical pastoral material some of the ways in which what has been discussed somewhat theoretically meets one in "real life." Though I find it impossible to categorize the wide variety of forms in which one might meet a problem in mourning in marital and family conflict, I will present some illustrations from my practice as a pastoral counselor which reflect the type of case that first called my attention to the role of grief in family conflict. The examples are divergent enough to give the reader a flavor of the subtle ways in which family symptoms may mask unresolved affective mourning and to provide a further base from which to draw some tentative conclusions.

As indicated, at this point one is not prepared to point to any particular family symptoms which might be indicative of unresolved grief in family conflict. However, in my experience, the sudden onset of family symptoms (and perhaps the sudden remission of conflict[12]) can often be traced to a significant loss by death, abandonment, or normal developmental separations which tend to reactivate unresolved separation problems and upset the family "balance." While many enduring personality problems may also have their roots in unresolved mourning, the precipitating events may be much more difficult to recover and, within the limits of most short-term pastoral counseling, beyond reach at an affective level.

Each of the following cases is marked by a rather sudden onset following a definable loss and were presented to the pastoral counselor as a family or marital problem.

> CASE 1: Mr. and Mrs. Alford sought pastoral counseling for a marital problem after a twelve-year marriage. Mr. Alford, for the duration of his marriage had been a "devoted family and community man." Seemingly without warning to his wife he asked her for a divorce. In a conjoint interview both he and his wife were unable to explain this reversal except for Mr. Alford's statement, "I just don't love her anymore." Further discussion revealed that Mr. Alford, now thirty-seven years of age, had remained subservient to a very dominant and successful father. Following his training he had accepted a position in his father's bank and submitted to his father's plan to make him wealthy and successful. Suddenly his father died of a massive coronary. His death signaled a release for Mr. Alford of his long-suppressed adolescent problems. He began to act out his sexual and aggressive feelings in a way designed to proclaim to his dead father, "I am a man after-all." Mr. Alford began, in what appeared to the counselor as a rather compulsive manner, divesting himself as his "past" and asserting his "new self," as he called it. Clearly what Mr. and Mrs. Alford stubbornly clung to as a "marital problem," and indeed it was, took root in the complex relationship between the father and his son and the particular form of the son's grief reaction to his father's death.

In this case, Mr. Alford had outwardly submitted to his father's authority by patterning his life in a way he believed would conform to his father's expectations. Mr. Alford's grief response included the emergence of latent aggressive trends bordering on sociopathy. While outwardly he "sang for his father," inwardly he suppressed deep hatred and love toward him and after his death suddenly "lost all feeling" for all those close to him.

> CASE 2: Mr. and Mrs. Brown present a similar problem with a much different result. They sought help from a pastoral counseling specialist at the suggestion of their pastor who described them as a couple with serious marital problems nearing the stage of divorce. While this assessment proved quite correct the peculiar dynamics of the relationship led directly to Mrs. Brown's unresolved grief over her father. Mrs. Brown

initially complained of a twenty-two-year history of quasi-alcoholism in her husband and the unhappy relationship they had maintained. Mr. Brown confirmed their unhappiness. He was mystified, however, by his wife's divorce suit at this particular time because he had "reformed" a little over a year ago and, as both agreed, had perhaps the best months of their entire marriage during this period.

Almost incidentally Mrs. Brown mentioned that her father died several months ago and that her husband did not understand her needs during the crisis. Mr. Brown described a long history of feelings of insecurity in relation to his wife's family and agreed that he had not been as sensitive as he might have been. The counselor was impressed during the interview with Mrs. Brown's lack of emotion in face of the divorce and in the wake of her father's death. She had not shared her grief with anyone and seemed unable to "let it in," preferring to deal with her feelings by rationalizations such as, "He had a good life," and "Though we had a bad relationship when I was young, he tried to make up for it in later years," and also by outright denial, "I don't feel much of anything about him." The counselor remarked at one point that this was surprising.

In the next several interviews the counselor moved further into her irrational feelings of guilt, hostility, and longing for her father. She rehearsed her regrets over a lack of a significant early relationship and stated with feeling finally that she was going to miss him a great deal. For the first time since her father's death, Mrs. Brown cried with her husband. He wept silently as well.

In the following interview Mr. and Mrs. Brown announced that they felt more hopeful about their relationship. Mrs. Brown invited her husband to move back home and allowed him to "come back into her life" emotionally. Her ability to risk living through her mourning allowed Mrs. Brown the freedom not to *have to* give up both the men in her life at once. A six-month follow-up revealed that they were doing well and in some ways enjoying life more than ever before.

In contrast to the Alfords, the Browns' affective mourning processes were more available. What began for them as a crisis of acting out their grief was resolved in their willingness to submit to their feelings and to be reunited on an affective level.

CASE 3: The Cones, a family consisting of mother (age forty-five), son (age sixteen), and daughter (age twenty), presented John, the sixteen-year-old boy, as the family "problem" or "patient." Whereas he had always been a "cooperative docile person," he had become recently almost incorrigible in school and at home. A review of the family history indicated that Mr. Cone, described by has wife as a "diagnosed paranoid schizophrenic," had asserted his "masculinity" through rigid, hostile control of John's behavior. Upon his unexpected death, a year ago, Mrs. Cone had felt relief.

At an emotional level Mrs. Cone was terrified of her husband and had enslaved herself to him. Now she cannot believe that she put up with all that she did during their many years of marriage. John reacted to his father's death by trying to shake off the restrictions his father had placed upon him.

Mrs. Cone, since her husband's death, had adopted a new mission in life—to mold her son, in a way that utterly failed with her husband, into an "acceptable, worthwhile person." She and her daughter formed a coalition to undermine the son's integrity, a strategy which invites his further delinquent behavior. Mrs. Cone identifies her son with her husband unconsciously and tells him in effect, "All men are no good in my book, and I'm sure you will prove me right. But I can work on you, because you are younger whereas your father was too big for me." The mother transferred her conflicting needs for dependency and control and her feelings of anger toward her husband to her son to deal with her irrational anxiety over the loss of her husband about whom she had no good word to say. While the casual observer would classify the Cones' marriage as quite destructive, it obviously made emotional sense in terms of their interlocking needs, and its abrupt termination created a state of intense disequilibrium against which the Cones' most available resources were mobilized.

The family problem in the Cones' case masked rather complex grief reactions. They chose to deal with these feelings by firming up existing family alliances and by exerting increasingly intense controls in order to forestall the emotional issue. Interestingly Mrs. Cone spoke of her religious faith as being a great support to her throughout the years and also in the present crisis but saw no connection between the Christian values of concern for persons above all else and her relation to her son. He had become for her a nonperson.

In reviewing my cases of the past two years I find numerous instances in which ineffective mourning has resulted in or exacerbated moderate to intense family or marital conflict. The pattern seems remarkably similar: a loss is experienced by one or more members of the family who are either unaware of the meaning of their anger, guilt, and anxiety or more or less consciously choose not to name the emotional difficulty. Instead, in a way which makes sense within his particular frame of reference, the individual begins to act out the irrational feelings of separation anxiety and their derivatives, hostility and guilt, upon those with whom he is most intimate. Invariably a positive result in counseling has involved newly shared affective mourning of whatever losses were most significant to the people involved. Whether the loss involves the death of a loved family member, close friend, a changing pattern of life, the movement of a child from the home, there is much to be mourned and the affects associated with mourning will have their day.

In working on this problem, the Biblical dictum "Blessed are those who mourn, for they shall be comforted" (Matt.5:4) has taken on a new meaning. While one may tend to limit the process of mourning only to obvious external loss of relationship, it appears that these processes are intrinsic to all of human existence. The fact that this dimension of life is so persistently ignored by workers in the field is a tribute to our collective resistances to seeing and experiencing our losses be they "real" or symbolic. It appears to be easier to face unacceptable sexual and hostile feelings than to mourn those relationships which have become idolatrous (fixations) for us and which encapsulate the power of the human personality. What we so often meet as pathological in individuals and families are not mourning processes per se but rather the persistent defensive avoidance of the natural process of grief over giving up what has been. Theologically, mourning is the continuing, necessary, painful, emotional, and personal process of crucifixion and humiliation that must precede every new growth in the power of the self. Without mourning in intimate relationships there is no life and no final blessing. The way of life, as one perceives it in his practice as a pastoral counselor, is the way of mourning.

## Implications for Pastoral Care

Though the preceding presentation of theoretical and clinical material is by no means exhaustive, reasonable confidence in the accuracy of these observations encourages one to draw out some of their possible implications for pastoral care and counseling. In my experience the greatest gap in the pastoral care of the bereaved person comes in the failure to follow up on the longer-range impact of loss. In the period of dramatic personal reactions and public exposure pastors typically do their job. But what of the period, often years afterward, in which losses are being integrated and affective mourning accomplished? There is a real temptation in the face of overloaded schedules to condense one's pastoral care (be it lay or professional) into the immediate crisis situation and to believe that in the quiet withdrawal which often follows loss that mourning has been accomplished. The clinical evidence presented here would indicate that family and marital symptoms may be one way in which persons "make noise" about their pain. Persons may speak loudly in the form of family or marital conflict about their own "pain" over losses which have never been resolved.

The parish minister, priest, and rabbi are in an especially good position to make efficient use of this observation. For they among all the professional "helpers" can not only observe but have access to persons and families over time. The sensitive clergyman may be able to make the diagnostic link up between grief and family or marital conflict rather rapidly, whereas the isolated specialist may spend months of painstaking work to get to the real issue. In his consultations for family and marital problems the pastor will want to inquire not only into the patterns of communication and role relationships which exist in the family but will want to become aware of the history of the conflict. When one uncovers a related experience of loss, it is sometimes possible to make a direct inquiry, to be a catalyst for the process of unresolved affective mourning.

Though one may expect rather strong resistance to the painful feelings associated with loss, such sharing of pain is often necessary to the restoration or discovery of the bonds of tender love. While the pastor will want to exercise his responsibility as a helping person so as not to violate the trust of those with whom he works, and while one will never be able to lead persons where they are not ready to go, one will often find that a gentle nudge into an area of pain will be accepted and utilized by persons for their benefit. As in every area of pastoral work, the pastor will feel comfortable with mourning processes in others to the degree that he has accepted these feelings within himself.

In addition to the personal relationships of pastoral care and counseling, the public areas of preaching and worship, to cite briefly and incompletely some other areas of pastoral work, offer possibilities for stimulating healthy mourning processes. How often one has observed in serving the Lord's Supper the quiet grief expressed at the chancel rail. Particularly important for many persons is the commemorative aspect of the Communion which symbolically brings the past into the present. (This dimension of experience may also account for the dramatic drop in attendance in many Protestant churches on the day of the celebration of Communion.) Though maudlin sentimentality in religious services is to be avoided, one might easily overlook the personal values which obtain in the worship experience. Much of the hostility of lay persons today to the neglect of personal dimensions of religious experience comes from the overly rational, action-oriented approach to religion taken by many educated clergymen which too often truncates the needful "regression in the service of the ego" which is facilitated by the total impact of religious symbol and practice. The reality of the emotional dimensions of the human self including inevitable reactions to loss and change can be taken into account by those planning worship experiences without falling into the trap of totally "subjective" worship.

Since all of us have been raised in a somewhat plastic culture, it cannot be expected that we clergymen are exempt from the influence of a culture which seems bent on affirming the permanence of the temporal and the unreality of ever-present experiences in human life. One such reality is the necessity of dealing with the pain of loss, be it person, function, or fantasy, and the forward movement of life toward new growth. It behooves us to reconsider the fundamental realities of human life and to see a large part of our pastoral responsibility as helping persons deal effectively and affectively with "all the changing scenes of life." There is always much to mourn—and much to rejoice. In our work with individuals and families we need always to consider that we deal with human beings in almost constant movement between these two poles. It may be that our incorporation of this truth may offer a significant clue to understanding and assisting persons experiencing the "dark nights of the soul" and the hell of separation in relationship.

# Notes

1. See G. Gurin, J. Veroff, and S. Feld, *Americans View Their Mental Health* (New York: Basic Books, Inc., Publishers, 1960). Also compare with M. Taggart, "A Review of Research in the Non-Pastoral Journals," *Journal of Pastoral Care*, vol. XXIV, no. 4, pp. 246–260.

2. See D. K. Switzer, *The Dynamics of Grief* (Nashville, Tenn: Abingdon Press, 1970), especially Chaps. 4 and 5.

3. *Ibid.*

4. F. Lake, *Clinical Theology* (London: Darton, Longman & Todd, 1966), stresses the critical role of separation anxiety in the developmental process. R. May, *The Meaning of Anxiety* (New York: Ronald Press, 1950) presents an existential approach to the study of human anxiety, stressing the component of the threat of loss of self and relationship in all anxiety and symptomatic efforts to ward it off.

5. N. Paul, and G. Grasser, "Operational Mourning and Its Role in Conjoint Family Therapy," *Community Mental Health Journal*, vol. 1, no. 4, pp. 339–345.

6. *Ibid.*, p. 340.

7. *Ibid.*, p. 341.

8. S. Kopp, "The Refusal to Mourn," *Voices*, vol. 5, no. 1, pp. 30–35. Kopp states: "To some extent each of us still lives in the darkness of his own unfinished past. The refusal to mourn the disappointments and losses of childhood, to bury them once and for all, condemns us to live in their shadows" (p. 30).

9. N. Paul, "The Role of Mourning and Empathy in Conjoint Marital Therapy," in *Family Therapy and Disturbed Families*, eds. G. Zuk and I. Borzormenyi-Nagy, (Palo Alto, Calif.: Science and Behavior Books, Inc., 1969), pp. 186–205.

10. J. Hilgard, M. Neuman, and F. Frish, "Strength of Adult Ego Following Childhood Bereavement," in *Death and Identity*, ed. R. Fulton (New York: John Wiley & Sons, Inc., 1965), pp. 259–271.

11. S. Sherman, "The Concept of the Family in Casework Theory," in *Exploring the Base for Family Therapy*, ed. N. Ackerman, pp. 22–24.

12. J. Friedman, and D. Zaris, "Paradoxical Response to the Death of a Spouse," *Diseases of the Nervous System*, vol. 25, no. 8 (1964), pp. 480–483.

# 17

## Consoling The Bereaved In The Weeks After The Funeral
### — WALTER DEBOLD

Sometimes the clergy are blamed for neglecting the mourners after a funeral is over. Whether the deceased person was young or old their passing leaves many pains of the heart that are not healed in a day. But are clergymen unmindful of this? Is it true that the clergy, like other people, hurry from the gravesite to other concerns of their own? Do they, too, overlook the opportunity to be a genuine neighbor to the sorrowing?

It may be unfair to generalize about any category of people in this regard, but let us look at the situation as objectively as we can.

When the clergy hear criticism of themselves they become defensive. That is hardly surprising; they are human. "Taken from among men," as the scriptures say, they can be expected to defend their own image. However, in the face of the charge that he fails in the role of consoler, the clergyman may hurry somewhat more quickly to his own defense. He is aware that he has a special duty, a high calling. And he is aware that society expects a great deal of him. If he cannot vanquish Death, his flock expects that he will, at least, face it with them. Beyond that, they look for such fortitude in the clergyman that he is expected to bear criticism with a much greater degree of humility and meekness than the next man. Nonetheless it ought not be surprising if he raises his verbal guns in his own defense if he is accused in an area so central to his vocation.

At any rate suppose that the charge is true, that the clergy do not "follow through" after the day of burial, that they appear to forget all too quickly the mourning of those left to live on. What might be some of the reasons that could account for this shortcoming? Listed below are some possible explanations of a minister's inadequacy in the role of consoler:

1. He or she is clumsy with words. . . .

2. The minister's parish is too large, and he or she is too busy. . . .
3. Moral support for the bereaved should come from the faith community as a whole. . . .
4. Some clergy have a lack of imagination or are simply thoughtless.
5. Some of the clerics are shy and hide behind the stereotyped liturgical roles concealing their inability to be simply "human."
6. Some ministers place too much confidence in ritualistic ministration, misunderstanding its purpose or its power.

The fact is that this last reason may be the most important one to reflect upon. It is no doubt true that most of the criticism directed toward the clergy under this heading may spring from modern man's passion for authenticity.

Whether it is a revolution or a revival that religion is going through today, it is beyond question that modern man has a great hunger for sincerity. Instinctively he senses that love of the divine requires, as a prior condition, love of what is human. Love of fellow men requires that we communicate with them using meaningful symbols. As a nation's currency requires that it be backed up by some precious metals so also must man's symbols be backed up with meaning in order to have any value. Man's symbols must be backed up with life, with heart, precisely because man lives by symbols. None of the burial rites that man devises for any religion are guaranteed to "make all things right." None of these ceremonies work automatically. There are broken hearts still among the mourners. There are losses unrestored. This tragic event stands between man and his hope of understanding God.

## Clumsiness in Condolence

Awkwardness about expressing sympathy is a common human failing. There are extraordinary moments in life, whether of joy or of sorrow, that call for appreciation by poets or artists. Most of us cannot do justice to those moments and so we are mutually tolerant over one another's fumbling efforts. We value any sincere gesture which communicates fellow-feeling. Religiosity or affected piety are distasteful, but any other humble gesture is redeemed if it incorporates sincerity. And funerals seem to elicit sincerity. Death is a leveler; each of us is touched by its mystery. Everyone is humbled in the face of that mystery. There is something in the atmosphere that brings us to the same lowliness. The death of a loved one is a fresh reminder of our own mortality. This is a time for authenticity. The bereaved are grateful—beyond words—for our presence. No need to be overly concerned about how well our sentiments get to be verbalized.

## When the Clergy Are Too Busy

A second defense for the failure of the priest, minister, or rabbi to follow up in his ministry to mourners is expressed in the word *busy*. And this single word may fairly describe the reality. The parish may be too large, the flock too numerous, or the members of the synagogue too dispersed for the shepherd to be in as close contact with everyone as he would like. In spite of the fact that we are all a little suspicious of our neighbor's hiding behind the word *busy*, we ought to be prepared to accept the fact that it is often a valid excuse.

"Quantity threatens quality"; sheer numbers of people tend to diminish the possibility of a truly personal relationship. Very often the pastoral opportunities and demands are too much for one person. There are many wise scriptural cautions against our judging our neighbor. We are warned that we, ourselves, are to be judged; if we would obtain mercy we must win the right to it by our tolerance for the imperfections of others.

It might be noted that the expectations which people have of their spiritual leaders may vary somewhat from one denomination to another. At times, however, the expectations and the clerical performance seem to vary more on the basis of geography than of theology. The urban clergy, for example, might be expected to visit their families more frequently simply because it seems to be more feasible physically. Many observe, however, that the opposite turns out to be the case: the rural clergy often cover more ground and maintain more of a personal bond with a widely scattered flock. This conclusion may warrant a more systematic study before it can be taken seriously, but at least it suggests that there are avenues offering some interesting psychological exploration. Happily, most of the members of either the urban or the rural congregation seem to be prepared to make charitable judgments about the pastor's busyness. Nevertheless, there is no doubt that the pastor whose compassionate zeal is evident is the one whose name is revered. There is nothing that the faithful appreciate more than sympathy shown at the time of bereavement.

## Faith Community Should Give Moral Support

J. B. Morton, in one of his travel books, this one on Ireland, described his feelings as an Englishman among the Irish. He acknowledged their warmth and cherished their hospitality but he sensed something in the air that seemed to say, "All these people share something that is hidden, they are members of a secret society, as it were, and you are an Outsider!" Perhaps what he sensed was even some unity among them that sprang from their shared faith. Our purposes here do not demand verification of that. But what probably can be agreed upon is the fact that a people who share a vision are more able to share one another's life, to support one another's burdens and celebrate one another's joys. No doubt the religious community ought to contribute moral support to one another in time of trouble. To put it this way may be to state an even more fundamental imperative than to state the obligation to contribute to the maintainence of the physical plant where one is taught these moral obligations!

While granting that the whole congregation has the "duty" of showing loving concern especially for those of its members who are grieving, one is aware that this duty is going to be carried out concretely by individuals responding to the call of the Spirit in the concrete situation. The pastor, especially, will be the one who most often becomes aware of the special needs on each unique occasion. Moreover, he is the symbol of the loving community. For the family that is bereaved it is true that his concern betokens the concern of all of the communicants. In the face of death there is no time to dawdle over the duty of demonstrating charity. The Judeo-Christian tradition ought to lead to love with spontaneity and enthusiasm lest one drain all life out of neighborliness. No one should be surprised to discover that a shared responsibility is often a responsibility that does not weigh very heavily on anyone. "The best committee is a committee of one." How often we will find that verified!

## Lack of Imagination

At first, it may seem strange to hear this failing imputed to the clergy. But it is true, they can suffer from it as well as anyone else. And it may be a way of accounting for another fault that sometimes appears among the clergy: thoughtlessness. Either of these may seem a strange excuse for the pastor or rabbi who fails to follow through after his parishioners are bereaved. But he may just not have the imagination to recognize that the shock of a loss can leave people stunned for a long time afterward—and that this may be especially the case when a death is sudden, without forewarning or preparation.

The family, whether stunned or not, is still in the position of having to pay bills, make decisions, and plan for the future. The approachable minister can be a source of support even if only as a sounding board enabling others to make their own decisions. Obviously this role calls for discretion; since the clergy are not lawyers, doctors, or psychiatrists, they must have the prudence to defer to the professionally competent. But very often their people can put trust in them as if they were "one of the family." The minister's availability will be seen as a "blessing" when families undergo deep anguish; those are the times when people realize the simple truth in the words of Genesis: "It is not good for man to be alone."

# Shyness

We mentioned timidity as a possible excuse for a minister's failure in the role of consoler. One, somehow, expects the clergy and professional people to have a sufficient amount of savoir-faire for just about any situation that they could be thrown into. Maybe we trust too much that education automatically supplies this. But, "taken from among men," ministers may be expected to be fairly representative of the sons of Adam. Some are bashful, shy, inarticulate. The younger ones may appear more awkward than the older. Sometimes their seniors have developed idiosyncrasies which only conceal their lack of self-confidence. In an age of specialization the theologically trained person is only too aware of his or her limitations. Although probably grateful to not be living in a culture which expects the local guru to be endowed with omniscience, the clergy must often be uncertain about just what expectations their flock really does have of them.

# Overconfidence in Ritualistic Ministrations

This chapter began with a list of a half-dozen reasons that might account for the occasional inadequacy of the clergy in the role of consoler. The last one may be the most important even if it is the most embarrassing to acknowledge.

Suppose that the priest or minister or rabbi were to content himself with the ritual prayers for the dead? Suppose he were satisfied that his task is fulfilled by voicing the petitions of the mourners to God? Suppose he develops a skill in speaking to God but proves inept in speaking to men? Suppose he is institutionalized as the chief mourner and can look to the grave but not to the grief of men? Suppose that he turns from the grave as a barber from his chair to say, "Who's next?" The very thought is blasphemous.

Disdain for the sensibilities of the living does not serve to honor the dead. If the clergyman came to be such a professional pray-er that he could proceed through the ritual in an impersonal way, then he would seem to be leading his people into the realm of magic. A community of faith surely ought to be more than a crowd mumbling some meaningless jargon. They must be more than a group who gathers to fulfill some empty public observance, retreating from there to private worlds where they hide from death and from neighbor—and from reality.

The dread of this kind of inauthenticity is probably what is behind most of the complaints about the clergy today. It is not that they are actually guilty of these faults in any great measure so much as it is feared that they might become more so. Everyone is engaged in a combat against depersonalization in this busy, crowded world. However history describes the religious attitudes of this age, however it evaluates the changes in the churches, it will surely note twentieth-century man's passionate concern for authenticity.

## Benefits from Sincere Compassion

All the foregoing reflections might appear to take it for granted that the charge is simply true when it is said that the clergy neglect to follow through with a compassionate concern for the bereaved. But perhaps one ought not to convict those accused all that easily. One may slander a whole class of dedicated men and women without sufficient evidence. It may be too easy to find stories repeated to the disadvantage of a whole group of people, while the good they have done may be "interred with their bones," as Shakespeare might say.

Man has a responsibility to serve the interests of justice by acknowledging that much good is accomplished by many good men and women who are continually doing what is called for: they do follow through in a truly fraternal way after the burial. They try to be good neighbors to those who mourn. Everyone can probably recall examples of this. It does take a little more effort than to recall the complaints, because, as in the case of the newspapers, the bad news tends to crowd out the good.

Countless rabbis, ministers, and priests make it a practice to visit a bereaved family a week or so after a funeral. It is one way of reassuring them that the community's public demonstration of sympathy was more than a passing thing. One priest, a chaplain at a large city hospital, spends a fair amount of his time visiting the homes of bereaved relatives when there are especially tragic cases that come through his emergency door. Then he informs the local parish priests of special needs.

Another clergyman is the head of a large institution where a young man was tragically killed. Meeting the parents at the funeral home and again at the grave the clergyman discovered that the father, particularly, was unreasonably blaming himself for what happened to his son. The clergyman was the best one to cope with this situation and he went out of his way to visit that father and gently but persuasively lead him out of his dark night of self-torment.

In another case a young mother lost a child and then, in a few short months, her husband. Each death was totally unexpected. The first loss was extremely difficult to bear, but when the second one followed so quickly it was impossible for the woman to conceive of a God anywhere in the cosmos who could be merciful or loving. The minister who sees a parishioner through such difficult days is wise to tolerate the expressions of anger against God. He, himself, may prove to be the target of much of the resentment. He must be willing to endure this. Days will come when it will be more feasible to discuss the mysterious ways of God with men. In this particular case there happened to be such a wise and understanding minister.

In the months and years after being widowed the senior citizens need more elaborate programs to occupy them. Some churches have facilities that lend themselves to this need. Some programs involve little more than bus rides or bingo games. In other cases there are sewing circles or art courses or craft instruction. To these ongoing activities the clergy are able to introduce people who are beginning to recover from some deep sorrow. Each case of grief is unique, but there are enough things common to the human experience to make it possible for us to communicate some tangible evidence of fellow-feeling.

Sometimes when death visits the home of a childless couple, it seems that the anguish of loss is greater than in the larger family where there are so many more to fall back upon. The bereaved spouse can, when he or she is without children, feel that the whole reason for being is taken away; now the bereaved may lean toward death himself, looking forward to it with longing. The clergy need to have a sensitivity to these special problems. Indeed, it seems that they usually do; and here they can do great good, for they are irreplaceable when it comes to patiently working toward the discovery of new vision and new life projects that justify "going on."

One often hears it said, more likely than not by older women, that "it is harder for a man to manage by himself if his wife dies first and he is the one left alone." Observation seems to bear this out. The man was not conditioned to be the homemaker, so he grows careless about the house and its appearance. Overcome by his loneliness, he lacks the incentive to look after the things that form his daily environment. Then it gets to be a vicious circle; the gloomy, unattractive surroundings promote an unhealthy atmosphere of death. It can happen that only a clergyman can invade this private world of death and open some windows.

Truthfully, one hears more and more examples of sincere compassion being shown by the clergy individually and in organized ways by the faith community. Both the compassion—and the occasional complaints over the lack of it—seem to arise from the same ground: we all experience a certain holy anxiety that humanness may die from our world. The evolution of society presents new problems and challenges to test our love of neighbor. We will continue to contribute to the humanization of mankind if we cherish the words of the scriptures: "Precious in the eyes of the Lord is the death of his faithful ones!" (Ps. 116:15) We may be confident that no one more highly values humanity than God who invented it.

# 18

## *The Grief-Work Cycle in Judaism*
### — STEVEN MOSS

The grief-work cycle is the basic mechanism of bereavement. E. Linde-mann and others point out that if this mechanism is not made to function actively and speedily by the mourner, then illness will result. This illness can be of both a psychological as well as of a physical nature.

Postponement of the grief-work cycle appears to be the natural direction a mourner would at first take, because grief-work calls for a direct confrontation with the reality of the death of the "other." The readiness to shun such a confrontation is typified by the common statement by the mourner, "I can't believe he is no longer here." The first step of this grief-work cycle also calls for a letting go of all pent-up emotions and thoughts. It is necessary to let the floodgates be opened. This too is difficult for the modern mourner as our society fosters stoicism, especially for the male sex, in the face of tragedy. These human and cultural factors allow the mourner to alter the course of normal grief reactions and thereby bring on what Lindemann calls "Morbid Grief Reactions." J. R. Hodge writes:

> "One of the big obstacles to this work seems to be the fact that many patients try to avoid the intense distress connected with the grief experience and to avoid the expression of emotion necessary for it." Through active engagement with the grief work, the bereaved must come to an acceptance that the loved one is actually gone. . . . If the grief work is not actively pursued, the process may be fixated or aborted or delayed, with the patient feeling that he may have escaped it. However, almost certainly a distorted form of the grief work will appear at some time in the future.[1]

While various authors have outlined detailed patterns of the grief period, the grief-work cycle can be described in a general way by two steps. The first step was mentioned above. It is the realization that the loved one is gone, is dead, and nothing can change this state. It is a direct confrontation with reality. It forces the mourner to look at the hard, cold facts.

In the Bible, Jacob demonstrated such a reaction to what he believed was the death of his son Joseph when he lamented: "No, but I will go down to the grave, to my son, mourning [Gen. 37:35]." And to the possibility of the death of his other son, Benjamin, he cried: "My son shall not go down with you; for his brother is dead, and he only is left; if harm befall him by the way in which you go, then will you bring down my old age with sorrow to the grave [Gen. 42:38]."

This sense that the mourner is going down to the grave, that he is placing himself beside the dead one, is the first step of the grief-work cycle. It calls for a letting out of all emotions, be they a sigh, tears, a moan, anger or laughter. It calls for a temporary separation from the activities of the living and of life, so that there is an actual "going down," an identification with the dead loved one. All sadness and sorrow, and the sense of the nonexistence of death are experienced by the mourner.

The second step of the grief-work cycle is a "coming up" from the depths of the "grave." In this stage the mourner must gradually begin to form his ties again with the living and with life. He must slowly begin to establish relationships and take on responsibilities. It must be noted that a part of the mourner will always be in the depths with the dead loved one; this is the open wound so often mentioned. Within time this part will be less and less of a weight retarding the mourner from living. It is these depths that are fathomed at the times of unveiling of the tombstone, at *Yizkor* (Jewish memorial services for the dead) and at *Yahrzeit* (the yearly anniversary marking the day of death). The reality of this part of the mourner, which is always in grief, must be acknowledged by the mourner, family, friends, and minister. If it is not, confusion, embarrassment, and guilt will accompany the shedding of tears when the loved one is recalled during the forthcoming years.

## The Bereaved's Relationships With Others

This grief work cycle of going down and of coming up needs to be applied in two areas. The first area, whose importance is recognized by all writers in this field, deals with the mourner's relationships with friends, relatives, and society. These relationships are severed by the mourner, as these relationships are severed for the one who has died. For both the mourner and the one who had died there is

> no commonality or community with other men. The qualities and charac-
> teristics of a living human being are suspended. According to the Mi-

drash [a collection of rabbinic commentaries to the books of the Bible] death is one of the aspects of human life which likens man to a beast. In death, man has witnessed the ultimate opposite of life, of God, and of man, and he cannot now summarily leave death behind him and return quickly and easily into the land of the living.[2]

As Judaism recognizes that the person touched by the experience of death, which is antilife, becomes less of a human being in his relationship to his fellow men, the period of *shiva* (the first seven days after burial) is marked by various customs by which the mourner breaks his ties with the living around him. These customs include: (1) no cutting of hair; (2) no washing of clothing; (3) no washing or anointing of oneself; (4) no marital relations will be conducted; (5) no wearing of shoes; (6) no work will be conducted; (7) no scripture will be read except Biblical books such as Job and Lamentations; (8) no greetings of hello or well-being will be said; and (9) there will be no sitting on either a soft bed or couch but rather on the ground or hard benches. While these various customs of mourning have exceptions based upon specific circumstances such as when mourning comes during a holiday or sabbath, they do bring the mourner through the first stage of his grief-work cycle. He is forced to face the fact of the other's death directly and realistically.

The goal of these customs is exemplified by the statement from the tractate of the Mishnah (the authorized codification of the oral law which developed during the second Temple and down to the end of the second century of the common era) entitled "The Sayings of the Fathers" in which it is written: "console not your associate in the hour when his dead lies before him (Pirke Avot IV: 23)." The first step of the grief-work cycle is to let the mourner face his grief head on and alone.

The mechanism of the second stage is put to work once *shiva* begins. The first meal upon returning from the cemetery is prepared by friends. The mourner cannot even use his own food for this. While this custom is part of the first stage of the grief-work cycle, in that the mourner cannot participate in such an activity of life as preparing his own food, it does point toward the second stage in that he is bolstered and supported by the community.

After the burial and throughout *shiva* condolence calls are made on the bereaved. While he himself cannot answer the phone or open the door (which if possible should remain unlocked during this period), friends and relatives are with him to do so. Each night a *minyan* (ten men, which is the minimum number of people needed for communal prayer) meet at the mourner's home to say *kaddish* (the memorial prayer for the dead). And if ten men cannot assemble at the home, the mourner must attend synagogue services himself. All these customs and others show the mourner that as he is going through the first stage of grief, as he is in the depths, the community is ready to lift him up and to form new relationships with the living once again.

The Jewish customs of mourning allow the mourner to move through the second stage—the *sheloshim* period (the first thirty days after burial) and the first year—as those customs by which he severed his relationships with the community are dropped by the wayside and he begins to develop his life with the living.

## Man's Relationship With God

The second area in which the grief-work cycle must be applied is that of man's relationship with God. While I believe that more people than those who admit such a relationship do have some type of relationship with God (and I will leave this term open to individual definition) prior to a death in the family, death does sever such a tie. Mourners many times ask: "Why has God abandoned me?" and "Why has He done this to me?" Feldman writes:

> Death desacralizes man because it is the end of the dynamic interaction with God which can take place only in life. Death removes man from an intimate relationship with God. . . . The image of God in man has been affected by death and *tum'ah* [defilement] have 'de-imagized' man who was created in the image.[3]

As Judaism recognizes that death also severs one's relationship with God, the customs of mourning also allow the mourner to go through the two stages of the grief-work cycle in this area.

As to the first stage, Feldman states:

> The laws of the *onen*—the initial period of mourning immediately following death but prior to burial—offer further support for the concept of death as estrangment from God. For example: the *onen* is exempt from wearing of phylacteries [ritualistic items used during morning prayers]; he does not recite the benediction before or after meals; he may not repeat the *amen* when he hears the benediction; he does not recite the normally obligatory *shma* prayer; he is exempt from all positive Biblical precepts; and, based on Lev. 10:19, a priest who is an *onen* is forbidden to eat of sacred food. It is precisely when the mourner is an *onen* and is existentially experiencing death at first hand that the *halakhah* [Jewish law] exempts him from performing the precepts. When death enters, man's relationship with the divine is temporarily suspended.[4]

This then is how the Jewish tradition (in its normative legalistic sense) helps the mourner into the first stage of his grief. But the work entailed in the second stage is begun even as early as the interment service itself. This work is the realization that, while death eats at one's relationship with God, as the mourner returns to life again his relationship with the God of life and death must also be renewed.

With this in mind, before the funeral service, while the mourner's garment is torn as a sign of his mourning, he declares: "Blessed is the Lord, the truthful judge." And after the coffin is lowered the rabbi recites the prayer *Zidduk ha-Din* of which Baeck writes:

> In accordance with this conception the phrase "blessed be the name of the Lord" was made part of the prayer of suffering; and coined especially for this by the language of that age was the term *Zidduk ha-Din*, the acknowledgment of the judgement. The term signifies the commandment of God in his days of suffering, and thereby to acknowledge his God. And as in the first phrase so in this one is stress laid on that suffering which death entails. More than anything else death seems to destroy the value of life and to deny its dignity; it is an irrationality, it is negation. The man who sees and suffers death seems to have his belief engulfed by meaninglessness. But in the face of death there prevails the "Thou shalt" as a triumph over the "Thou must" of fate; there prevails the moral freedom that is always available to man, the "acknowledgement of the judgment" which is his acknowledgment of the commanding God.[5]

The prayers during *shiva* help the mourner to realize that while he senses his relationship to God has been severed, actually it has not been severed at all. During the grace after meals the mourner is not allowed to recite all of the paragraphs, as a sign of his broken relationship with God, but the friends and relatives present say all the paragraphs in order to help renew his relationship with God. As it is written in the medieval mystical work *Maavor Yabok:*

> Therefore those who have come for the purposes of comforting the mourner would say all the blessings in order to shower upon the mourner and upon themselves blessings from God without end; blessings which flow from the tributaries of the pure river which flows through the spheres from the God without end.[6]

And the *kaddish* said each night during *shiva* and on each day during the year after the burial of a parent also helps the mourner to reestablish this important relationship with God.

## Conclusions

Commenting upon the Jewish tradition's attempt to help the mourner through his grief-work cycle, Rabbi Maurice Lamm writes:

The Jewish tradition has thus provided for a gradual release from grief
. . . with its own laws governing the expression of grief and the process
of return to the normal affairs of society. It fits so closely the normal
cycle of bereavement that some have maintained that the laws of mourning are descriptive rather than prescriptive.[7]

The areas of the grief-work cycle mentioned above should be imple-
mented by friends and by clergymen of all denominations. More attention should be paid to the area that speaks of man's relationship with
God than has been done up until now. As I have discovered many
times during my own ministry to the bereaved, if the ties between the
mourner and God remain severed by death, the person's emotional
and intellectual life, which was fostered by certain conscious and unconscious religious influences, will forever remain adversely affected.
While death snatches the physical presence of a loved one from a
person's midst, it does not also have to permanently destroy a person's ties with God, life, and society.

If these ties are to be properly knitted, the grief-work cycle must be
conducted actively and speedily. The healthy going down and coming
up need the service and constant help of ministers, physicians, and
friends. As bereavement is experienced not only when death is experienced but also when loss of any kind is felt throughout one's life, the
more adequate the grief-work cycle, the better will be the reestab-
lished life with God and society.

## Notes

1. Dr. James R. Hodge, "They That Mourn", *The Journal of Religion and Health*,
   vol. 11, no. 3 (July 1972).

2. Emanuel Feldman, "Death as Estrangement: The Halakah of Mourning,"
   *Judaism*, vol. 21, no. 1 (Winter 1972) pp. 62–63.

3. Ibid,. p. 64.

4. Ibid., p. 66.

5. Leo Baeck, *The Essence of Judaism* (New York: Schocken Books Inc., 1961)
   p. 137.

6. Aaron ben Moses Berechaiah of Medina, *Maavor Yabok* (B'nai Berak, Israel:
   Yashpha, 1927) p. 249

7. Maurice Lamm, *The Jewish Way of Death and Mourning*, (New York: Jona-
   than David Publishers, 1972) p. 78.

# 19

# The Bereaved in the Hospital
## — CARLETON J. SWEETSER

When death occurs in a large hospital, the patient's problems are finally solved, but often immediately on the scene is an individual or group of people with great problems and needs—the newly bereaved. They are people who may have suffered the greatest loss of their lives. They are shocked, disbelieving, sad, denying, angry, despairing, guilty, explosive, withdrawn. They may well have just embarked upon the hardest and loneliest phase of their own lives.

In a modern acute-care hospital there seem to be two broad categories of death and consequent bereavement, the first being the termination of life after long illness, a "normal" death that, at least to some extent, had been expected and awaited by loved ones. The other, which occurs frequently in a modern hospital, is sudden and unexpected death—the result of an accident or human violence, perhaps taking place in the midst of emergency-room pandemonium, or of a sudden cardiac arrest of a patient hospitalized for some other chronic condition (e.g., the completely unexpected late-evening heart arrest of a young man who, after several weeks in the hospital for tests, had been finally diagnosed to be suffering from a malignant brain tumor and scheduled for a craniotomy the very next morning; his family was present). It is the latter category I would briefly discuss first, because the need for ministry to the bereaved following an unexpected death seems to be particularly urgent.

## Unexpected Death

Sudden deaths in a hospital, resulting from traumatic and violent circumstances, often occur with family and loved ones present, they having been summoned in the emergency. When such a death of a loved one takes place, the immediate reaction is a state of great shock. A sense of unreality, disbelief, and denial is apt to predominate. The fact of the sudden terrible loss can't be comprehended as a reality or accepted as a natural part of life. The most instinctive response is to cry, inwardly or outwardly, that it isn't true. A bereaved person in shock may behave or react in ways that don't seem socially appropriate or acceptable—the young woman who smiled broadly and continually as she talked after the unexpected death of her husband; or the three teen-age girls who, on learning of the death from stabbing of their young brother, tore around the confines of the emergency suite, screaming at the top of their lungs, knocking over furniture, frightening patients, one of them finally throwing herself on the floor, writhing, kicking and screaming.

The suddenly bereaved may suffer loss of emotional and physical control and become hysterical. They can withdraw quickly into a state of numbness and isolation. They can react to their loss with bitterness and great anger which can be directed at others on the scene: two young men had to be restrained by guards from "beating up" the doctors on the intensive care unit because their brother's life couldn't be saved following an automobile accident. With respect to anger turned on others, ethnic and social backgrounds can be important factors: ghetto and other depressed peoples, all too familiar with social deprivation, often question that their loved one received first-class professional care in the hospital, and their anger can be expressed in suspicion, hostility, and confrontation with staff.

Shock, denial, a sense of unreality, guilt, loss of self-control, anger, despair, great sadness, a sudden sense of isolation and abandonment are the hallmarks of sudden and unexpected bereavement. Persons so suffering are in great need.

## Death of the Terminally Ill

Bereavement immediately following a more expected and awaited death, the culmination of long illness and perhaps considerable hospitalization, is a situation of different emotional tone and stage of intellectual acceptance. Genuine sadness and realistic comprehension of the loss are more apt to be the case, and the bereaved may already have started down the long road of expressing and working through grief. But even when illness is terminal, when the end of suffering is desired and death expected intellectually, the loss, when it occurs, is still great, and its actuality signals the beginning of a very bleak phase, possibly the worst, in the life of the bereaved. And shock, with all its component reactions—from denial and a sense of unreality to loss of control and anger—can be present here too in varying degrees. "While there is life there's hope" is deeply rooted in the human heart, and the loss of someone beloved, under any circumstances, is not readily received as a good and natural part of life's processes, particularly at the shattering moment of the loss. On the whole, "expected" loss is more likely to be marked by calmer circumstances and reactions and by genuine sadness and grief.

## Responsibility of Hospital Staff to the Newly Bereaved

The newly bereaved, then, are persons in acute distress and persons for whom a hospital and its staff have a moral responsibility, especially during the period between the patient's death and the bereaved's departure. People suffering in this state need the help of others and should not be ignored or abandoned by hospital personnel quickly withdrawing into routine activities (perhaps threatened by their own feelings about death), or left alone to walk through the corridors of the hospital, crushed, angry, numb, or dazed. The responsibility for them is an important one, and I believe should be so conceived by institutions that comprise the setting for the beginning of most of the bereavement in our society and which are inextricably bound up with its cause. This is one of the reasons why St. Luke's Hospital, New York City, maintains a twenty-four-hour resident chaplaincy program, why all deaths are supposed to be reported immediately to the chaplain's office, and why the chaplain on duty goes to the floor as soon as notified of a patient's death—Protestant, Jewish, other religion, "no religion"—irrespective of religious preference or designation. (Roman Catholic patients are served by priests on call from a nearby parish church.) Ministry to the bereaved would seem to be an integral part of ministry to the dying. It may begin before the patient's death (and if a chaplain who has been visiting the patient and his family is in the hospital at the time of death, he is specifically called); and a crucial part of that ministry is from the time of death until the bereaved leave the hospital.

What should be the approach to the newly bereaved? Hardly that of telling them that God is good and loving at a time when circumstances seem to be saying cruelly that such is not the case. Rather, it should be simply in terms of a ministry of *presence*. A concerned, friendly person to stand by, to share compassionately a bit of the shock and suffering, and possibly to serve as a calming link to the world of reality. One who will listen receptively and understandingly to poured-out feelings, who will gently guide, if necessary, through daze and confusion, who will offer immediate practical help if indicated—in short, who will *be with*—is the ministry or service needed at the crucial moment and immediately following. It may be the factor enabling another to take the first step in acceptance and real mourning, and it may communicate the reality of God's goodness and love in creation's processes in a way that verbalizing cannot. It is certainly a ministry which can and should be shared by doctors, nurses, and attendants, but is one for which the chaplain is a powerful symbol and for which he should be peculiarly fitted. When a patient dies, the book is really closed for all those whose professional responsibilities were the improving of his health and extension of his physical life. But the chaplain is one who is also concerned with helping people die and accept death, and thus *to some degree* working in an alien environment and at cross purposes with other hospital professionals. He is the right one to come at the time of death and be with the newly bereaved while they are in his institution.

The offer of commendatory prayers, frequently accepted by the bereaved as they join the chaplain at the bedside, can be a powerfully helpful action, a seemly and spiritually fitting benediction to the course of an earthly life. I note that it is a concluding act often appreciated by nurses, and among the bereaved can certainly be a nurse or a doctor who had long struggled in behalf of the patient's life. In pointing so directly to the existential finality of physical death, bedside prayers, when meaningful for the bereaved, help toward a sense of the reality of and acceptance of death as part of the life process. In addition to its theological significance, it can be a helpful and healing act.

An invitation to the newly bereaved to the chaplain's office or some quiet place away from a scene of trauma and confusion serves the purposes of the nursing staff still charged with the care of a floor of living patients as well as the immediate needs of the bereaved. A place to be alone to collect themselves or with a friendly concerned fellow human being to whom they can express present feelings, the use of a telephone for calling others they want to notify, even the offer of helping with preliminary funeral arrangements if people are ready for or anxious about them, staying with them until others arrive, and seeing them out of the hospital and into taxis are some of the ways a ministry of presence can be expressed during a short but sometimes crucial period in peoples' lives.

It is a crisis ministry in a hospital—from the death of the patient to the departure of the bereaved—that may be only of a few minutes duration. Or it may call for hours of the chaplain's time, as it did when early one morning an out-of-state couple arrived just as their college-age son died from the injuries of a motorcycle crash the previous night. A friend of the boy's, who had accompanied the parents on the trip, unaware of the seriousness of the situation, disappeared with their car until well after lunch. The six hours spent in the chaplain's office, pouring out feelings and some guilt, reliving the boy's life, contending with their feelings of the injustice of the tragic loss of the promising life of their gifted son (about to enter college on a full scholarship), were both a painful and a healing time for the stranded parents. Two people who early in the day had staggered away from the intensive care unit, shocked, numb, and disbelieving, walked out of the hospital in the afternoon deeply and sadly aware of and sorrowfully accepting the loss of their son. The chaplain is the only one in a hospital who can give priority to this kind of care.

The time of the death of a loved one is a critical period for human beings, and the experiences immediately associated with it, I believe, can well have lasting effects on people for good or ill. (I think of a woman who, in spite of the doctor's orders permitting her, was prevented by a seemingly cold and uncaring nurse from seeing her sick husband outside of visiting hours. Moments after the refusal he died, and for years she could not drive past that nearby hospital without suffering feelings of great bitterness.)

Concern for and care of people at this time would seem to be a logical and moral reponsibility of those institutions of *healing* in which people so frequently become the newly bereaved.

# 20

# *Bereavement: A Pediatric View*
## — RUDOLF TOCH

The composite dictionary definition of *bereavement* is "to deprive or dispossess of life, hope, etc; to leave desolate, especially by death, orphaned, or widowed." In this context the pediatrician meets, and has to cope with, bereavement in a variety of situations affecting the whole array of people centered around a child. He also has to deal with the child bereaved and with his own sense of loss. The following statements are not an attempt to deal with the subject exhaustively but are a few remarks about some of the situations encountered by one physician in some twenty-five years of caring primarily for children with cancer as well as severely damaged, multiply handicapped children doomed to institutional life.

## The Professionals

Perhaps the proper starting point would be a brief explanation of the means by which the health professional may learn to deal with his own bereavement which will follow the loss of every patient and to which no one becomes wholly inured. By necessity this is a personal statement, but I hope that it is applicable to others. Each one of us has to learn to adjust consciously to the fact of death (the inevitability of it we all acknowledge intellectually but often deny or refuse to face emotionally). My advice from personal experience is to make a concerted effort to think about death as it may affect you, honestly searching your own mind and heart in an effort to explore what your own death means, and then what the deaths of those dearest to you mean, forcing yourself to face these contemplations without letting your mind wander, exploring your strengths and weaknesses, sources of internal and external support, particularly the role your religious beliefs and philosophy of life would play when challenged by death. Next, learn to talk about death freely and shed the current practice of making it a taboo subject in polite society. In discussing the death of children I am aware of the reversed status of death and sex as fit subjects for social conversation. Whereas sex used to be off limits, it is now a popular topic of conversation; while death used to be talked about freely as little as twenty-five years ago, it is now impolite to mention it at all. This reflects not only social mores but mirrors clearly the individual's desire to deny, or at least ignore, death. The trend that includes death and dying as a topic for discussions and seminars in the education of health workers shows a growing concern that people involved in the care of the sick must be taught about death, because they no longer develop an awareness of, and proper attitude toward, death in the course of their own growth and development. The very fact that a national organization such as the Foundation of Thanatology is obviously filling a heretofore unmet need illustrates the need for greater individual awareness and action.

In every hospital there is need for more discussions and informal talks to help individual staff members come to grips with their own fears, attitudes, expectations, and aspirations. This may be one time when familiarity does not breed contempt but reassurance and a sense of greater competence.

## The Parents

In his encounter with the likely death of one of his patients the pediatrician must be willing to prepare all concerned for that eventuality and then help with the various problems that attend the event. Since most children die in hospitals, he most likely will not be alone in this but will have the competent cooperation of experienced social workers and nurses. Though the physician has the traditional role of being primarily responsible, there may be others on the health care team with greater expertise, born out of experience, who can be of more help and comfort to the bereaved. The care of the bereaved must not be left to chance. It must be carefully planned, and every member of the team should know his proper role. Often the discussion of the likelihood of death is unconsciously ignored in the press of lifesaving or at least life-maintaining procedures so that when it does occur the people who are present at that moment may face a problem for which they are not adequately prepared. Not only must the family be helped to anticipate the event by those whom they have known best in the course of the child's illness, they must also know the people who will actually be present when death does come. It is patently impossible for every physician, social worker, or nurse to be on hand at that time, but continuity can be maintained by preplanning, even if it involves only a telephone conversation when the time of day or other factors make a personal presence impossible. Foreseeable death from an illness should be carefully preplanned by those who are responsible for the patient to ensure that its impact on the bereaved will not be compounded by ad hoc measures and confusion. The adage of forewarned being forearmed is true for the family that has been carefully and sympathetically prepared for the loss of their child. They will bear up better than those who must meet "death unprepared for," from which even the litany in the Book of Common Prayer asks deliverance.

I do not intend to imply that talking about death will eliminate the shock and grief of a death, but it will lay the foundation for each individual's working out his own grief reaction, guilt feelings, resentment, and any other reaction that the bereaved will have to manage before returning to full functioning.

Death is not the only cause of bereavement. Loss of hope is equally difficult to bear; the parents of hopelessly damaged and handicapped children need help with their bereavement. The reaction of such parents, be it at the time of birth or later in the child's life after illness or accident, varies from excessively lavishing emotional and material resources on the child to virtual abandonment of him. Skilled sympathetic counseling, with as full an explanation as feasible of causes (when known), probabilities of future development or restoration of functions, complications to be expected and how to avoid them, and in general what parent and child may expect to happen, will help some parents. Other parents act in seemingly irrational ways, which to me indicates their grappling with unresolved guilt feelings that require professional help of greater intensity and depth. Parents of handicapped children, sometimes for good and sometimes for ill, often resort to exertion of political pressure to obtain assistance from state agencies and facilities, long trips to distant medical or religious meccas, unproved methods of therapy, and aggressive demands for public and private support for research in specific afflictions. Sometimes families break up. It is my impression that bereavement will strengthen only those family bonds that are basically sound, while it will lead to irreparable dissolution of the family when preexisting stresses and tension become aggravated by mutual blaming and accusations. The high incidence of separations and divorce in the face of having to cope with a hopeless situation is distressing. It takes the combined efforts of physician and social workers to help parents face the problem and adjust to it. Fortunately there are resources available, though seemingly never quite adequate, that can be utilized by and for people in need, but it requires experienced social workers to know where to find them and how to direct those in need to them.

Added to the sense of loss of hope for their child, parents are faced by the worry that they may have to cope with the problem alone and, particularly when it involves older children and consequently older parents, what may become of the child when they are no longer able to cope. Whenever possible the professional team should be aware of these concerns and help ease the burden. The conflict between individual responsibility and public obligation is far from resolved, and legislative attempts have so far been inadequate in furnishing the one antidote to this form of bereavement: reassurance that the damaged child will be cared for competently and permanently without being an excessive financial burden on the family.

## Children

How does one help a child who loses a parent or sibling when old enough to comprehend the loss? I have found it of little use to try preparing a child for impending death, though it is essential that the child be made to feel a part of the family all through the illness of the dying member. So often it is assumed that a child must be protected against the concerns associated with illness; consequently he is excluded from information or even lied to. Even young children sense trouble and know when they are being shut out; the younger ones become insecure while the older ones resent it. It is impossible to keep children from learning the truth as long as it is known to others, since chance remarks overheard will often inform them of the very facts they are being "protected" against. The advisable course to follow is to be honest with each child to the extent of his ability to comprehend. The feeling of being treated fairly and with openness is often more important than the details of information imparted. Questions must be answered simply and to the point; elaborate explanations will usually be forgotten.

We must remember when advising on the manner in which a child should be told about death to stress that the demeanor of the informant is as important, if not more important, than the words used. Children learn about the meaning of death not from what we say but from how we say it. It is advisable that the saddening experience fit within the range of emotions that the child has learned to expect. Any drastic or excessive emotional display may very well impart a fear of death to the child which a more controlled reaction might avoid. Every child should be told about the death in as simple and direct a manner as possible. Circumlocutions and paraphrases, though kindly meant, will only confuse, cause resentment, or create fear. There is no place for: "He fell asleep and did not wake up," or "God took him to live with him," or variations on these themes, because children take adult statements literally and usually have not yet learned to interpret euphemisms. Every child must be given an opportunity to react to the news in his own way which may take seemingly inappropriate forms, including lashing out physically or verbally, denial, or even laughter.

Often a child will not cry and will be considered heartless by those inexperienced in the way children may react. The feeling of loss and occasionally of guilt may last a long time, even when outward signs of it are lacking, and will require sympathetic support (though never pity).

It is also useful to stress that making the child ventilate his feelings about death will usually fail and probably result in withdrawal. We must never seem to pry but must always be open to the child's overtures. He will talk to us when he can. In the meantime he must be made to feel that we respect his sorrow and want to help but on his own terms. Only rarely will he need formal psychiatric help to cope with his bereavement.

## Other Causes of Grief for Children

Bereavement may come to a child without anyone's dying. The family destroyed by divorce leaves children bereft and in need of specific help which they only too often do not get. Here again compassionate honesty will accomplish much. In no case should the child be placed as a pawn between the warring parents and forced to take sides. Because no illness is involved, the health professionals may ignore this very potent source of childhood trauma, and others, for instance the clergy or teachers or at least concerned family members or friends, must step into the breach to avoid aggravating the harm done the child.

The changing pattern of sexual activity of younger girls has brought the pediatrician increasingly into contact with the unwed pregnant adolescent who experiences a definite sense of bereavement more complex than that evoked by the death of a parent or sibling. With the readily available resources for abortions few of these pregnancies now go to term. The young girl who needs an abortion usually has special psychological problems.

Not only does she have to face an often hostile family but she may have to cope with her own loss of self-respect and recriminations. Added to this are the feelings of responsibility for the budding life and the awareness that parts of our society condemn abortion as murder. Occasionally she will be exposed to divergent advice and even placed in the middle between warring factions of our society. All this enhances the sense of guilt and bereavement, and it is not surprising that contemplation of suicide is not uncommon when the child is not being helped compassionately by people who can place their concern for her above their own prejudice. Studies show that girls who want abortions usually suffer no lasting emotional damage, and it is surprising that many can hardly remember the whole event after a few years. Even these seemingly well-adjusted (at least to the abortion) youngsters need a sympathetic ear that will help them sort out their feelings and adjust to the changes the pregnancy made in their lives. The children who do not want abortions and who with immature, unrealistic arguments try to persuade all involved that they should be permitted to keep their babies (even at age thirteen), but who nevertheless do have abortions will show excessive grief reactions and will often need skilled psychiatric help to work out their much more complex and usually preexisting psychiatric difficulties.

The most intense problem with bereavement occurs in girls who have their babies and then give them up for adoption. I believe that giving up a child is a traumatic experience that the mother really never overcomes; she needs a lot of emotional support, in spite of the facade she may put on. I know of no simple approach to easing the sense of guilt and loss that these girls feel. Here again a skillful, compassionate social worker may achieve more than the physician, if she can spend the time necessary to gain the girl's trust and to listen. Platitudes are of very little help, though usually invoked. Time is probably the only healer.

By pointing out some aspects of bereavement as this pediatrician sees them, I hope I have stimulated those interested in the problems to explore them more fully in discussions, because only through very open and often personal sharing of experiences, attitudes, and concerns can the individual grow to a better understanding and thereby greater skill in helping those in need of help.

# 21

# *Divorce and Grief*
## — JOHN FREUND

Heads were nodding in recognition that someone had put into words things they had been feeling but were unable to articulate. Neglected, to say the least, in some instances made to feel outcasts in their faith community, often unable to sort out their own feelings, these divorced and separated men and women had been coming together one Sunday afternoon a month over the past year for what amounted to an "R and R" (rap and relaxation) program with others who shared their situation. Entitled "A Program of Concern" and sponsored by the Sisters of the Cenacle in Lake Ronkonkoma, it is a welcome, if long-delayed, recognition by some religious leaders of the needs of those who, whether through their own fault or that of another, have lost a significant other in their lives by divorce or separation.

## Coping with Loss

Heads were nodding because many of the people there were recognizing a description of their own experiences in coping with loss. For some there had been a welter of hostile feelings toward a spouse who had wronged them. For others it meant the confusion of adjusting to a new life in face of the painful blow to their self-esteem that occurred when persons they trusted walked out of their lives. Others were still numb to recent losses in their lives. Still others were asking a hostile and rebellious "Why me?" or a constructive "Why?" and "What does this mean?"

Influenced by the growing literature on people's reactions to the actual or anticipated loss of a loved one through death and struck by the suggestions that these reactions might apply to other situations of loss, I decided to present some of the ideas of Dr. Elisabeth Kübler-Ross on the stages people tend to experience as they grapple with the fact of their own imminent death. I had intended to present what she had learned from her dying patients and then try to set up some parallels with what these divorced people might be experiencing.

I never got to the second part of my presentation. It was unnecessary. Although I was still talking about peoples' reactions to their own
death, I quickly became aware of the nodding heads. There was no
need to explain the parallels. Each seemed to be off and running with
a sense of "I know that feeling" or "That's where I am now."

The rest of the presentation quickly changed into a dialogue with
the speaker as well as with each other. Much of the dialogue centered
on how to cope with their emotional reactions at the various stages in
their adjustment to the loss of their spouse, welcome as it may have
been in some instances.

The dialogue had been greatly facilitated by at least two factors I
could identify. The first was the fact that someone had put into words
what they had been feeling but could not sort out. This is what Henri
Nouwen refers to as serving others by being an "articulator of inner
events." The other factor seemed to be a sense of relief arising from
the fact that, if someone had been able to notice a pattern of response
similar to their own in people who were grief-stricken, then they were
not alone. They were not in as bad shape as they thought they were.
It seemed to be a much needed ointment to their confused emotions
and badly wounded self-images. They were able to see themselves
more clearly and had a frame of reference. "Naming the demon," as
Rollo May might describe it, seemed to give them a measure of
strength in coping with it.

## Need for Support from Others

Toward the end of the discussion, I was reflecting on the differences
as well as the similarities between their own loss and the loss of a
significant person through death. What seemed to have terrific impact
was the fact that while there are an increasing number of social sanctions and rites that facilitate working through the death of a loved one,
almost the opposite has been true of their experience.

A good number of relatives and friends usually rush to the side of
a woman who has just lost her husband through accident or sickness.
Granted there has been much anesthetizing of the emotional reactions
of grief with comments such as, "Don't cry. He wouldn't want you to.
Be brave." At least people have made an attempt to support the
woman and be at her side. They have been able to recognize the need
to help her take care of many practical details in adjusting to life
without her husband.

The situation of people, especially women, who have just been divorced is in most cases startlingly different. Instead of being met with
an understanding of the type of struggle she must face and support
she needs, she is often met with hostility, rejection, or fear. She often
finds herself as a second-class citizen in the community and church.

Many of her friends disapprove of what she has done or has had happen to her. Others view her with distrust and fear, for she is often, even if unconsciously, seen as a threat to their own marriage. There is the frequently unspoken question about the ways in which she contributed to the breakup of the marriage. People do not consider it a failure or the wife's fault if her husband dies. But if there is a divorce, silent suspicions often are present, whether they be with or without foundation. Added to this, the person who has been through the divorce often suffers from a sense of failure or guilt. (This applies to men as well as women, though I have chosen the feminine pronoun in these descriptions.)

The grief suffered by a divorced person thus goes unrecognized and the working-through process is not supported. In so many subtle ways it is also aggravated by the rejection and suspicion of those who would be in a good position to help.

As a result of this, the working-through process is not only prolonged and made more painful, but the chances for a successful outcome are diminished. Unable to understand her grief and its components of anxiety, hostility, and guilt—and unsupported by those around her—confusion, loneliness, depression, and sometimes panic are intensified. It becomes very difficult for her to learn from the experience. She rushes into destructive situations and responses.

Marriage counselors have long recognized the rebound phenomenon. Desperate for support and understanding, it is often difficult for her to be objective about the first person who shows the least sensitivity to her. She can be blind to the danger signals in the relationship. While not claiming this is a universal occurrence after divorce, I have been troubled by the frequency of cases I encounter where people make the same mistakes in marriage after marriage. I offer it as one example of the kind of thing that can happen when the grief involved in the breakup of a marriage is not recognized or supported. An example in the opposite direction is the woman who retreats into a shell and nurses a combination of fear of being burned again and bitterness toward all men.

I do not mean to imply that a severe grief reaction is present in every case of divorce. The concept of anticipatory grief may be just as operative here as in situations of loss through death. The emotional divorce may have taken place long before the legal divorce.

## Failure to Deal with Grief

I would like to suggest one other parallel between the problems involved in death and divorce. One of the more striking things Dr. Kübler-Ross discovered when she began her project of interviewing dying patients with the theological students who had requested her help was that, much to her amazement, each floor of the hospital she visited had no dying patients. No one in the hospital wanted to admit that people were dying.

There has been much writing in recent years about the fact that the whole thrust of medical training of the doctor or nurse is geared to saving lives. Death represents so often something of a defeat to the medical profession. No one likes defeat, so there is the frequent avoiding of death by the professional staff of the hospital. Only recently have medical schools and nursing schools begun to address themselves to an inescapable fact of their profession.

I wonder whether such a parallel exists in the field of marriage counseling. I am not implying that divorce is as inescapable a fact in marriage counseling as death is in the medical profession. Nor am I implying that most professionally trained marriage counselors are so committed to saving a marriage that they never handle divorce situations. Most recognize that sometimes the best thing for both children and parents is a recognition of the destructiveness of a relationship. (Even many of the strictest religious traditions recognize some sort of bill of divorce. The question for them is one of remarriage.) But a silence of sorts does exist.

A quick look at the index to the *Journal of Marriage and Family* shows that in the period between 1939 and 1962 there were a scant sixteen articles with divorce in the title. This averages out to less than one a year. Many of these were statistical, sociological, or legal studies. In the period between 1963 and 1969 there were eight. This is better than one a year, and the titles show a greater tendency to deal with the emotional problems of the divorced. But it is still surprisingly little for a country with a divorce rate as high as ours. The index of the *Family Coordinator* for the five years between 1968 and 1972 had only one article on divorce.

It may be unfair to draw a conclusion from one or two journals, especially since they are dedicated to promoting family life, but I do think it is fair to raise the question about whether there is a hesitancy to come to grips with something that affects more than one out of four marriages. Perhaps greater attention to postdivorce counseling might lessen the number of people for whom love is not something better "the second time around."

Looking at another aspect of the literature on divorce it may be interesting to note that in an article that appeared in *The Family Coordinator* at the beginning of this year Esther Oshiver Fisher[1] spoke of many of the elements that appear in the literature on grief, such as separation anxiety, adjusting to a new identity, displaced hostility, etc. Yet she failed to identify the relationship of these elements with grief.

A step in this direction is taken in the book *Divorce and After: An Analysis of the Emotional and Social Problems of Divorce*.[2] Two entries in the index refer to grief explicitly and represent a few short, even if pertinent, paragraphs in a 350-page work.

> Emotional divorce results in the loss of a loved object just as fully—but by quite a different route of experience—as does the death of a spouse. Divorce is difficult because it involves a purposeful and active rejection by another person, who, merely by living, is a daily symbol of the rejection. It is also made difficult because the community helps even less in divorce than it does in bereavement. . . . Divorce is even more threatening than death to some people, because they have thought about it more, perhaps wished for it more consciously. But most importantly—there is no recognized way to mourn a divorce. The grief has to be worked out alone and without the benefit of traditional rites, because few people recognize it for what it is.[3]

In the other section it points out that all parties concerned in the context of divorce may to some degree experience an emotional loss and grief.

> The marriage as an entity may have been closely interwoven with one's pattern of pursuit of emotional supplies, gratifications, supports, and feelings of emotional security. The divorce means that this is excised. At least, a considerable reorganization of patterns of relationship has to occur. When there is bitterness between the divorcees leading to alienation, friends are confronted often with a conflict over allegiances. Intense emotional conflicts can result for all concerned. The redistribution of allegiances may mean a loss of an emotionally significant friend. The friends of the divorcees, as well as the divorcees themselves, may have to experience a period of grief and undergo a process of mourning for what is felt to be lost.[4]

Two things strike me at this point. One is that there may well be a lacuna in marriage and family-life literature and research with regard to coping with the emotional problems of those involved in divorce. The fact that the *Family Coordinator* sees the need to present an article in January, 1973, on some fundamental guidelines for divorce counseling as well as the relatively few references to divorce counseling in the extensive bibliography put out by the Minnesota Council on Family Relations[5] seems to support my impression.

The second thing that strikes me is that as more attention is paid in the literature to the special problems of divorce counseling, it may very well be profitably influenced by the growing literature on grief. The study of the dynamics of grief may assist greatly in helping the people who become the numbers that make up our divorce statistics.

No one enjoys looking at the present rate of marital failure. It represents too many damaged lives. But it is a fact, and these people need the best help we can offer.

## Notes

1. Esther Oshiver Fisher, "A Guide to Divorce Counseling," *The Family Coordinator* 22 (1973):55–62.

2. Paul Bohannan, ed., *Divorce and After: An Analysis of the Emotional and Social Problems of Divorce* (New York: Doubleday & Company, Inc., 1971).

3. Paul Bohannan, in *Divorce and After: An Analysis of the Emotional and Social Problems of Divorce*, pp. 42–43.

4. Arthur Miller, in *Divorce and After: An Analysis of the Emotional and Social Problems of Divorce*, pp. 77–78.

5. Minnesota Council on Family Relations, *Family Life Literature and Films: An Annotated Bibliography (1973)*.

# PART IV

# CLERGY AND THE MEDICAL PROFESSIONALS

*Clergy frequently feel isolated and unsure where they fit with other professionals involved in caring for the dying and bereaved. Often clergy are not called until the end of life is imminent, and then they exercise their ministry unrelated to what the rest of the health care team have been doing.*

*Effective teamwork between clergy and medical professionals requires that all involved move beyond the stereotypical pictures they have of each other to an understanding of those concerns which are unique to each group, as well as those they have in common. The psychological issues for clergy and doctors in their different ministrations to the dying and bereaved are quite similar. It is sometimes forgotten (or denied) that the professionals who care for the dying experience grief when their patients die. A team that communicates with each other can also minister to each other in their shared grief.*

*The chapters in this section address the issues involved when clergy work with medical professionals in the care of the dying and the bereaved. Chapter 22 outlines some problems and solutions in the minister's relating his role as representative of a religious institution to the values and procedures of the health care institutions. Chapter 23 describes some unique functions that clergy can exercise in the health care setting. Chapter 24 is addressed to physicians in their role in caring for the dying, pointing out how they share common ground with the minister—a role seen quite differently by the author of the previous chapter.*

*How we understand our professional responsibility has an impact on how useful or helpless we feel, and therefore how emotionally available we are to patients. In Chapter 25 a professor of nursing emphasizes the roles still available to the health care team when cure is no longer probable and how these roles can be shared by clergy. The importance of non-professional staff is the theme of "Learning to Talk with the Cancer Patient," Chapter 26.*

*Educational programs to help people face death and bereavement are described in Chapter 27. Chapter 28 deals with ways to pull together a multidisciplinary team and the need for mutual ministry to one another within the team.*

*Clergy can improve the total context of care by facilitating communication among the care givers, developing ways for professionals to care for each other in their grief, initiating educational programs for both professionals and lay persons, and extending the care and communication into the homes and communities of patients and families.*

# 22

# *Problems Which Confront the Minister*

## — EDWARD F. DOBIHAL, JR.

What, then, is joy? What, then, is sorrow?
Time alone can decide between them,
When the immediate poignant happening
lengthens out to continuous wearisome suffering,
when the laboured creeping moments of daylight
slowly uncover the fulness of our disaster,
sorrow's unmistakable features.

Then do most of our kind,
sated, if only by the monotony
of unrelieved unhappiness,
turn away from the drama, disillusioned,
uncompassionate.

O you mothers and loved ones—then, ah then
comes your hour, the hour for true devotion.
Then your hour comes, you friends and brothers!
Loyal hearts can change the face of sorrow,
softly encircle it with love's most gentle
unearthly radiance.

Dietrich Bonhoeffer
*Letters & Papers from Prison**

Often for clergy the ministry to the dying and bereaved seems to be a repeated drama that leaves us "sated, if only by the monotony of unrelieved unhappiness." Far too often, we appear to be loners confronting the processes of dying and of bereavement with no support for the personal questions, feelings, and emotional drain that this ministry entails. In addition, the institutional system of which the clergyman is a part, the Church, has largely ignored the practical issues of death that he must live with, though it has made abstract theological statements about life and death which may be more unhelpful than helpful. Finally, the health care system, particularly as demonstrated by its institutions—the general hospital and nursing homes—tends to be a closed system that makes the parish clergyman feel like an outsider. Thus, when his parishioner and the family are within that system, the clergyman often feels like a fifth wheel, unclear as to how his ministry is to be integrated with the machinations of scientific medicine that seem to be rolling on in their own inexorable way.

This chapter is concerned with three topics: problems of the minister's person in relation to dying and bereavement, problems related to the institution of the Church, and problems related to health care institutions. Though the chapter is "problem centered" it is presented with the hope that by confronting the problems, growth and more effective ministry might result. I hope that clergymen will not "turn away from the drama disillusioned, uncompassionate." By confronting all the starkness of drama dying, and bereavement, we clergy will come to see that, in Bonhoeffer's words, "Then your hour comes, ye friends and brothers! Loyal hearts can change the face of sorrow, softly encircle it with love's most gentle unearthly radiance."

## Problems Which Confront the Minister's Person

Being a clergyman does not protect the individual from confronting a variety of anxieties when facing the issue of death. Too many seminarians and clergy quote too soon such scriptural statements as, "Death is swallowed up in victory. O death, where is thy victory? O death, where is thy sting?" They seem to have in this statement, followed by the message of Christ's triumph, a solid foundation, a proclamation of hope; and yet when it comes from an abstract theological formulation it collapses in the face of the actual situations of the suffering of the dying, or of angry, depressed, and miserable mourners. Or worse yet, it may not collapse. The clergyman can stay apart from actual involvement in the pain and suffering. He can utilize his academic theology to stand aloof, ritualize his quoted comfort to the mourners, ritualize the funeral service, and only be dimly aware that he has isolated himself from "being" with his people. Often this is accompanied by anger directed at the cold physician who isn't being a true family physician-friend and who is heartlessly prolonging life. But professional pots calling professional kettles black assist neither the living to include dying in life, the dying to do so with dignity and respect, nor the bereaved to work openly and healthily through their loss. If the clergyman is to be of assistance, he must first confront the reality of death and his own personal response to that reality. Death does not make a mockery of his theology any more than it makes a physician a failure, though that is often the latter's fear.

Over the past few years I have met with many small groups of lay people, clergy, and seminarians who have considered at some depth the issues of death and bereavement. Many have begun by saying that they saw death as a reality and have not been "bothered by" the concept. When asked, however, to write down the answers to the following questions, the discussion became more real: "If you could choose, when would you choose to die? If you could choose, how would you like to die and how would you not like to die? If you could choose, in what order would you have death come for yourself, your wife or husband, your children, and why?"

These questions often led to the kind of discussion that the partici-pants had not engaged in before in a really open way. Death was confronted as the enemy of the young person or older person who still had dreams, plans, meaningful life activities to work out. The fear of dying was confronted with the following ramifications: possible long suffering, fear of physical or emotional pain, fear of loneliness, fear of people being dishonest or too honest, fear of depleting the family's resources, fear of not dying bravely or in control and thus seeming to have weak spiritual resources, fear of expressing emotions in tears or anger or withdrawal or misunderstood joy and peace, fear of dying with one's secret life or of being open and naked in confession, fear of leaving meaningful relationships with loved persons for an unknown voyage to be taken alone. I have used the word *fear* purposely, for although these discussions often at first caused feelings of discomfort, difficulty in concentrating, an urge to change the subject, and a sense of blueness, these symptoms of anxiety changed as the actual known fears that people had were articulated and were accepted and echoed by others in the group.

Such programs demonstrated that clergy need to begin to consider this problem by first considering the personal ramifications of dying and bereavement. They are often called upon for their professional services or to be an expert in discussing the topic. This can lead them to the assumption that they, therefore, must have all the answers and that the human doubts, fears, frailties, and questions are not allowed them or at least can never be voiced aloud. This attitude was stated by the dying wife of a clergyman who said, "Chaplain, my biggest fear is that I won't be able to carry this off, that I won't be able to die bravely enough and I'll show a lack of faith and bring shame on my husband."

Faith can and does contain doubt. Being a clergyman or clergyman's wife does not mean that one is less than or more than human. Clergy-

138

men often decry being placed in some superhuman role but they should be aware of how they may create this image in the eyes of others by always being the strong one, always being serene in the faith, always having the ready answer for someone else's question and problem. To dare to express one's own humanness and to personally confront the issues of dying and bereavement is the first task. Such a confrontation should not be merely introspective but should be shared openly with others. Then ministry can come from the person and be inclusive of the meaningful elements and statements of the faith. Without such a personal pilgrimage ministry is too often wooden. It shuts off the suffering, the confusion, the variety of feelings of the dying or bereaved, for though these may be intellectually understood they are emotionally intolerable.

## Problems Related to the Institution of the Church

Because the Church is an institution, it can dehumanize individuals in the same ways that any other institution can do. Though it seeks to witness to God's presence in the world, to care for the suffering and the burdened, it needs to consistently exercise judgment on its service and even then it errs in the practice of what it proclaims. Two particular problems have stood out as I have observed our ministry to the dying and bereaved. First, we have tended to ritualize our ministry, making that ministry wooden, and impersonal. Second, we have tended to inhibit emotional expression.

First, let it be said that this is not a criticism of all ritual. However, it is a criticism of that ritual which is automatic, used as a tool by the ministering person, and is more an expression of the need to control the situation than to respond to needs that are being expressed.

Some examples of this may be observed in those visiting the terminally ill patient. On the one hand, hope is seen as important, as it is, and therefore, the visit always stresses encouragement, jokes, cheerful remarks, positive prayers, etc., as though this "ritual" instills hope. On the other hand, reality is seen as important, as it is, so the mood tends to be more somber, even if the patient's mood isn't. There are probing questions such as, "You must be worried?" or "Are you sure you're not feeling bad?" or "Isn't there something you want to talk about?" The ritual of always facing reality is brought into the sickroom by the pastor rather than by his perceiving what is there in the person he is visiting. Finally, spiritual care is seen as important, as it is, so there is a focus on prayers, sacraments, the scriptures, with the emphasis on being sure the sick person is "right with God."

Other illustrations could be cited, but the significant fact is the set of mind of the helping person that causes him to determine his ministry within his own mind, apply it, and keep his mind closed to the messages that would come to him through careful listening. Messages, verbal and nonverbal, are missed. These messages would convey the needs of the sick person, allow for the development of a meaningful relationship in the midst of the crisis, and then permit a ministry to develop with flexibility within the uniqueness of every situation.

Another related issue is demonstrated by the observation that visiting the sick, including the dying, is most frequent when there is acute distress or a sudden crisis and hospitalization. Chronic illnesses, long hospitalizations, being moved to a nursing home or confined to one's own home, mean a decrease of visits from pastors and church visitors over time. We become busy with the new pressing issues of the day, we respond to the new crises, and the sustaining relationships needed by the chronically ill lose out to the ritual of our crisis orientation.

The same phenomena are seen in relationship to the bereaved. At the time of death the ministry of the pastor and the church community are focused. There is a particular ritual act, the funeral, to be performed. It is interesting that in discussing bereavement with pastors their first emphasis will be on the funeral and only with effort can they move from this ritual to consider the total process of grief and mourning. Yet when you talk to the bereaved, they place much less emphasis on the funeral which comes at a time when they are often numb and confused. They stress the loneliness of weeks, months, the first year, when they are confronting their loss, feeling the pain, establishing a new life, and needing a continuity of care that is seldom offered.

In summary, the first need for the dying and/or the bereaved is to be listened to with great care. Then we can discover the unique ways in which they are coping with their crisis, allow them this opportunity as we stand with them, and assist them to discover their strengths and some realistic supports for their weaknesses. Then rituals which are meaningful to their lives can support them in faith and not be perfunctory or unrelated exercises or ineffective defenses against the reality which they are willing to include in their living.

The second problem in ministering to both the dying and the bereaved is the tendency to inhibit emotions. Though we sing of joy and sorrow, tears and hope, despair and love, we have become accustomed to identifying feelings with words and hiding them in our lives. Somehow the Church seems to give the message that faith, the Spirit, the religious life, are demonstrated by a calmness and an ability of the individual to bear his own burdens. Within the institutional framework the liveliness of the Word, the dancing and singing and joyful noise, the weeping and gnashing of sorrow and despair, the anger and cursing, all Biblical realities and expectancies of life, have become taboo. Thus there is a distance among us, for what is real must be hidden. We relate through layers of pretense, and support can only be partial, for it is restricted to indirectness meeting indirectness.

An illustration of this would be the fifty-year-old man sitting at his dining-room table talking to me of the death of his wife three years before. He leaves the table and returns some minutes later with refreshments, a pleasure at serving me, but also a redness to his eyes. We eat, drink coffee, continue to talk, and suddenly the tears are there. He starts to leave, I place my hand on his arm, and the sobbing begins. When the sobs subside, he says, "I haven't cried in front of anybody in three years. I was ashamed, men don't do that, but I often cried alone." Society gives such wrong messages sometimes, and too often the Church supports or helps build these ideas.

Countless bereaved men and women have told of staying away from religious services because of their fear that "I might not be able to control myself. I might break down." They were not only ashamed of this themselves but were trying to be considerate of the congregation saying, "I saw how awkward it made people feel, they didn't know what to do." (These were mainly Protestants. Perhaps it would be different for other faiths, for some Jewish and some Roman Catholic practices encourage emotional expression.) This is strange testimony about the people of God, the caring ones, the ones joined by love. I'm not being sarcastic at this point, for there are many who care, many who love. They bring food, they call on the phone, they invite the widow or widower out, they express concern in doing. But they have difficulty *being with* the person, living through feelings with them, and too often cut off the expression of feelings with kindly meant words: "It will be all right," and "You have to control yourself or you'll make yourself sick." How far that last statement is from our understanding of personality dynamics and yet how often it is used in a society that is fearful of feeling!

Similar illustrations could be given with regard to the dying. Some go toward death angrily fighting. Their anger might be directed toward a doctor, nurse, the pastor, or God, and too often it makes us uncomfortable. The person isn't being a "good Christian," a "good patient," and we have trouble living with someone who fights because he hates leaving this life. Or we sense that a person is "down" and so we offer words of cheer and encouragement. This is not to say that such words are inappropriate or that hope should be dashed. But when they are uttered to protect the helper from the feelings of depression of the terminally ill, the patient perceives this, and the possibility of sharing his reality is lost.

This practice of inhibiting feelings is beginning to change. More clergy are seeing that feelings are real and that their expression can be helpful. Educational materials, preaching, small groups, and expressive worship are all encouraging the bringing of feelings into the open. This change is strange, sometimes fearful, for clergy and lay people. It is different and doesn't quite seem religious. And there is room for some caution, for as the pendulum swings there can be a false worshipping of feelings, a faddish or slavish response that is certainly not liberating. This can also become a problem in ministering to the dying or bereaved if we become convinced that every person must have certain feelings, a certain way of handling his crisis, and our expectations don't allow individuals to deal with their reality in their own way. Perhaps these words of a patient will illustrate my point: "You know, Chaplain, I feel uncomfortable with him. He looks so serious and keeps asking me what's on my mind, and am I sure there isn't something bothering me. It's like he's not listening to what I'm saying but wants something else." Trying to get a patient or a grieved person somewhere may prevent us from getting somewhere with the person. It's his world we want to experience with him, not an image world of our own that we must lead him to.

## The Minister and the Health Care Institutions

Since most people, 70 per cent in urban areas, now die in hospitals or nursing homes, the clergyman must have ready entrée to these facilities if he is to minister to the dying. His entrée to his parishioners is usually well accepted, but very often he then feels isolated within the facility. For hospitals are often closed systems. They have their own jargon, their own hierarchy of relationships, their strange procedures and rules, their internal communication system, their protective defenses against anyone seen as an outsider. Enough has been written about hospitals existing for personnel needs rather than patient needs, for patients and not families, to enable the minister to see that he isn't the only outsider. However, he experiences particular problems in carrying out an effective ministry. One problem could be called the simple lack of trust. Both hospital personnel and clergy contribute to this.

### The Patient's Experience

General hospitals exist primarily for the treatment of acute medical problems that cannot be cared for outside the facility. Even patients with chronic problems only enter the general hospital for relief of an acute problem or some relatively brief, supportive therapy. The hospital staff has a high sense of responsibility and often seem to become possessive of the patient as they diagnose and treat the disease. Patients and families feel a loss of responsibility for their own lives as

they become dependent upon the hospital staff in surroundings per-
vaded with a sense of mystique. The patient is in a strange room that
is something like a bedroom but with differences like oxygen outlets
and other peculiar gadgets; the voice that can come out of the wall
speaker saying, "What is it, Mr. Jones?" or "Have you had a B.M. this
morning Mr. Jones?"; the menu that may be restricted and the food
that is bland and may have to be eaten in bed; the stiff nightshirt that
may have to be worn and that has an opaque front but missing ties so
that one's flank is always exposed; and the bedroom seems to have a
revolving door through which countless people—apparently without
names, since they seldom introduce themselves—come and go, usually
without knocking.

The patient can begin to feel exposed to the world but then he
senses from various subtle and not so subtle hints that there is a
distinction—not the whole world, just the hospital world, and he is
not to worry about that. "We're here to take care of you so have
confidence in us. We know you don't know about all these tests and
procedures, but believe us, have faith in us. Look, don't let the nudity
or seminudity, the inquiries about your bathroom habits, the rides
through the hall in a wheelchair or stretcher to various strange rooms
for various strange tests worry you. We do this all the time, it isn't
personal, it's just part of being a patient. Have faith in us, we know
what we're doing." Those are the implied attitudinal messages conveyed to the patient and family. The patient who is sick, needing
help, uncertain in this strange world, does need to have confidence in
those caring for him. Most often they are kindly, confident in their
knowledge and ability, and for many patients it becomes easy to be
dependent, even to regress and become demanding of more attention
and care rather than demonstrate more initiative and responsibility.
The message has been received: "Let us take over and we will be able
to make you well."

The hospital staff, with its realistic sense of responsibility for an
individual while diagnosing and treating a disease, can develop a
sense of protectiveness, often overprotectiveness, for their patient. A
wife will be asked to leave when the nurse gives her husband a bed
bath, a curious interpretation of modesty and privacy. Ninety-nine
percent of the doctor's notes, and all too often the nurse's notes, neglect the fact that a patient has a social history, that some of the
patient's patterns of living might affect the treatment and the patient's
future, that the patient has a religious history that might be significant, or psychological dynamics that might be particularly relevant to
his functioning. All too often it's as if the patient's life began on his
admission, except for the previous physical symptoms that brought
him to the hospital, and will end on his discharge.

These feelings of ultimate responsibility, of being *the* caring ones,
and the definition of this hospital time as the essential time make the

hospital a closed system. The staff get to know each other, develop complimentary expertise, have their own language and communication shorthand. There are tensions within the various structural lines of the subspecialties of medicine, nursing, social work, chaplaincy, psychiatry, etc., but there is also a sense of belonging, of being part of the hospital staff. The sense of belonging is enhanced by keeping "outsiders" out—be they family, clergy, friends, agencies, even medical and nursing personnel—though this is seldom consciously seen. There is a distrust in sharing responsibility, for this would diffuse control among people who are unknown. To overstate the case, this type of omnipotent power cannot be shared if it is to be sustained. To share it would quickly demonstrate its delusional quality and threaten the "closed system" which is in reality more "closed" by the staff than the patient. They simply are more expert at keeping out the realities of life which the patient, families, and other outside persons are left to deal with on their own even if they are among the most significant of the illness.

All of the above has particular and tragic implications for the terminally ill person, because he does not fit the treatment model. His disease is defeating the essential focus on diagnosis and treatment, and most hospital staffs have not been trained to see that there are other ways of caring than to cure. For example, pain which is often useful in diagnosing an acute illness serves no useful purpose for a patient whose disease is known and who is terminally ill. For that patient pain is awaited with fear; it robs him of attention to more important activities and depletes his energy. Yet, in this country, worrying about addiction, we give medication on demand (usually too late, for by then the pain is present) and make patients feel like cowards or babies if they tell us too often that they hurt. We have done little to preventively control pain in ways that would leave patients alert to do their other important work: saying good-by to life in their own way.

Patients do need to end their lives in their own way and they need to do so with their kinship family and their family of friends. Both of these facts go counter to institutional health care at this time. As already mentioned, patients are seldom given much responsibility in their hospital care. Also, patients' families are seen as outsiders to be treated with kindness at best, tolerated at the worst, but not very significant in the treatment program. For the terminally ill (and many other patients), these attitudes are detrimental. The terminally ill patient needs to be listened to skillfully and then spoken to honestly with great appreciation for his integrity and methods of coping with life. This takes time and the great amounts of time that were spent in *doing for* the patient now need to be spent in *being with* the patient and family. Unfortunately, the "efficient" use of time is not conceived of in this way in the general hospital nor are many staff trained to "be with" in addition to "do for" patients. Thus, the terminally ill demand a different kind of attention, a new kind of care, and this means a change in the system. That is one cause of anxiety. Also, hard-working, often overworked staff, receive rewards for making people well, for curative treatment, and for research into new types of cure. Personnel have received very little education regarding care of the terminally ill and are at least as anxious, some research says more anxious, about death as is the general society. With this anxiety and with their rewards coming from other types of care it is not surprising that the terminally ill in most hospitals are either isolated or treated with heroic measures as if death must be defeated. It would be an error to say, however, that hospitals are satisfied or comfortable with this state of affairs.

To an extent this can be changed by additional training and open discussion of the long-neglected area of caring for the dying patient. However, we know enough now to realize that a new type health care facility is needed for patients who are dying from severely debilitating chronic illnesses. Such facilities as St. Christopher's Hospice in London where they are specialists in providing this kind of care are urgently needed as service, educational, and research facilities in this country. That is why a model of this type facility is being developed in the New Haven area.

## Stereotypes and Symbols

*Clergy enter the hospital world from the outside; as "outsiders" they are often stereotyped.* That is their first problem. They symbolize a great many things for the staff, often not very realistic, and this is a second problem. They may be seen as judging persons. If the staff is anxious and uncomfortable about their care of the terminally ill person and the family, they are not overjoyed by the outside judge. Or clergy are seen as the miracle workers when the muscles of medicine have failed. I've often heard the words, "Well, we've done all we can. It's in your hands now." That is usually an introduction to a wasted, comatose patient, on a respirator and filled with innumerable tubes, whose family is torn between "Help her to live" versus "For God's sake let her die." Or clergy are seen as the antithesis to scientific medicine— to the real world. They are the contemporary magicians, the worshipers of "pie in the sky," the ones who won't admit that God and religion are really crutches and should die. Here the attitude is one of disdain, or perplexity—"Why should those fellows be involved"—leading to avoidance. But there are also many positive attitudes from staff who have seen how patients and families welcome and appreciate a ministry and from staff who are active participants in some religious community.

Problems, but also opportunities, exist for clergy because of their being seen in some symbolic way. Around the crisis situations of terminal illness they have the opportunity to minister in a world that is different from their parish. This causes anxiety so often that clergy tend to confine their ministry to the parishioner who is sick and to the family. Many times they may hear complaints, be unclear as to what the patient knows or doesn't know, feel the isolation of the patient and family, and therefore they identify with their parishioners. They feel their "outsiderness," are angered by this, wonder why their importance hasn't been seen, why they haven't been included on the team. They make very valid comments such as "I've known this woman and her family for ten years. I know she is a lot stronger than they think she is. Doesn't anybody care about that information? I'm her priest but I can't even find her doctor to talk to him." Two worlds, both too closed, have met, and it becomes clearer how we have divided people up, divided functions up, developed in-group communication but little communication among groups. The minister is saying, "These people are my parishioners. I am their priest—pastor—rabbi, I'm concerned for them and responsible for them." The doctor is saying, along with other hospital staff, "These persons are my patients. They have entrusted their physical lives to me. I am concerned for them." The authorities of "two worlds," meeting over the crisis of terminal illness, unfortunately seldom meet with mutual understanding. Each ministers from his own world, and the patient and family must integrate the two. If they are inconsistent with one another, the task is difficult.

It is unrealistic to expect an immediate change in the attitudes that have developed, because the clergyman is seen in various symbolic or stereotyped ways and because he also conceives of "the doctor" or "the hospital" in a stereotyped manner. The problem of stereotyping can only be resolved when there is an effort to eliminate the false images through encounters that let persons, not conceptions of roles, be seen. This breaking down of false images can begin with the clergy if they enlarge their ministry to include more of the hospital world than simply their parishioners. Most hospital chaplains have encountered the same type of stereotyping, but it has been broken down when they have become known and accepted as persons. The question is how this can happen for the clergyman visiting the hospital.

## Practical Problems

*Clergy often maintain their isolation.* The administrator of the large medical center where I work said to me shortly after my arrival, "You know I've wondered why in the three hospitals where I've been an administrator no new clergy in the community ever came in to meet me and ask me about the hospital where his parishioners would be coming for treatment." This man was an active layman and would have appreciated being of help to the clergy as well as turning to them for help if he knew of their interest. The Department of Religious Ministries of this medical center now holds orientation sessions for new clergy, and the hospital occasionally sponsors luncheons and dinners for all clergy of the area to provide a time for their questions and ideas as well as a program on some new developments within the hospital. Though it is helpful to have a chaplaincy department to develop such programs, many could be fostered by a community ecumenical clergy group in collaboration with the hospital administration. The care of the terminally ill patient would be of utmost interest to clergy, and at many hospitals they would find the administration, medical staff, and nursing staff willing to engage in such a discussion.

The most useful encounter can occur around a minister's parishioner who is also a physician's patient. Many clergy have said to me, "I don't know what the doctor has told the patient and this really handicaps me." When asked if he has seen the doctor, the answer is usually, "I've looked for him when I've been in but I've never seen him." I've then asked, "Have you left a message?" to which the reply is generally something like, "No. I didn't want to bother him. I thought I'd check the next time I was in."

Unfortunately the clergy seldom connect the reason for their visiting their parishioners in the afternoon—their own schedules plus that being the time a patient is most available—with the reason he seldom sees the doctor. The doctors' and the clergy's schedules are designed differently and, therefore, they will most often miss each other. For the minister to casually encounter the physician he should be in the hospital between 7:00 and 10:00 A.M., and even if he were there then, it might be awkward for a conference because of the rush of planned activity. Another time is often between 5:00 and 7:00 P.M., but that is awkward for the clergy who are often eating prior to going to evening meetings. Somehow the clergy seem to reflect the same general awe that keeps schoolchildren distant from teachers and adults distant from doctors. They need to overcome such timidity with medical authorities, pick up the telephone, and arrange a meeting or have a telephone conversation. Physicians are not always saving lives and they are not all so closed mouthed (some are) that they will not cooperate with other persons who are trying to be helpful to their patients.

In a conversation with a physician who is unknown to the clergyman it is important that the minister do some listening. A physician recently stopped in my office to blow off steam saying, "I had a call from Rev. B. today about my patient Mr. C. He started right off giving me hell for not telling Mr. C. more about his illness, what the treatments were for, what the prognosis was. I couldn't even interrupt. When he finally calmed down I told him that I had spoken very clearly to Mr. C. about all those things; at the time he heard me, but a day later it was as if nothing had been discussed. I tried to be polite in telling Rev. B. about anxiety and denial, but, hell, haven't these guys ever heard of these things." Most clergy have but when they are in the anxious situation of terminal illness, when they are the recipients of the patient's anger, depression, and bargaining, when they are feeling left off the team and perhaps over-identifying with the patient, they can act out of their anxiety rather than seek information that will clarify the situation. The minister who is accustomed to running the whole show in his parish, of being the authority, has to learn how to collaborate with another authority in this situation. One way is to guard against assumptions, to ask clear questions, to listen carefully to answers, and then to articulate how he sees himself carrying out his own role, with an openness to receiving a response.

One of the clergy's greatest allies in their ministry to the terminally ill and the family is the head nurse and her nursing staff. This again means that the clergyman must develop relationships. It is amazing how many clergy, even those not wearing some distinctive garb, think that they are automatically recognized as clergy. It is more amazing to see how many clergy, when they have been identified as to role, think that then everyone automatically knows and accepts what they are doing. This could be called the "messiah image," which implies that the wearer of the cloth can do no wrong. If the clergy want to over-come their role as loners, if they want their ministry to be seen as important and integrated with the total care of patients and families, then they need to introduce themselves to the nurses responsible for the floors where their parishioners are located. More than that, when they have had significant contacts with a terminally ill patient or his family, they need to talk with the nurse to see if this has produced data unknown to her and important to her and other staff. This means that the minister seriously considers the limits of confidentiality, his pride in his own ability to handle tough situations alone, and his fear of sharing his fears and mistakes. This takes a high degree of trust, but only as the caring individuals—nurses and clergy—come to know each other can a realistic determination of the degree of trust possible be determined.

Finally, if the clergyman (or clergywoman) is to effectively minister to the terminally ill and their family, he must plan how he can be available to them when he is needed. Since most deaths now occur within hospitals, he must plan with hospital personnel. He should educate his congregation to the fact that he is not only available at times of crisis, but that he wants to be called. He should let the family of a terminally ill person know that he is always available to them or to the patient, *if* he really means that. Families will often hesitate to call a clergyman at 3:00 A.M. where a nurse won't. A nurse is accustomed to people being available twenty-four hours a day. If a minister has a significant relationship with a terminally ill parishioner and/or his family, then being present at the final stage of life and the moment of death can be very important. The nursing staff need to know that he wants to be called, his telephone number needs to be written down, and he must be sure to be available when called. This requires some planning that few clergy have done. When it is necessary, how can they be reached on a twenty-four hour basis? What priority would such a call have over a meeting, a service of worship, or a class?

I hope this kind of questioning will bring us out of an abstract discussion of death, or of an academic discussion of such questions as, "What should the patient be told?" Terminal illness is a reality, and people are living through it. Bereaved families exist and some of them are now sitting in hospitals anticipating the death of a loved one and already experiencing the loss and grief. Death occurs and at a moment in time this life does cease. How close does the minister want to be to these realities? How present does he wish to be to the patient and the family? It is difficult to walk through this valley, but in my experience the minister can be more than counselor, can be more than personally supportive; he can be part of a relationship in which the reality of the presence of God is experienced. But does he really want to take this journey with his parishioners?

## Conclusions

The three types of problems that the minister has in relating to the terminally ill—problems which confront the minister's person, problems related to the institution of the Church, and problems of being outside the health care institution—wherever they really exist and are recognized, are possible of solution and offer opportunities for change and a more effective ministry. These solutions include confronting the minister's personal anxieties about death, making rituals relevant to specific situations and relationships, including the expression of emotion within the life of the Church, making death and bereavement meaningful topics for congregational reflection and response, and developing ways of being more included in the care given a parishioner who has become a patient. Finally, we must ask ourselves whether we use these problems to keep us away from a very difficult task. If so, they usefully serve a hidden motive and will continue to exist, though clamored about, because we really don't want them solved. To remove them would necessitate a very demanding ministry. Do we want that?

# 23

# The Clergyman as the Dying Patient's Agent
## — ROBERT M. VEATCH

In the beginning it was commanded that man should subdue the earth and have dominion over every living thing. With the technological revolution, for the first time we really have the power to re-engineer the nature of man. And with this awesome power comes the responsibility over man's own life and death. Now we can freeze man so that we can wait for a cure for his particular disease. It is our faith in technology that leads us blindly to believe that someday we shall learn how to thaw him out again. Now we can keep a creature's cells alive virtually indefinitely through the use of artificial respirators, artifical cardiac pacemakers, and intravenous feeding with artificial food. Some people would say this gives rise to what we might call an artificial human being. Now a surgeon with skill, a bit of nerve, and some luck can and has removed the heart from a living human being and maintained him for 65 hours on mechanical devices while he waits for a suitable heart for transplantation.

This new potential for controlling life and, therefore, for controlling death has brought a tremendous number of theological and ethical questions to the foreground. As we discover new means for life, we are discovering anew the meaning of death. There is simultaneously a horror and a fascination with the subject of death. This is what the English scholar Geoffrey Gorer had in mind when he called death "pornographic."[1] Like sex was for the Victorians and still may be for many of us, there is simultaneously an obsession and a compulsive concealment of the phenomena of death in our culture. Death is taboo, to use a religious term. This simultaneous preoccupation with and avoidance of the subject reveals that even the most secularized of us will still treat death as a sacred event. Is not that really the meaning of sacred—something which is elevated to ultimate significance, which at the same time is viewed with dread and awe? As we come closer and closer to controlling our biological processes through new biological, technological breakthroughs, death stands as that ultimate abyss, as a great unknown, much as it has since the creation of the human species. Certainly we have overpowered a few diseases, polio, pellagra, and even the plague. These are diseases which used to snuff out life prematurely, but there is not one piece of medical research that has ever told us a thing about death itself. It stands before us as, from the scientific point at least, the great unknown; probably more awe inspiring than ever before. We have not even changed significantly the average life expectancy of an infrant born in this world in the last twenty years.

This chapter will deal with a few of the ethical issues which these medical advances have brought into being, and will be limited to three topics: first, the definition of death; second, the ethics of allowing a dying person to die; and third, the ethics of what to tell a patient who is about to die. These topics will be examined particularly with respect to the clergy's role in caring for the dying patient.

## The Definition of Death

In 1968, a sixty-two-year-old man named John Stuckwish received a transplanted heart from Dr. Denton Cooley and his team at St. Luke's Hospital in Houston. The donor was a thirty-six-year-old man, named Clarence Nicks. Nicks' brain had been damaged beyond any possibility of returning to its normal functions by a beating he had received at the hands of a group of attackers. There were no signs of electrical activity in the brain and there was no spontaneous respiration. It is critical, however, that his heart continued to beat for some time. Dr. Cooley and his team took the heart from Nicks' body and placed it in that of Mr. Stuckwish. The ethical questions arise when one begins to reflect on the relationship of the surgeon, the donor, and the donor's attackers. The people who beat up this donor have now been arrested. They pleaded in their defense that Nicks was not dead at the time the heart was given; his heart was still beating. The attackers even went beyond that to accuse the physician who removed the heart of murdering Nicks. To complicate matters, one physician had pronounced Nicks dead at the time his brain stopped functioning and his respiratory function stopped, while another physician specifically disagreed.

### Criteria for Brain Death

What is it that constitutes life and what constitutes death? A committee of distinguished physicians, lawyers, theologians, and scientists was established at Harvard to formulate new criteria for determining brain death, growing out of conflicts such as the one we just described. Four criteria were put forward by this committee.[2]

1. Unreceptivity and unresponsivity
2. No movements or breathing
3. No reflexes
4. Flat electroencephalogram

Dr. Beecher, who is really the prime mover, argues that the electroencephalogram itself is not absolutely necessary to establish brain death by these criteria. Rather, it is confirmatory evidence. These tests are to be repeated in 24 hours. There is one further proviso: individuals under central-nervous-system depressants and those with internal temperature below 90 degrees are specifically excluded. Now, what are the ethical questions resulting from these criteria? Two very serious disputes have arisen.

The first is the charge that those who are proposing the new definition of death are promoting the termination of life of an individual for a social benefit: transplants. Many of those who are arguing for the new definition of death are quite explicit in stating that this, indeed, is their motive. Henry Beecher, for instance, has said that "there is indeed a life saving potential in the new definition for when accepted, it will lead to greater availability than formally of essential organs in viable condition, for transplantation."[3] Beecher goes on to ask, "Can society afford to discard the organs of such patients if they can be used to restore health to salvageable patients?"

But the question that philosophers and theologians such as Hans Jonas and Paul Ramsey are asking is: "Is it ethically acceptable to bring this kind of a consideration into the discussion?" Paul Ramsey says, "If no person's death should, for this purpose, be hastened, then the definition of death, itself, should not, for this purpose, be updated."[4] Hans Jonas, in informal discussion, has asked what I think is an even more embarrassing question: "If the need for organs justifies a new definition of death, then why not define everybody over 65 as dead for the purpose of giving organs, or, why not define every criminal or every socially undesirable person as being dead?" It is rather embarrassing that we have become interested in the definition of death just at the point in history where it is useful for us to take organs from a dying or recently dead cadaver and give them to another individual. In essence, we are putting the good of the collective society over against that of an individual. The need for organs can in no way ethically be introduced as an argument for a definition. We cannot go about adopting a particular definition solely because it serves the function of providing organs.

On the other hand, it is more plausible to argue that because, for the first time in history, the exact specification of what death means now has crucial social significance, we can, for this reason, look at what the meaning of death is in our society and begin to refine it with more precision than we ever needed before. Whenever we get to the position of arguing that a new definition of death should be adopted because it would provide organs, we have made an unconscionable violation of an individual's right to life. On the other hand, if all we are saying is that we should look at what we have always meant by the concept of death and make it more precise because, as a by-product, we are able to serve a social function, then I find no fault with that position.

Now to the definition of death itself. There are three questions that have been conflated under the rubric of the definition of death. These must get sorted out immediately because they have a great deal to do with separating the role of the clergyman and theologian on the one hand and the physician and other scientific specialists on the other. We must ask first, what is the proper concept of death? Second, where is the locus of death? And third, what criteria are to be used for death?

## Concept of Death

The concept of death is purely theological and philosophical. In asking what our concept of death is, we are looking for some quantum change in the character and status of what is essentially significant in an individual. There is a quantum change in the way that person is treated, the rights that are attributed to him, and the meaning of his existence. There is a change in the sacred character of an individual life. I think it should be completely clear that we are really talking about a theology of the nature of man, and as such there is very little that scientific research can contribute. There are several alternatives for what is this ultimate significance that changes dramatically at the point of death. Probably the most traditional formulation of it is that death occurs when the soul leaves the body. In black music, there is soul when there is life or spirit. Soul is really a shorthand phrase for that which is ultimately valued. But another formulation, which has dominated Western thought for many centuries, is that death occurs when there is a cessation of the flow of vital body fluids, specifically blood and breath. Breath has been associated with life from early days of the Judeo-Christian tradition. The theological phrase is "the breath of life." Another concept is the loss of capacity to integrate body activity. Death means an irreversible loss of this capacity. This concept of death is rapidly gaining ascendancy. It is now reflected in the law on death in Kansas and Maryland and is the concept that many of us would now use. This neurologically based concept of death, however, places ultimate value on a wider set of functions than is at first realized. Would we consider a man dead, for instance, who possessed the capacity to spontaneously integrate respiration and who yet would never have the ability to think, feel, or interact socially? This is the basis for the suggestion of a fourth concept of death, one which focuses specifically on the body's capacity for consciousness and social interaction. Some are now beginning to propose that we must go beyond the broader neurological concept of death to isolate this one capacity as that which is essential to man's humanness. The important thing to realize is that all of these are attempts to state theologically or philosophically the nature of man. They are clearly theological and philosophical questions.

## The Locus of Death

There is a second question wrapped up in the notion of the definition of death. Once we have given attention to the theological question of the concept of death, then it becomes time to look at the locus of death. After we have determined the nature of man and the concept of death, that gives us a basis for looking at what parts of the body we should examine if we want to determine whether a man is living or dead. If blood and breath are the essence of man, then apparently we look at the heart and the lungs. If the soul is the essence of man, then we look for the seat of the soul and perhaps, if we are to believe Descartes' anatomy, the pineal body of the brain. Others find it in the heart or in the breath. If bodily integrating capacity is the essence of man, then, on the basis of present scientific knowledge, we would say that that is the central nervous system and, specifically, the brain. The question of the locus of death, unlike the question of the concept of death, is largely, but not totally, a technical question. There is really, at this point, an interacting of the theological and technical.

A third question that is incorporated into the discussion about the definition of death is the criteria for pronouncing death. It is at this point that we are clearly in the realm of the technical. We need to have criteria for determining when those critical organs which we have established under the discussion of the locus of death have irreversibly ceased functioning. The Harvard Committee listed criteria for determining when the brain had irreversibly ceased functioning. These criteria are technical measures for making the prediction that the brain will not resume functioning. It becomes clear that these are purely technical questions when we reflect on what would happen if next week someone produced evidence that we needed not these four, but perhaps five or six, criteria, and that these five or six criteria were better predictors of irreversible coma and loss of neurological integrating capacity than the four listed by the Harvard report. No one would hesitate for a moment to adopt the new list of criteria on the basis of the new scientific evidence. On the other hand, the position that irreversible loss of consciousness as the concept of death which we consider on the basis of our theological and philosophical tradition to be the meaning of death can in no way be tested empirically. I can conceive of no scientific research which would in any way impinge upon that theological and philosophical proposition. There might be clearly scientific research which would change the locus of death. If we suddenly learned that consciousness was in the legs, we would all then begin focusing on the legs in the search for the seat of consciousness.

We have then three questions bound up in what is sometimes passed off as the discussion of the definition of death. If one claims that brain death is death indeed and that the list from the Harvard Committee report contains the criteria for death, then he is arguing three things simultaneously. First, he is telling us what technical functions to look at to determine when the brain is irreversibly ceased; that is a technical question based on the criteria of pronouncing death. Secondly, he is making a statement about the concept of death—that death is the irreversible loss of neurological integrating capacity. Thirdly, he has made a statement, which is simultaneously technical and theological, that the locus of this activity we consider to be essentially human is in the brain. There are three different propositions. Only by separating those which are technical criteria questions from those which are theological and philosophical will we be able to grapple adequately with the ethical problems related to the definition of death.

## Clergy Roles

Now having made these distinctions, what is the clergyman or clergywoman's role in the issues related to the definition of death? I see the clergyman as a central figure in what, at first, might have appeared to be a purely technical medical problem. I see the clergyman as having four functions. The first function is his classical *teaching function*; he must serve as the theologian making clear what the nature of man is. At the parish level, the clergyman must communicate this theological understanding to his congregation, helping each individual to work out his own theology of the nature of man. There is no one else equipped to do this kind of a job. It is utterly beyond the scope of the scientist. And no one else is doing this kind of job. William May, chairman of the Religion Department at Indiana University, has said that if the clergyman is suddenly overcome with the feeling of tongue-tied irrelevancy when he enters a sickroom, he gets exactly what he deserves if he has not worked out the problem of the meaning of death with his congregation with a series of sermons or with a series of work sessions with lay groups.[5] He must also teach the congregation that within the definition of death there are both these technical and theological questions, so that a layman in his congregation when he becomes a patient in a hospital is not trapped into the situation of saying, "Doctor, I'm sure that you know best what should be done for my condition so I will leave it totally up to you." We are dealing here with a question where a patient has not only the right, but the duty, to express his own ethical and theological views. It is only through training by the religious and philosophical leadership of the community that the patient is going to be prepared to carry out this awesome task.

In addition to the teaching function, there is a second function, a *counseling function*. When the clergyman has adequately prepared his congregation and is dealing with a dying patient, that patient desperately needs counsel and guidance in the formulation of his conscience. The physician is particularly poorly equipped to serve this role. In the first place he has absolutely no expertise or experience on the theological questions. He has probably not thought them through in these terms although he may have thought through the technical aspects in great detail. Secondly, he is psychologically not equipped to counsel his patients. The physician whose patient is dying has just failed in what he thinks is his life's work. His patient is dying. He is absolutely unprepared in such a condition to serve as a counselor for someone who has just presented him with an ultimate failure. In addition, the psychologist, Herman Feifel, has shown that physicians have more anxiety and are more afraid of death than the layman.[6] He suggests that physicians often enter the field of medicine because they do have such fear and fixation about death. Thirdly, he may not be equipped ethically to serve the counselor function because he, himself, may be committed to a professional ethic which is summarized as "preserve life at all costs." If that is not our more universal ethical norm which grows out of our religious and theological tradition, the physician is placed in a very embarrassing position of affirming a particular ethical responsibility of preserving life and at the same time having to counsel a patient whose dying perhaps should not be prolonged according to his own religious and ethical values.

The third function for the clergyman is the *listening function*. Elisabeth Kübler-Ross has shown that listening to the dying patient is one of the most needed and one of the most kind acts one can perform.[7] The physician is poorly equipped to fulfill this function as well. The physician is a doer. He is used to giving the patient "orders," not listening to him. The usual phrase is the "management" of the dying patient. The relationship between the physician and patient is an authoritarian one that just does not lend itself to the role of listening. The physician sees himself as the patient sees him, in a position of authority. The dreadful analogy often used is that of his relating to the patient as a parent does to a child. The listening role is not the appropriate role for the pysician to be placed in. But it is the kind of role that the clergyman can serve. The clergyman stands in a relationship of "covenant" with his congregation. He is able to relate to the parishioners of his congregation not only as teacher, but also as peer and equal. As such he is able to listen to the patient when the patient most needs to be listened to. The covenantal relationship establishes a bond of mutual trust, responsibility, and community.

There is a final function which is related to the word *minister*. The Latin word for minister means "servant." The *servant function* is, at least in some cases, the role of advocate. Whereas the physician is not in a position to serve as the patient's advocate, in some cases the clergyman is and more so than anybody else. This may mean caring for the dying as opposed to trying to cure him. It may also mean serving as the patient's agent or spokesman. At the present point in the debate about the concept of death and the locus of death and the criteria for death, the patient should have the right to be declared dead if he has clearly communicated that he wants to be and the criteria for "brain death" are present. On the other hand, he should have the right to be kept alive if he wants to be. The physician who disagrees places the patient in a very awkward position. This is a situation where the patient needs an advocate, and the clergyman is often the only person in our society who is equipped to serve this role. For some decisions which must be made in the care of the dying patient, the next of kin is legally delegated to serve as patient's agent. This is true in decisions pertaining to the donation of organs under the Uniform Anatomical Gift Act in the situation where the deceased has not specified his wishes. But even in cases where a relative is available to exercise judgment about the care of the patient, someone is needed with the informal authority and know-how to see that the patient's interests are protected. The clergyman in some (but unfortunately not all) cases has the moral legitimation to play this serving role. His activity on behalf of the patient may be rejected, but it can hardly be ignored. The claim, by the clergyman, that the patient's moral rights and responsibilities are in jeopardy must have some impact. Not only does the clergyman have moral legitimation, he also has something approximating peer status with the medical authorities in the community. He has a professional education and social standing which, while not necessarily equal to that of the physician, is probably as close as any class of individuals who is likely to have knowledge of the patient's interests. Finally, the clergyman frequently has access to and a working knowledge of the hospital structure. He is expected to be present during the dying process; he may know his way around the hospital floor; and may know how to "work the system." No one else close to the patient can approach the clergyman as an effective servant of the patient's interests.

## Allowing the Dying To Die

The second area of the ethical issues that I wanted to deal with is the question of allowing the dying person to die. There has to be a clear separation between the question of the definition of death and that of allowing a patient to die. Some of the members of that group who would flatly oppose pronouncing a man dead who had the criteria for brain death established, but a heart still beating would still argue that nothing should be done for that patient which would impede the dying process. These are two totally separate questions. Cystic fibrosis is a disease pertinent to this discussion. A 10-year-old girl had had cystic fibrosis from birth. This child had been admitted to the hospital many times throughout the course of her life, and this time the disease was very near its termination. She had been given from days to months to live. The physicians continued to use every heroic measure possible to squeeze a few more breaths out of this dying body. The mother pleaded with the physician just to make the girl's life comfortable, but to do nothing to continue the agony of the gasping for breath. Yet these physicians committed to the preservation of life at all costs could not bring themselves to cease the introduction of those heroic measures. It was not solely a case of blindly proceeding on what they had been taught. Particularly the nurses involved in the case had become very fond of this girl. It was out of a real sense of humaneness that they could not bring themselves to refuse a procedure which would continue her life for a few more minutes or days. Dr. Kübler-Ross tells of a twenty-one-year-old girl who was hospitalized with acute leukemia. She describes the agony that this girl and her parents went through.

We interviewed this patient in November and she left the hospital soon after to come back to our treatment center New Year's Eve of the same year. At that time she was not expected to live through the night. When I went to visit the parents in the waiting room outside the intensive treatment unit, the father was in so much agony and pain that he was unable to relate. He sat numb and immobilized and could not enter into a conversation between the patient's mother and myself. . . . [The mother] had related two strange incidents to me at the time when her child was dying. When I listened to my own emotional reactions to these incidents, it suddenly occurred to me that both of them represented people as insensitive, imperceptive and cruel. I asked her if something cruel and insensitive happened right now to her child. At this moment the father lifted his head up and started to cry and the mother pointed with her hands in the direction of the daughter's room. When I visited the patient I realized what the parents tried to relate. She lay there half naked on the bed hooked up on infusions, tubes, tracheostomy, on a respirator and staring desperately around the room. My first impulse was to cover her with the bedsheet when a nurse approached me and

said, "Don't bother—she will push it off again in a minute." Approaching the patient, she held my hand and pointed to the ceiling. I looked up
and asked if the light was bothering her. She grabbed my hands and
kissed them, thus communicating that my impression was correct.
When I asked for the lights to be switched off, the nurse came again and
reminded me of the rules and regulations of the intensive treatment
unit. Then I asked for a chair for the mother to sit with her child. I was
told that they could not give her a chair anymore because the mother
stayed more than five minutes during the previous visit. This girl died
eight hours after the physicians had informed the parents of her imminent death—she died with the noon light in her eyes, tubes in the
mouth and veins and the parents sitting outside in the waiting room.[8]

There are two ethical questions arising from the question of allowing to die. The first is separating allowing to die from positive euthanasia and both of these from suicide. One study asking physicians their
attitudes about preservation of life revealed that 59 per cent would
practice "negative" euthanasia if authorized by a statement, whereas
27 per cent would practice "positive" euthanasia "if changes occurred" permitting it.[9] This suggests that if a patient wanted treatment
stopped, even if there were a written statement confirming it, the
chances are only slightly more than fifty-fifty that his wishes would be
carried out. Unfortunately the study does not address itself to the
actual behavior of physicians in response to the attempt of the dying
patient to exercise his existing legal right to refuse treatment. If a
patient desired active ending of his life and there were "changes" to
permit this, the chances are apparently less than three in ten that he
would receive it. Even more troubling is the unanswered question of
what happens if a patient did not want euthanasia (active or passive)
and were unconscious in front of a physician who does favor it? The
physician, according to one dominant interpretation of professional
ethics, is committed to the preservation of life, often stated as the
preservation of life at all costs. Lord Brock, who was a distinguished
British physician, has argued that the physician has a special ethical
duty which requires that he avoid euthanasia in either its positive or
negative forms. Brock says:

> As an ordinary citizen I must expect that the killing of an unwanted can
> be legalized by an Act of Parliament, but as a doctor I must know that
> there are certain things which are part of the ethics of our profession
> that an Act of Parliament cannot justify or make acceptable. . . . We may
> accept the need for euthanasia on social grounds but we cannot accept
> that doctors should implement it.[10]

The clergyman is once again placed in a position of serving as the
patient's teacher and counselor and listener and advocate. If the patient is pleading with the physician that a dehumanizing procedure be

stopped and the physician refuses to hear or act, then it is the clergy-man's role along with the family's to act as the patient's advocate. It's an awesome responsibility, but one that no one else could fill. If one considers the alternatives of injecting an air bubble into the bloodstream, cutting off the intravenous feeding tube, and refusing to perform a major piece of heroic surgery, there is a continuum between an action which would bring about the death by an agent who would not otherwise be responsible for the patient's death and an omission of an action which causes a death which would have occurred in any case. George Fletcher has argued that the critical difference is between ac-tions (or which one is legally responsible) and omissions (for which one may or may not be responsible depending upon the established rela-tionship).[11]

While the distinction is complex, we may be able to reach some consensus on a general conclusion. First, if given a choice, in the case of a terminal patient who is not suffering, between injecting an air bubble and simply turning off a respirator, virtually all would opt for turning off the respirator as the morally preferable course of action. Secondly, in spite of the moral preference for allowing to die, there may be cases, theoretically at least, where action to end life is morally preferable. This would be the case where there is prolonged, intract-able suffering. Thirdly, these cases are extremely rare, especially if one considers morally justifiable the giving of pain-killing drugs even if the indirect side effect is possibly the hastening of death. Finally, we must consider that even if there might be rare cases where active killing of the dying patient is morally acceptable, it might be an un-wise policy to make such actions legal if the risk from abuse and misjudgment is considered too severe.

It seems to me that the important dimension is the extent to which a patient's freedom is preserved and the extent to which his humanity and dignity are maintained. I would favor legislation establishing clear procedures for patients to consent to or refuse to consent to procedures where they would be allowed to die and in which the patient's appointed agent or next of kin would have the right to make such judgments when the patient is judged to be incompetent and has a specific, progressive, terminal illness. The physician may, upon occa-sion, be called upon to be the patient's agent in such cases. But far more often he should play the role of teacher and counselor preparing the patient to make such decisions. In those cases where the patient or the patient's agent has made the awful decision to refuse further death prolonging treatment, the clergyman may once again have to serve the patient as advocate of his legal and moral rights protecting him from unwanted intervention or unwanted cessation of treatment.

Pope Pius XII issued a very important pronouncement called the "Prolongation of Life," in which he stated his position clearly: "Nor-mally, one is held to use only ordinary means. Ordinary according to the circumstances, the persons, the places, the times and the culture. That is to say, means that do not involve grave burden to one's self or another."[12] The Protestant denominations have not spoken as clearly as Pius XII has. While the distinction between ordinary and extraordinary means is common, it is terribly confusing. The classical view of the technologically oriented person, including many physicians, is that the reference point is not to the individual patient but to the procedure per se. An I.V. drip is an ordinary procedure, but a heart transplant or hemodialysis or the freezing of a body is considered extraordinary. A second way of using the terms *ordinary* and *extraordinary* is seen in the less technologically oriented. The papal statement says that ordinary is used according to the circumstances of persons, such that the procedures do not involve any grave burden on one's self or another. Here extraordinary takes on meaning specifically with reference to the individual patient's condition, not the status of technology. The clergyman may have to serve as a spokesman for this perspective in the technological hospital environment.

This still leaves open the meaning of the terms. One usage apparently derives from common language. The distinction is made between usual and unusual treatments. This has the disadvantage of making normative those practices which may be common but still morally questionable. A second meaning of the terms rests on the distinction between useful and useless procedures. This seems to be incorporated into the papal position. Yet there may still be those procedures which would be considered useful (in maintaining life) and yet still morally elective. A patient on a hemodialysis machine must be attached for a period of eight to twelve hours at a time, two to three days a week. Through the use of this machine, it is possible that the person may live for many, many years. A patient recently decided that if he did not get a kidney transplant within a specified time he would withdraw voluntarily from the use of the hemodialysis machine because he found the machine dehumanizing, making his life so miserable that even though it would preserve his life in the medical sense, it destroyed it in a psychological and moral sense. Many, myself included, would consider hemodialysis extraordinary in the sense of being morally elective. Thus the distinction really reduces to those procedures which are morally elective and those which are not. For us, morally elective procedures are those which are useless or which impose great burden on the patient.

## What To Tell The Dying Patient

The third and last area to be considered in which the clergyman must confront the biological revolution in the case of the dying is that of what to tell the dying patient. A fifty-four-year-old woman had been hospitalized for two weeks with severe abdominal pain. She was examined by a medical student, and by the attending physician, and the chief resident in the hospital. And on a Wednesday morning she had exploratory surgery and the findings of that surgery were that she had stage IV cancer of the cervix with a five-year survival rate of between 0 and 20 per cent. The medical student who was dealing with this woman wanted to discuss his findings with her, sharing with her as gently as possible that, while there was hope for new treatments and that they would do everything they possibly could in the way of radiation therapy and drug therapy, her outlook was not good and that realistically the chance of survival for more than five years was very small. The student, before he discussed this with the patient, decided to check with his chief resident, and was told very forcefully that "We never tell a patient that he has cancer." Cancer is a word that is not to be used in the medical context. The physician's duty was to do all that he could to make the patient's life as comfortable as possible and that perhaps he should tell her that she has a neoplastic lesion with secondary metastatic growth, but above all he should never tell her that she has cancer.

Physicians and laymen have very different reactions to this case. Clergymen seem to be particularly at odds with the medical professionals. One study has shown that 88 per cent of physicians follow the usual policy of not telling their patients that they have cancer.[13] Yet 98.5 per cent of patients being examined in a cancer-detection center reported that they wanted to be told of the diagnosis. Among patients with cancer, 89 per cent said they preferred knowing and 82 per cent of a group of patients with no known cancer seen in a hospital outpatient department said they would want to know.[14] The polarization between the groups could hardly be greater, and the clergyman will often be the only one with the knowledge and resources to protect the patient's interests.

Yet the physicians who were discussing the case above were making a similar claim. They held that it was the physician's obligation above all to do no harm to the patient. These physicians sincerely believed that ordinary people such as this patient could not handle the bad news that cancer is present. Thus even if the morally relevant consideration is limited to the consequences for the patient, there will be serious disagreement about just what benefits the patient and keeps him from harm. While the medical professional seems to feel that the patient will be happier if he is not told, many laymen would argue quite the reverse. The anxiety generated by conditions of uncertainty produce far more suffering than the awful knowledge of the terminal diagnosis. It prohibits responsible decision making and freedom on the part of the patient, producing a pain far greater than the agony of the truth. Clergymen seem to share this weighing of the utilitarian calculus. To the extent that they share the patient's perspective, they

are in a far better position than the physician to advise on what
should be told.

But the ethical argument may turn on a quite different form of
reasoning. There are, according to this position, formal right-making
characteristics of actions including the obligation to speak truthfully
on matters which may reasonably be expected to be meaningful or
useful to the patient and the obligations which arise from the contrac-
tual or covenantal relationship. There is a moral dilemma when a
patient whose ethical position emphasizes these characteristics encounters a physician whose normative ethics emphasizes consequences
pure and simple. This arises over and above those conflicts between
patient and physician who might weigh relative consequences differently. If different ethical norms are operating or different weighings
are given to the consequences, the two could hardly be expected to
reach the same moral conclusion.

Patients must participate in decisions as much as possible if they are
to overcome the feeling of loss of control. All these things will lead to
the conclusion that if one has to keep from doing harm to a patient,
the patient must be told and dealt with in truth and dignity. At least
from the perspective of many patients, honesty and trust in the pa-
tient-physician relationship is extremely important. It is demoralizing
for everyone concerned to be stuck with a lie. Life tends to get organized around it. Of all the kinds of lies that one might get stuck with,
the lie to one's self is probably the worst of all. This is the big lie—
thinking to one's self that he has done his ethical duty by telling his
patient that she has a neoplastic lesion with metastatic growth.

What is the clergyman's role in the case of what to tell the dying
patient? The four roles are education, counseling, listening and finally,
advocacy. That there is a close relationship between truthfulness and
human dignity; that hope need not be limited to hope for a cure; that
harm comes from the anxiety of mistrust as well as from the hearing of
bad news: all of these are things that can often best be brought out by
the clergyman. There is a need for counseling, to convey this information to the patient and to alert him to the fact that he often has to
pursue information he might want. There is a need for listening to the
patient so that a patient's position will not be interpreted solely by
one individual. Those who have studied the dying patient say that
patients deny for those who want denial and they accept death openly
for those who accept it. The physician may be hearing denial when a
clergyman is hearing acceptance. It is the clergyman's role to listen to
the patient's position and communicate it to the physician and others
when necessary. Finally, the fourth function of the clergyman is sometimes to be the advocate for the patient. This puts the clergyman in a
very difficult situation. There are times when the clergyman might
know that the patient is being lied to and yet he is hardly in a position
to break the confidence between the patient and the physician. But he

must live boldly, become the advocate of the patient, and insist that the patient's interests be protected even if it means a very hard task of telling the truth to the dying patient. This is an awesome task for the clergyman, but one he must often undertake. There is no one else who can.

# Notes

1. G. Gorer, *Death, Grief and Mourning* (New York: Doubleday & Company, Inc., 1965).

2. Harvard Medical School Ad Hoc Committee to Examine the Definition of Brain Death, "A Definition of Irreversible Coma," *Journal of the American Medical Association* 205 (1967): 337. See also "Refinements in Criteria for the Determination of Death: An Appraisal," a Report by the Task Force on Death and Dying of the Institute of Society, Ethics and the Life Sciences, *Journal of the American Medical Association* 221 (1972): 48.

3. H. Beecher, "The New Definition of Death: Some Opposing Views" (Paper presented at the meetings of the American Association for the Advancement of Science, December 1970).

4. P. Ramsey, "On Updating Procedures for Stating that a Man Has Died," in *The Patient as Person* (New Haven, Conn.: Yale University Press, 1970).

5. W. May, "The Sacral Power of Death in Contemporary Culture" (Paper presented at the meetings of the American Association for the Advancement of Science, December 1970).

6. H. Feifel, S. Hanson, R. Jones, and L. Edwards, "Physicians Consider Death," Proceedings of the American Psychological Association, Seventy-fifth Annual Convention, 1967.

7. E. Kübler-Ross, *On Death and Dying* (New York: The Macmillan Company, 1969).

8. Ibid.

9. N. K. Brown et al., "The Preservation of Life," *Journal of the American Medical Association* 211 (1970): 76.

10. Lord Brock, "Euthanasia," *Proceedings of the Royal Society of Medicine* 63 (1970): 662.

11. G. Fletcher, "Prolonging Life," *Washington Law Review* 42 (1967): 999.

12. Pius XII, "Prolongation of Life," *Observatore Romano* 4 (1957): 393.

13. D. Oken, "What to Tell the Cancer Patient: A Study of Medical Attitudes," *Journal of the American Medical Association* 175 (1961): 1120.

14. W. D. Kelly and S. R. Friesen, "Do Cancer Patients Want to Be Told?" *Surgery* (June 1950).

# 24

# The Physician's Ministry to the Dying — JAMES A. KNIGHT

Dark mother always gliding near with soft feet
Have none chanted for thee a chant of fullest welcome?
Then I chant it for thee; I glorify thee above all;
I bring thee a song, that when thou must indeed come,
Come unfalteringly.[1]

—Walt Whitman

The physician, as a dedicated adversary of death, has to confront death in at least three different ways: first, as a healer, fighting for his patients' lives; second, as a helper, easing the way when death becomes inevitable; and third, as a mortal human being, eventually, also to die. All three of these tasks will be easier for the physician who has come to terms with his or her own feelings about death. In his work with his dying patients, the physician is forced to recognize, at some level of his consciousness, the interrelationship between the anticipation of death and the conduct of life. Also, his work with the dying offers a special legacy in that one "can enhance the meaning of being alive by touching the edge of a life that is slipping away."[2]

## Tendency to Withdraw from the Dying

A physician is trained to outwit death whenever possible, and this is still an essential element in the medical and psychological care of patients. He is a protagonist of health who believes that disease and death are his enemies.

In spite of his limitations as a healer, the doctor can help to prevent lonely and anguished deaths. To do so, he must be not only available but accessible as a person. He can then maintain respect for his patient, because his primary antipathy will be directed only toward the cause of suffering, not toward the person who suffers.

The care of terminal patients arouses some of the most pervasive

164

fears in man—extinction, victimization, helplessness, passivity, aban-donment, disfigurement, and above all, loss of self-esteem. The physi-cian who treats such patients is also subject to these fears. Since he is bound to a patient who is dying, the physician must also face an exacerbation of his own sense of failure, guilt, and intimations of personal mortality. In such a situation, there is a tendency to with-draw from the dying. Walt Whitman challenges us through his words: "The faithful hand of the living does not desert the hand of the dy-ing."

## Sensitive Response to the Dying

The medical student is no exception in wanting to withdraw from the dying patient. If he recognizes this tendency in himself and works to understand and neutralize it, he will be able to keep company with and minister to the dying as the good physician should. He must learn early in his training that he can be an instrument of therapy. Mankind has known from the beginning of time that healing and comfort come from human relationships. This is often forgotten in today's emphasis on drugs and surgical procedures.

The dying patient experiences a penetrating type of loneliness and aloneness. He needs a shoulder to lean on as he becomes oriented to his new situation and works out some kind of solution to his approach-ing fate. The family also has its burdens. If those who tend the sick form a true community of spirit with the dying patient, the feelings of isolation and separation accompanying death are neutralized or mini-mized. He leaves the prison of his aloneness and feels united again to others.

The terminally ill patient often has an unconscious fear of being "untouchable." The touch or caress is the most basic nonverbal com-forting technique we possess, and it communicates a solace to the disturbed or frightened patient that words can never produce. Thus the routine back rub or massage given by the nurse engenders both physical and psychic well-being. The clergyman places his hands upon the patient in prayer. The physician examines with his hands the part of the body in pain. These are all ministries which the dying patient desperately needs.

No patient should ever be treated as if he had no future. Although a patient is terminal, he should be encouraged to plan for himself and his family, particularly his children. Children are living defenses against the fear of being blotted out, and terminally ill patients can derive comfort and satisfaction from the visits of their children and from helping them plan their future.

Many feel that to neglect the question of whether the patient is dying often causes his sense of alienation and profound loneliness to increase. Patients usually feel alienated from the family that avoids or distorts the truth or outright lies about it—especially a truth that is suspected or known by the patient. This was a major point emphasized by Leo Tolstoy in "The Death of Ivan Ilyich."[3] The dying Ivan Ilyich was tormented by the deception of his family. He was forced to participate in the deception and thereby had to live all alone on the brink of an abyss, with no one who understood or shared in depth his feelings.

The final days and hours can be a very meaningful experience for both patient and family. C. S. Lewis, in a vivid account of how he moved through stages in his grief after his wife's death, gives us these memorable words: "It is incredible how much happiness, even how much gaiety we sometimes had together after all hope was gone. How long, how tranquilly, how nourishingly, we talked together that last night."[4]

The road of truth is not always the easiest road to follow in ministering to the dying, but it is the road which can lead to fruitful encounter and a sense of community in the life of the patient. Such a course of action demands an attitude of sensitive response, of entering into the feelings of the patient rather than avoiding or directing them.

A sensitive response to the patient is dependent in part upon a solid understanding of the stages through which a patient passes in coming to grips with his feelings about his imminent death. Elisabeth Kübler-Ross has outlined these stages and discussed them in detail in her splendid book *On Death and Dying*.[5] The first stage is denial, followed in the second by anger and resentment. The third stage is one of bargaining for an extension of time for a specific purpose, or possibly for a few days without pain. Most of the bargains are made with God and are kept secret. Depression, reactive and preparatory, constitutes the fourth stage. The reactive depression is related to those who have been dependent upon the patient. The preparatory depression is actually anticipatory grieving for the impending loss by the dying person of all his love objects—his life, family, possessions, work, and friends. The fifth stage is acceptance and the final rest before the long journey.

## Handling the Truth with the Dying Patient

How anxious patients are to know the truth about their illness is a topic often discussed with more passion than insight. At times a patient asks everybody except his own doctor (the doctor in charge) what his prognosis is, when he actually knows already, at some level, that he is close to death. Such a patient is frightened of just this verdict from his own doctor. The doctor in charge is less approachable on this subject exactly because he is the keeper of desolate truths. By the same token, others caring for and around the dying patient are more accessible because they bring no final verdict. The doctor's reticence to discuss the patient's impending death cannot be written off solely as a question of his own fear of death or his concern over his professional self-esteem. The dimensions of death are too awesome to admit of easy professional solution. The problem of isolation and fear of abandonment of the dying patient cannot be solved by handing out truth like a pill, for the truth can be both disturbing and isolating.

While a patient may know that death is imminent, he may prefer to hide this truth for a very crucial reason. If his family and friends know that he is near death, they may flee his presence and leave him alone and isolated. Although hiding the truth may interfere considerably with deep relationships or meaningful communication, it may forestall abandonment which the patient dreads about as much as death.

All of us share the common difficulty of being inhibited in our talk with the dying because the alternatives in language appear so limited. Too often we assume that the only form of truth telling is direct, immediate, and blunt. Such a frontal approach seems to be the only alternative to evasive silence or circumlocution. This need not be so. The explicit discussion of diagnosis or prognosis with every patient in clinical detail would be foolhardy. At the same time, the alternative to blunt talk need not be double-talk, a condescending cheerfulness, or a frightening silence. As William May points out, there is such a thing as indirect discourse in both love and death.[6]

Many patients instinctively question the doctor in an indirect fashion about their own death. They may ask for example, should they buy a house, go on to graduate school, get married, or have plastic surgery done on their faces. A quick yes or no would interfere with further discussion. When the doctor responds in such a way that he conveys to them somehow that he recognizes the importance of the question, it becomes possible for the patients to discuss their fears, uncertainties, and anxieties. Sharing then takes place between doctor and patient.

A fine example of communicating meaningfully by indirection involves the great physician William Osler at the bedside of a little girl. The mother of the little girl wrote of the interaction:

> He visited our little Janet twice every day from the middle of October until her death a month later, and these visits she looked forward to with a pathetic eagerness and joy. There would be a little tap, low down on the door which would be pushed open, and a crouching figure playing goblin would come in, and in a high pitched voice would ask if the fairy godmother was at home and could he have a bit of tea. Instantly

the sick-room was turned into a fairyland, and in fairy language he would talk about the flowers, the birds, and the dolls who sat at the foot of the bed who were always greeted with, "Well, all ye loves." In the course of this he would manage to find out all he wanted to know about the little patient. . . . The most exquisite moment came one cold, raw, November morning when the end was near, and he mysteriously brought out from his inside pocket a beautiful red rose carefully wrapped in paper, and told how he had watched this last rose of summer growing in his garden and how the rose had called out to him as he passed by, that she wished to go along with him to see his little lassie. That evening we all had a fairy teaparty, at a tiny tea table by the bed, Sir William talking to the rose, his 'little lassie', and her mother in the most exquisite way; and presently he slipped out of the room just as mysteriously as he had entered it, all crouched down on his heels; and the little girl understood that neither the fairies nor people could always have the color of a red rose in their cheeks, or stay as long as they wanted in one place, but that they nevertheless would be very happy in another home and must not let the people they left behind, particularly their parents, feel badly about it; and the little girl understood and was not unhappy.[7]

A distinction should be made between accepting the "facts" regarding one's condition while still acknowledging their tentativeness or penultimacy. Gabriel Marcel emphasizes the point that a too ready consent to the impending death of another may constitute a betrayal, since it is in effect giving him up to death.[8] In fact, it seems that a doctor's surrendering a patient too quickly and too readily to death would strike at the very heart of the doctor-patient relationship and jeopardize or destroy it. Thus one may accept a provisional prognosis without consenting to it as inevitable. Further, the manner in which those around the patient respond to the prognosis may be of greater importance than how and to what extent they communicate the specific terms of that prognosis.

The physician's role in caring for the dying has been defined by Samuel L. Feder: "I don't have any idea how we help a person to die; but I am sure we can do much to help a person to *live* until the time of death."[9] Hopefully, whenever the truth is told, the relationship between doctor and patient is marked by sufficient trust and confidence to support and affirm the dying regardless of what the truth might be.

The doctor, like everybody else, may be able to do very little in the face of death, for deeds are no easier to come by than words in extremity. T. S. Eliot once said that there are two types of problems faced in life. In one case the appropriate question is "What are we going to do about it?" In the other case, "How do we behave toward it?" The more searching problems in life are of the latter kind. In a profession tinged with messianic pretension, the doctor is accustomed to tackling problems in terms of the first question and is left somewhat bereft when the question is inappropriate to the crisis. The doctor has a hard time learning that while he may not be able to do anything about a tragedy, this inability need not altogether disable his behavior toward it.

Because death was terrible to Cicero, desirable to Cato, and unimportant to Socrates, it should be obvious that before telling the dying person anything, one has to know who he is and the mechanisms he uses to cope with difficult and insoluble problems. More to the point than what to tell the patient is an understanding of the doctor's relationship to him and how best to keep in touch with the patient along his course so that he is free to raise issues as he chooses.

## Spiritual Resources of the Patient

The doctor will be working with patients whose religious faith ranges from zero to profound commitment. The doctor's yearning for rationality must make place for religious faith in larger meanings as he works with his patients. A tremendous resource for a patient is a deep-seated faith that he is not suspended over an abyss. While agreeing with the existentialists that awareness of personal death brings greater intensity and clarification to life, the patient may simultaneously hold the conviction that death as an occurrence holds, also, the promise of a greater fullness of Being.

## Prolonging Life or Prolonging the Act of Dying

After George Washington, dying of edema of the larynx, had suffered repeated bleedings, purgings, and blisterings—then current methods of scientific medicine—he implored his persecutors: "I pray you to take no more trouble for me. Let me go quietly."

George Washington's physicians were diligent to the end because in his case they thought they were prolonging life, when actually they were prolonging the act of dying. With our modern scientific skills and drugs we can prolong the act of dying to frightening lengths. Often we hear statements today, usually regarding the elderly, that science will not let people die naturally, even when they are ready and longing for death. This "scientific" attitude is often considered respect for life, but one wonders if it is not, in the words of Martin Buber, "man's lust for whittling away the secret of death." The good physician trains himself to prolong life, but not to prolong the act of dying. The terrifying dilemma which often confronts him is "Which am I doing?"

If it has been established beyond any doubt that the patient is *in extremis*, if the physician and his associates are in unanimous agreement, and if there is no question in anyone's mind about the prognosis, are extraordinary measures indicated to keep the patient alive a little longer? Only rarely would the patient's wish be known in this matter. Usually the relatives would not want to prolong the act of dying. No voices representative of the Roman Catholic or Greek Orthodox Churches or of the Jewish or Protestant faiths have suggested that physicians should try extraordinary means to keep life going when every process of the body is determined to die. Pope Pius XII issued an encyclical during the last year of his life which stated the official position of the Roman Catholic Church as not requiring extraordinary means when only suffering and certain death lie ahead.

Traditional moralists draw a distinction between "ordinary" and "extraordinary" medical or surgical procedures. This view was restated well by Pope Pius XII in an allocution to physicians in November 1957. "Ordinary" would mean considerably more than normal treatment and includes whatever treatment a patient can obtain and undergo without imposing an excessive burden on himself and others. A sick man and those who care for him are bound to employ the available means of preserving life and restoring health. "Extraordinary" treatment has been defined as "what is very costly, or very painful, or very difficult, or very dangerous." A patient is not bound to submit to extraordinary treatment, nor is the doctor bound to apply such extraordinary means in cases where the patient cannot be consulted.

This reasonably clear traditional distinction does not exactly fit a number of dilemmas in patient care today. Many of the mechanical procedures now in use ought perhaps to be regarded in their proper function as temporary. Their purpose is to win time for the restorative measures to take effect. If, after these mechanical measures have been given a fair trial according to the circumstances of the case, it becomes evident that the patient can never be restored to functioning on his own, it may be said that the mechanical procedures have failed in their purpose. All they are accomplishing is keeping the patient in a condition of artificially arrested death, and they should therefore be discontinued.

We must learn to desist from those useless technological interventions and institutional practices that deny to the dying a good end. This purpose could be accomplished to a great extent by restoring to medical practice the ethic of allowing a person to die.[10] Life being what it is, there frequently comes a moment when it is good to die and therefore good to allow another to go unvexed to death.

One of the complicating factors today is the relentless determination to push back the frontiers of medicine. There is generally present in patient care the operative, but unspoken, assumption that any death is a medical defeat. Consequently, responsible patient care dictates the use of every conceivable device and stratagem for the prolongation of life. In the physician's therapeutic zeal, he must not forget that death comes to all, and that while medicine is dedicated to life and health, it is not to be abused by forcing upon a patient *in extremis* extraordinary measures when only suffering and certain death lie ahead.

The problem with the medical student and physician is that they do not perceive the healing task in existential terms, but rather in death-defensive terms. Of course, the sick person aids and abets the doctor's view of his task by making a silent plea to the doctor, "Don't let me die." If we cannot pretend that we defeat death, we give in to frustration and dissatisfaction. We cannot remember that all treatment is in a sense a delaying action. We need constantly to be reminded of one of medicine's most famous maxims: To heal rarely, to relieve often, and to comfort always.

## Ethical Issues in Terminal Care

Many disturbing ethical issues related to the terminal care of patients are emerging. Chief among these is euthanasia.

When family and patient request death, and prognosis indicates no hope, is the doctor morally free to perform the necessary task? To what extent does a physician have the right to assume a position of conscious arbiter over life and death? Although a doctor deals daily on the boundary of life and death, the fundamental orientation of his life remains the protection and enhancement of life.

Another category of euthanasia has to do with instances where it is not requested by the patient, for example, because of unconsciousness. The question may be asked, "Of what use is such a life?" The concept of the sanctity of life not only has served to protect the helpless and weak from destruction, but quite as importantly, has served to keep men from becoming inhuman in their treatment of one another. At the same time, the sanctity-of-life concept may be used as a screen to hide behind, thus obscuring our true commitment to the quality of life, to human life.

The recent capability in organ transplantation has brought to the front the matter of "sacrificial" euthanasia, so that organs may be used for tansplantation. The positive hastening of death for such an organ-procurement purpose courts many dangers and perils. At the same time, the opportunity to have one's death be the occasion for possible new life for another does offer a means of transcending the negative aspects of death.

The ethic of allowing a person to die should be based solely on a consideration of the welfare of the dying patient himself and not on a consideration of the benefits that accrue to others. It is one thing to take one's bearing from the patient and his interests to protect him against the onslaught of new technologies and institutionalized loneliness; but quite a different thing to take one's bearings from the interests of, or costs and benefits to, relatives or society. Kass has stated the problem succinctly: "The first is in keeping with the physician's duty to act as the loyal agent of his patient; the second is a perversion of that duty, because it renders the physician, in this decisive test of his loyalty, merely an agent of society, and ultimately, her executioner."[11] In his relations with individual patients, the physician must serve their interests. The medical profession cannot retain trustworthiness or trust if it does otherwise.

The ethics of medical practice has always distinguished between allowing to die and deliberately taking some positive step to hasten the termination of life or speed its downward trajectory. In allowing to die, or avoiding prolonging the act of dying, the intent is to desist from engaging in useless "treatments" precisely because they are no longer treatments and to engage instead in the positive acts of comforting and keeping company with the dying patient. In taking a positive step to hasten death, the doctor does become involved in killing. The agent of the death in the first situation is the patient's disease; in the second situation, the physician. It is hoped that medical ethics will preserve this distinction.

It seems reasonable, however, that in certain unusual conditions the notion of a good death with dignity may encompass the right to have one's death directly hastened. In time, acts of mercy killing may be legalized. If they are, two qualifications should be insisted upon. The first is that the hastening of the end should never be undertaken for anyone's benefit but the dying patient. The second qualification is that the physician not participate in the hastening, for this would violate a cardinal principle of medical ethics.

Because of financial burdens upon a family or intolerable suffering, a patient without any chance of recovery may want his life taken or, if able, may want to take it himself. Possibly, for financial and emotional reasons, the patient may be justified in taking his life. But would his family see it that way? For example, if a family felt some measure of genuine affection for their terminally ill husband and father, would not his taking his own life become an indictment upon their loyalty and love?

Many have found comfort in the option that they could terminate their lives if circumstances became intolerable. Nietzsche has expressed this concept clearly: "The thought of suicide is a great consolation: by means of it one gets successfully through many a bad night."[12] Sir Thomas Browne, in *Religio Medici*, expressed a similar idea: "We are in the power of no calamity while death is in our own."

Arthur Koestler, while incarcerated in a Spanish prison where daily killings were numerous, felt himself at the end of his tether. While scouting around his cell to identify anything that could be used for suicide, he discovered a splinter of glass in the window frame of his prison cell. Now he possessed an instrument for committing suicide, and its possession brought him utter comfort.[13]

Much of the conversation regarding euthanasia centers around liberation from intolerable suffering or a physical state worse than death. In the event the patient is physically unable to carry out the suicide act, then he would want others to perform the act for him. This kind of available option seems to bring comfort to certain people.

The philosophical concept of double effect would apply to a person wanting to terminate his life because, for example, of intolerable pain. His primary intention is to relieve pain. Another consequence, the termination of his life, would be secondary.

## Conclusions

We must ever remind ourselves of the dignity and profundity often attained by an individual in his final hours. Such a reminder is contained in a letter from a soldier to his wife, written in the last hours of a combat mission, knowing he would not survive:

> It is strange that people value things only when they are about to lose them. The vast distance is spanned by the bridge from heart to heart. . . . As long as there are shores, there will always be bridges. We should have the courage to walk on them. One bridge leads to you, the other to eternity; at the very end they are the same for me. Tomorrow I shall set forth on the last bridge; give me your hand, so that crossing it won't be so hard."[14]

## Notes

1. "When Lilacs Last in the Dooryard Bloom'd," in *The Pocket Book of Verse*, ed., W. E. Speare (New York: Pocket Books, Inc., 1940).

2. A. D. Weisman, *On Dying and Denying* (New York: Behavioral Publications, 1972).

3. Leo Tolstoy, "The Death of Ivan Ilyich," *Selected Tales* (Washington, D.C.: National Home Library Foundation, 1935).

4. C. S. Lewis, *A Grief Observed* (New York: Seabury Press, Inc., 1961).

5. E. Kübler-Ross, *On Death and Dying* (New York: The Macmillan Company, 1969).

6. W. May, "The Sacral Power of Death in Contemporary Experience," in *Perspectives on Death*, ed., L. O. Mills (Nashville, Tenn.: Abingdon Press, 1969), pp. 168–195.

7. H. Cushing, *The Life of Sir William Osler* (New York: Oxford University Press, 1940).

8. G. Marcel, *Homo Viator: Introduction to a Metaphysic of Hope* (New York: Harper & Row, Publishers, Inc., Harper Torchbooks, 1962).

9. S. L. Feder, "Attitudes of Patients with Advanced Malignancy," in *Death and Dying: Attitudes of Patient and Doctor* (Proceedings of the Group for the Advancement of Psychiatry Conference, 1965).

10. Paul Ramsey, *The Patient as Person: Explorations in Medical Ethics* (New Haven, Conn.: Yale University Press, 1970), pp. 113–164.

11. L. R. Kass, "Death as an Event," *Science* 173 (1971): 698–702.

12. F. W. Nietzsche, *Beyond Good and Evil* (IV. 157), *The Philosophy of Nietzsche* (New York: Modern Library, Inc., 1954), p. 468.

13. A. Koestler, *Dialogue with Death*, trans. T. and P. Blewitt (New York: The Macmillan Company, 1960), pp. 74–75.

14. *Chicago Daily Tribune*, Oct. 7, 1961.

# 25

# *Alternatives to Cure in Ministration to the Dying*
## — JOSEPH R. PROULX

Counsel, care, and cure are three essential components of the helping process. In actual ministration to the dying, the cure component remains predominant, while counsel and care play subordinate roles. It would seem logical to suggest that counsel and care should supersede cure in any comprehensive program aimed at the terminally ill. An assumption central to this idea is that elements of both counseling and caring are inherent in the roles of chaplains and nurses. It is to this combination of professional roles that we turn our attention.

## Counseling and Caring

Chaplains and nurses have a great deal to offer the dying out of their special preparations and selected clinical experiences. Moreover, as these professionals move away from their isolated bases of knowledge and toward more common ground, the effects of their ministrations become synergistic.

Although the chaplain's mission is fraught with theological overtones, and often the dying do view this person as a mediator between themselves and God nonetheless, the contemporary chaplain represents even more, a counselor. What the dying person may want and need is a concerned, listening presence; the comfort, strength, and support of another *human* being. In the throes of the struggle, the dying patient is frightened of the unknown which lies ahead. He is tormented and reduced by the impersonalization of the institutional setting. He has lost confidence in himself, his fellow beings, and his God, if he believes in one. Under such dire circumstances the chaplain's visit may help to restore to the patient a sense of worth and dignity.

In addition, the chaplain may bring to the confrontation a sense of authentic understanding. This type of understanding undergirds any definitive, interpersonal contact, for in essence it deals with being. It is the relationship of one human with another; it implies trust, sharing, and concern. The relationship embodies the mystical virtues of Faith, Hope, and Charity. It is the man of God working as the man of Man.

What is being suggested is a transformation of role, a "going on" and "going beyond" the traditional clerical dimensions. No longer need the terminally ill fear the chaplain's presence, for what is offered now is a humanitarian ideal, a bond of sharing, an affinity of one for the other. Although this may seem to be a somewhat idealized perspective, it would also seem to represent a feasible goal for all concerned clergy who would endeavor to minister to the dying and the bereaved.

What modifications may be prescribed for the professional nursing role? Although the nurse is in an excellent position—owing to temporal and spatial factors—to interact with those under her care, the availability of sheer physical presence does not always mean that satisfactory interpersonal relationships will follow. Many nurses have not been given the opportunity to explore their own feelings in relation to such crucial issues as death and dying. In attempting to escape from this deficit, members of the nursing staff may withdraw from communicating with patients who are experiencing crisis situations. The stereotyped image of the nurse—starched, efficient, and aloof—suggests health workers who do things to people without actually relating to the people. Although efficiency and capability on the part of the nurse are desirable attributes, they are not synonymous with the nurse's ability to share herself as a person.

The professional nurse role has inherent positive factors, mentioned previously, which, if used effectively, may help the nurse transcend traditional practices in the care of the dying. However, the nurse's presence, associated with knowledge and skills to alleviate physical suffering and promote bodily comfort, and the occupational restrictions of time and place are but a part of the caring role. The essence of the truly professional role indicates that what is needed in addition is concern and commitment—again, the humanitarian ideal as evidenced in the relationship of one being for another and *with* another.

The implication here is that the professional nurse is one who has faced up to her own difficulties about death and dying, and that she is someone who would be able to communicate the message to the patient: "You are not going to die alone."

What is suggested is that both chaplains and nurses alter their traditional perspectives. The former by lowering their gaze from ethereal regions, and the latter by raising their eyes from the mere physical. Where these lines of vision meet is the focal point of a new relationship between two key members of the health team.

One last word of caution is necessary. By no means is it implied that the chaplain should forsake completely his spiritual ministry, nor should the nurse totally abandon her attention to physical concerns. Rather, the objectives of both team members should be combined in work with the terminally ill.

## A Synergistic Approach: The Possibilities

Possibilities for chaplains and nurses to join forces may be briefly outlined under the following rubrics: awareness, sharing, and creativity.

Sarosi defines awareness as "a unitary process, a passive state of openness, a sensitivity to things, nature, people, and ideas."[1] Before chaplain and nurse become aware of their proposed joint role, it is necessary for each to become sensitive to the other. This implies a mutual appraisal of the other's role with its attendant assets and liabilities. In addition, an appreciation of the other's goals for the patient, the means of attaining these ends, and the obstacles encountered in fulfilling these ideals could bring individual endeavors more in line with the group focus.

Sharing is involvement. It suggests a give and take between persons. The self is transcended and a partnership is formed. The crux of sharing is a meaningful relationship. Both chaplain and nurse may avail themselves of the relationship to chart new directions in patient welfare utilizing the best from both disciplines: biological, emotional, social, and spiritual components of care. Movement in this direction with medicine as an ally has recently appeared in the literature.[2]

Creativity suggests new ways of doing things, of coping, of being. It is especially important when death is imminent. The professional person becomes a sounding board for the dying patient to test the latter's hopes against the external realities which encompass him. Both chaplain and nurse must guard against proferring invalid objects of hope to the terminal patient. Working together, then, chaplains and nurses may help the dying to create valid alternatives to desires, wishes, and dreams which are no longer within the patient's grasp. Work with the dying is a creative, albeit difficult, experience in the truest and finest sense.

## Some Implications

How may the possibilities of awareness, sharing, and creativity be developed and expanded? They may be explored along two avenues: formal education, which implies the professional schooling before actual practice; and programs in continuing education, referring to the ongoing development of personal and professional skills while actively engaged in practice. Since this chapter primarily concerns practitioners rather than students, it is to continuing education that the following remarks are addressed.

Part of the process of becoming a person—as well as a concerned professional—involves getting in touch with the inner self. The professional must explore his or her own feelings of anxiety, hopelessness, and loneliness. Therefore, objectives to be tested as plausible grounds for curricular adoption are: personal growth and development (the understanding of self, particularly the awareness of individual problems which may hamper effective interactions with others); development of existing interpersonal skills (the art of communicating with others, the capacity to listen effectively, the ability to detect nuances of meaning in shared communication, and the use of nondirective and other interview techniques); and, emphasis on selected human phenomena which have significant emotional overtones (the classic example is, of course, death and dying).

In the work setting, the means of accomplishing these objectives would be through the practitioner's use of self. The self may be probed and expanded by participation in individual counseling sessions or group work. Since the former is often seen as too time consuming and costly, the idea of group work appears as the most practical approach to the educational problem.

Small-group work especially provides opportunities for the professional health team members to identify their feelings, identify the feelings of others, and to interact or share these feelings with one another. For example, "The nurses involved find that the philosophies and techniques of the group training program do affect their nursing practice for the better. They report increased communication skills, increased awareness of their own feelings, a greater emphasis with patients on the here and now, and greater confidence in dealing with small groups on the ward."[3]

Ideally, the type of group which is recommended is the multidisciplinary group composed of professionals from all health fields. However, if this approach is not always feasible, it is suggested that chaplains and nurses form an interdisciplinary group of their own.

In the early phases of the educational program, group work might center on the development of self, personal awareness, and communication strategies. As the group members progress through the curriculum, emphasis might switch toward the sharing of clinical experiences, for example, the dying patient. The case study methodology of teaching might be used at this particular juncture. Lastly, group members may plan and promote clinically oriented, interdisciplinary case conferences which focus on the distinctly human aspects of practice and which may be shared with other professionals: physician, social worker, etc. Planned seminars and lecture courses on various topics led by various health team members could supplement the case conference.

As a final word about the proposed partnership between chaplain and nurse, I should like to quote Paul Tillich: "But an understanding of the differences as well as the mutual within-each-otherness of the dimensions can remove the conflict and create an intensive collaboration of helpers in all dimensions of health and healing."[4]

## Notes

1. Grace Mahlum Sarosi, "A Critical Theory: The Nurse as a Fully Human Person," *Nursing Forum*, vol. 7, no. 4 (1968), p. 360.

2. Granger E. Westberg, "Contextual Teaching of Pastoral Care in a Neighborhood Church-Clinic," in *Explorations in Ministry: A Report on the Ministry in the 70's Project* (New York: IDOC, North America, 1971), pp. 174–190.

3. Eugene F. Gauron, Shirlee A. Proctor, and Patricia J. Schroder, "Group Therapy Training: A Multidisciplinary Approach," *Perspectives in Psychiatric Care* 7 (November-December 1970): 267.

4. Paul Tillich, "The Meaning of Health," *Perspectives in Biology and Medicine* 5 (Autumn 1961): 100.

# 26

## *Learning to Talk with the Cancer Patient*
## — ARNOLDUS GOUDSMIT

As a member of a multidisciplinary team planning for a panel discussion on "The Comprehensive Support of the Patient with Advanced Cancer and His Family," I asked a representative of a nursing home association, "What are some of the problems which nursing home operators experience for which the panel might be able to present some helpful suggestions?" It appeared there were two questions: "How do you relate to the family?" and "What can we do about the maid?" The latter question referred to the fact that it had become apparent that the maid was the member of the nursing home staff most likely to react very emotionally ("go to pieces," as it was described) when one of the residents of a nursing home died.

The frequency and intensity of excessive emotional reactions in some of its staff are recognized as real problems by the nursing home community. The author had become familiar with a similar situation when, as chief of the oncology section of a Veterans Administration Hospital, he attended multidisciplinary, comprehensive, cancer-care conferences held at the hospital. The charge nurse, the social worker, the chaplain, and the clinical psychologist of the section also attended these conferences. Soon after this project was started I learned from the nurse about reactions on the part of some of the ward personnel to the death of certain cancer patients; about the crying, sobbing, and profound grieving among some of the involved staff; about the feeling of responsibility of the charge nurse and her closest associates to provide support, build understanding, and activate coping mechanisms for those overcome by grief reactions; and, finally, how almost exclusively the nurses' aides and the cleaning ladies, rather than the registered or the licensed practical nurses, exhibited the most conspicuous grief reactions.

The similiarity between these independently made observations makes one wonder whether there might not be some important underlying common factor operating in these two situations. And if so, might it teach us something about communication and thanatology, about learning to talk with the cancer patient?

Cancer patients represent something like a very special subspecies of human beings, different from most other individuals, at least in the contemporary United States. Most people go around taking life very much for granted and expecting that tomorrow will be just about like today. To be sure, they will be one day older, but in all probability they will not feel one bit older than they had the previous day. For all practical purposes people go about the business of daily living very much as if life would never end. Not so the cancer patient: the moment he receives the message of his diagnosis (by whatever means this should reach him) he knows that from this point on his days are numbered. He feels that what he has to look forward to is a steady decline of his capabilities and the development of progressive disabilities and discomforts. He finds himself segregated from the rest of mankind, not unlike the prisoner on death row. He is going to die, while the rest of the world will continue to live. As a matter of fact, he is well on his way toward death: he knows it, his family knows it, everyone knows it. So with all to end pretty soon, what is the use of these few more weeks or months still to be lived through without the perspective of a long-range future of glorious years, sights to be seen, events to be celebrated, relationships to be consummated? What is the use of it all? And the whole community appears ready to fall into line: as the news is related, the patient is regarded as virtually dead already. "He" has become different from "us." "His" problems are different from "ours", and communication, in the sense of honest sharing is stifled.

## Emotional Reactions to the Dying Patient

How about the maids and the cleaning ladies? There appear to be a number of reasons why they develop special attachments to advanced cancer patients. In the first place, these maids and cleaning ladies are, by and large, situated on the lower rungs of the socioeconomic ladder and have experienced the hardships, deprivations, and frustrations of such a position. Few would envy them; few would trade places with them. But now, exposed to the cancer patient, they see an individual who may have had more money, received a better education, enjoyed a less stressful marital relationship, and encountered fewer difficulties in raising children, but to whom all of these advantages at this time have little or no value. To have one's health, at least not to have cancer, that is worth more than all the riches and all the status symbols in the world. This realization, perhaps for the first time, of having something that someone might be jealous of, easily could induce rarely experienced sentiments of worth and power in those who serve in the lower echelons of the health establishment.

With their new-found status they find themselves able to talk with the cancer patient in a relaxed and down-to-earth manner. This occurs at a time when most of the patient's other conversations are limited to relatives and health personnel, all of whom have lifelong, socially structured roles to play as well as feelings of ambivalence, guilt, impotence, and grief to cope with. Thus it is easy to see how at this late stage in the cancer patient's life, with its deprivations and alienation, a new and genuine, open and honest relationship may develop. Unfortunately, because of the special features of the situation and the artificiality of the environment, many cleaning ladies and maids may not realize sufficiently their vulnerability to an emotional crisis when the patient dies.

Nursing, medical, and other professional staff are much less likely to develop the personal involvement with patients because their means of communication take place through the medium of medical and nursing signs, symptoms, activities, medications, and procedures. Because professionals have been told that what the cancer patient dreads most is not death or suffering but abandonment, they can be seen to engage all too often, not in genuine and caring inquiries, but in the more trivial and superficial aspects of the patient's existence. Parenthetically, most of the cleaning personnel have fewer, if any, assigned duties and organizationally structured relationships with the patients. Therefore, they are more free (and unprotected) in the development of their person-to-person dealings with them.

As they keep a safe emotional distance between themselves and a cancer patient, the friends, relatives, and health professionals too often fail to provide the empathy and understanding, the willing ear, and the open mind which could constitute the basis for vital support in depth. Too often there is no meaningful dialogue with the cancer patient. While this may be tantamount to a lost opportunity in other interpersonal relationships, for the patient with cancer, it compounds the ultimate tragedy.

Developing a satisfactory I-Thou relationship with the cancer patient can take place without any degree of formal, psychological, sociological, or theological sophistication. The interposition of cultural patterns and neurotic reactions leads to a repression of our native abilities to talk with him about his basic and existential problems at a level of full frankness and honesty. Recognizing, acknowledging, and understanding these impediments to better communication are the first steps leading to the recovery of our native ability to talk with the cancer patient in an open and therapeutic manner.

# 27

# *Ministerial Leadership in Thanatology*
## — J. WILLIAM WORDEN

Although death has always been a topic of interest, death as an area of formal scientific investigation is relatively recent. Interest now being manifested in the subject of death and in the care of those who are dying is attested to by increasing numbers of symposia; a proliferation of literature, including several journals and many books in the field of death and dying; the existence of centers for the study of death, dying, and lethal behaviors; and the inclusion of courses in the psychology of death in the curricula of various colleges, universities, and professional schools around the country.

Where will this interest lead us? Who is going to provide leadership and direction for proper growth and development of knowledge in this field? How much of this interest in death and dying is merely faddish and doomed to disappear in a few years?

It is interesting to note that at a conference in 1972 of the American Psychological Association (APA), there were no sections devoted to the topic of suicide, but there were several on the topic of death and dying. Several years ago, when the National Institute of Mental Health (NIMH) made suicide an issue of funding priority, there were a number of papers and presentations on suicide at similar meetings. With new leadership in NIMH, research interests have changed and suicide studies are no longer receiving funding. Will investigations in the death field be hampered similarly? Will they burgeon, only to wane in a few years as people go on to investigate other areas? Obviously, one cannot give definitive answers to these questions, but certain observations on the matter of *leadership* in this area can be submitted for speculation.

For the most part, the investigatory work and the innovations in this field currently are being made by members of the health professions or persons specializing in the behavioral sciences. There is an

absence of creative contribution from the clergy, with, of course, some
notable exceptions. Yet who is better able to give leadership in this
area than the clergy? Traditional professional roles give the clergy
access to the lives and presence of the dying and their families that
few others have. The minister is a natural to work in this field. Yet so
many of the author's clerical friends are content to sit back and decry
the growing secularization of our age and the irrelevancy of the
Church and its ministry to contemporary society. In doing so, they
completely overlook the possibilities for making a creative contribution. Many young ministers eschew the traditional clerical roles of
marrying and burying, longing for something exciting to do which is
socially relevant. What could be more socially relevant than giving
imaginative leadership to this field of thanatology while at the same
time having a rewarding personal ministry with the dying and the
bereaved?

I would like to suggest four areas where the clergy could and should
take initiative, in both investigation and innovation.

## Leadership in Death Education

At the annual meeting of APA in September, 1972, the author attended a panel on "Death Education" chaired by Edwin Shneidman of
the University of California at Los Angeles. On this panel were several
people who teach courses on death and dying at various universities
around the country. Dr. Shneidman himself, while he was a visiting
professor at Harvard in 1969 and consultant to the Omega Project
there, offered such a course in the Department of Social Relations.
There were only twenty chairs in his classroom, yet two hundred
students showed up on the first day to take the course.[1] People, especially young people, are interested in this topic and want to know
more about it. Interest, of course, is not just limited to youth.

On the aforementioned panel was another pioneer in the field of
death education, John D. Black, formerly head of the Counseling Center at Stanford University. Dr. Black has been conducting a senior
colloquium for ten years in which students gather at his home to read
and discuss such topics as suicide, euthanasia, abortion, capital punishment, and the like. Not only does this help them gain perspective
on what others think, but it also helps them to clarify their own feelings. It is Dr. Black's belief that the death-denying attitudes found
in our society make individuals less than human and that facing
these issues in their youth helps people to lead more effective human
existences.

Frances Scott from the University of Oregon was another member of
this panel. Dr. Scott and her colleagues combine their work in the

classroom with a very effective encounter group. During the weekends, small groups of students from the larger class gather for carefully supervised, intensive sessions of experiencing, encountering, and confronting their own feelings and reactions to death. The students have an opportunity to write their own obituaries, and each one is given a chance to hear his read aloud while he lies beneath a shroud. If anyone should think that this not an involving exercise, he should try it himself. (It should be noted that Dr. Scott uses this and other encounter techniques as part of a carefully devised and innovative curriculum on death and dying. An excellent documentary film has been made on this project which demonstrates its approach in more detail.)

Of the seven people on the APA panel, only one, Herbert Anderson of Princeton Theological Seminary, represented theological education. Dr. Anderson taught a course on death for the first time in the fall of 1971. Eighty students enrolled in this course for weekly lectures and small group discussions. This interdisciplinary course attempted to bring together psychological, sociological, and theological-ethical perspectives on death. Dr. Anderson had four specific goals for the course: (1) to help students become aware of their feelings about dying and death; (2) to help students learn the psychological dynamics of dying and grieving; (3) to enable them to become more sensitive to what is and what is not helpful in taking care of someone who is dying or who is grieving; and (4) to integrate the students' personal and clinical understandings of death with a theology that reflects the Christian tradition. In assessing the benefits of such a course, Dr. Anderson concluded that the students were "thinking about life with more freedom, had more willingness to invest themselves, and a greater sense of the urgency of time."[2]

Other courses on death are being offered at schools such as New York University, Wayne State University, the University of Maryland, Berkeley. There are even courses offered in medical schools such as the one for medical students at Harvard—a course which always generates greater interest among the students at the Harvard Divinity School than among those at the Medical School. But courses and education in death and dying should not be limited to the formal academic classroom. We need to bring such instruction to people of all ages, and one way to do this is in or through the Church.

An Episcopal clergyman, Herbert H. Smith, Jr., has been leading a creative program with his parishioners. Every year around the time of All Saints' Day, he devotes a week and a Sunday to helping the members of his congregation realistically face the possibility of their own eventual death. He discusses, in sermons to the whole congregation as well as with small groups of parishioners, such topics as funeral arrangements, the meaning of funerals, living wills, organ donations, etc. He has found that many people prefer a plain pine box to an ornate coffin but, realistically, unless they have made some advance provision, this wish is not likely to be granted. Not all of his parishioners have been excited about these discussions of their own mortality, but little by little the program is having a significant impact on the congregation.

Another clergyman who is making a positive effort in death education is Rabbi Earl Grollman of Belmont, Massachusetts. Dr. Grollman has written several papers on death and a book entitled *Explaining Death to Children*.[3] Deciding that death education should go beyond his own local congregation, he set up a program for the entire town of Belmont, a community of about 28,000 people. He held a series of three Wednesday evening seminars, led by competent persons in the field, covering such topics as: "What do we think of death and our own dying?" and "How does a family cope with the crisis of bereavement?" Imaginatively interspersed in the presentations were films, literature, and art related to death and dying. These seminars were well publicized and well attended.

Why should clergy be involved in death education? They have a natural entrée to the subject. People in our society expect a minister to talk about death and dying. It is part of his social role which gives him the right to be interested in people's deaths, that is, to ask people about their plans for death but not to inquire, as does the physician, about their bowel habits. In contrast, the physician has social sanction to inquire about one's bowels. However, if he begins to ask patients if they have made preparations for death, patients soon become wary or extremely anxious. Therefore, clergy should be encouraged to give some thought as to how they can take active leadership in death education, not only for people who are part of their local charge, but for the wider community as well.

## Leadership in Better Care for the Dying

It is doubtful whether anyone would quibble over the necessity of dignity at death or, if you prefer, the dignity of life prior to death. We want a dignified death for ourselves, for our families, and most of us want the same for other people. All one needs to do is visit some of the facilities for patients with terminal illnesses to see how great the need is for change in this area.

One of the most exciting concepts that directly encourages dignity at death is the "hospice" idea, initiated in England by Cicely Saunders and being transported to this country by Florence Wald of Hospice in New Haven, Connecticut. St. Christopher's Hospice is a Christian foundation located outside of London, England, which opened in 1967 for the care of patients with advanced and terminal malignant and neurological diseases.[4] Here, under the guidance of Dr. Saunders, patients are encouraged to preserve rewarding relationships, pain is managed in a creative way, and dignity is promoted right up to the end of a person's life.

St. Christopher's policy is to encourage patients to remain home with their families until home care is no longer feasible. After that, they reside in the hospice, and their families, including children, are encouraged to be with them as often as possible. Ailments such as pneumonia are not treated with a great deal of vigor because of the belief that respirators and similar equipment can interfere with the interpersonal relationships of a patient and his family. A shorter time with a significant relationship is to be preferred over a longer life without this advantage. Quality of time is more important than its quantity.

At the hospice, one does not find terminal patients hooked up to the assortment of tubes found in the standard hospital setting. Instead of utilizing intravenous feeding, the hospice encourages the more able patient to feed a less able patient with a spoon even though this might be a slow and lengthy task. Thus the enfeebled patient is helped to maintain a sense of dignity while the stronger patient is helped to feel useful even in the final days of his life. This adds to the dignity of both patients and to the sharing of life stressed at the hospice.

Religious expression at the hospice is interpreted as personal relationships between people who are prepared to give themselves to each other in the context of a common life. With this emphasis, the relationship between staff and patient becomes a close one. There is a chapel in the hospice with regular services for any patient who chooses to attend.

Management of pain is an important consideration at the hospice. At most facilities, pain medication is administered to a patient when pain becomes severe. At the Hospice, the staff tries to find the optimal pain dosage for each patient, and regular, optimal dosages of analgesics are given, helping to avert the threat of pain as well as the fact of pain. This not only keeps most of the patients pain-free, it deters them from concentrating on pain or the fear of pain as a major concern. Hence, the patient is free to concentrate on other issues deemed more essential, such as interpersonal relationships and the consummation of final wishes.

Dying persons are not abandoned at the Hospice. It is not unusual to find someone—a family member, volunteer, student, or some staff member—remaining with the patient right through to the end, alleviating the fear of dying alone that many dying persons have.

Obviously, everyone cannot run out and establish hospices for the terminally ill. But if there is merit in the hospice idea, and if we believe that the terminally ill don't fit the present hospital treatment model and that there is a better alternative to dying in a hospital or at home, then someone needs to assume leadership in promoting and developing this idea. I do not believe that such leadership will come from the medical community. It could come from the clergy if only we would life up our eyes to some of the exciting possibilities.

## Leadership in Creative Approaches to Bereavement

It is well documented that many persons themselves die following a recent bereavement. In addition to those who die, others fall ill, and this incidence of illness among the recently bereaved is a well-known medical phenomenon.

A study of bereaved individuals was done in the Boston area by the Harvard Laboratory of Community Psychiatry.[5] This investigation included sixty-eight widows and widowers under the age of forty-five. They were interviewed fourteen months after bereavement and compared with a matched control group of sixty-eight persons. The members of the bereaved group showed more evidence of depression and of general emotional disturbance, which was reflected by restlessness and insomnia, and difficulty in making decisions and remembering things. They consumed more tranquilizers, alcohol, and tobacco following their loss than they had prior to bereavement. They exhibited a marked increase in emotional complaints, anxiety, and tension, but not necessarily in physical ailments—a finding somewhat different from studies done on older widows which showed a significant increase in physical ailments. Many of these bereaved persons had spent part of the preceding year in a hospital and had sought the advice of a minister or psychiatrist. Those who had continued to show intense grief, anger, and self-reproach beyond a six-week period following their loss were found to be coping poorly with their bereavement a year later.

A number of programs have been established to help the recently bereaved with their grief. One such program was conceived by Earl Grollman. Rabbi Grollman and Dr. Phyllis Silverman of Harvard Medical School held monthly meetings at his temple for widows and widowers from his own congregation. Other rabbis in the area were encouraged to send such persons from their congregations.

A number of topics were considered during these sessions. These included:

Reorganizing your life: How to adjust to a new life with children, in-laws, friends, job, and daily routine.

Managing finances: Experts led discussions on ways of handling insurance, money, property, and investments.

Ways of dealing with the feeling of being a fifth wheel: How to reenter society without feeling unwanted or useless.

Interpersonal relationships: Should a widow or widower date? When? What about the reaction of children and in-laws?

The role of a single parent: How to deal with the demands and frustrations of this role.

The problem of remarriage: Should persons remarry? How long should one wait? Problems in second marriages.

The place of Judaism in the bereaved spouse's life: Getting over bitterness against God for taking one's mate. How to grow in one's faith, etc.

In addition to these monthly meetings, smaller groups also met over the period. These smaller groups gave individuals an opportunity to participate in special interests or hobbies, for instance, sports, music, lectures, and other community events.

One of the most significant results of this program was the widow-to-widow aspect where widows became involved in helping each other. The bereaved are the ones who best understand the various stages of a grief reaction and are least likely to tell someone glibly that he should "pull himself together." A bereaved person is able to offer realistic information to the newly grieving individual because his own experience has taught him how difficult recovery from grief can be.

There is no reason why similar programs cannot be established in other churches or communities. The growing literature on dealing with the bereaved presents many guidelines for this approach to bereavement.[6] Although most of the programs already established are relatively new and it is difficult to evaluate their effectiveness, early findings indicate that they will be judged effective on several levels, particularly their preventive effect on subsequent illness.

## Leadership in Ethical Decisions Related to Dying

A four-year, longitudinal study of terminal illness and suicide has made the investigators acutely aware of the ethical issues involved in the right to die. A series of cancer patients, a series of suicidal patients, and a series of cancer patients who attempted to commit suicide are involved in this project.

As medical technology increases, more issues regarding the prolongation of life will become relevant: how long to extend life; whether a dying patient has the right to take his own life; the quality of life which is to be extended. These questions are much more difficult to answer than is the medical-legal question of when a person is to be declared dead.[7]

Physicians and others in the health care field are acutely aware of these problems and of their complexity. These problems do not yield readily to facile answers. It is the author's opinion that physicians are open to "inputs" from outside of the medical community which will give guidance for making right decisions. Who better than the minister, with his strong commitment to the sacredness of life and his sensitivity to ethical principles, could assist in such decisions? But here a humble spirit is needed. There is no place for the platitude or the easy answer. There is a place, however, for the presentation of thoughtful principles which can lead to effective policies and humane practices.

## Conclusions

These are four areas for leadership by the clergy of vital importance and for which the clergy are eminently qualified to give leadership in investigation and innovation. However, we can lead only if we have faced up to our own mortality. The closer we are to our own mortality, the more defensive and clouded are our observations and judgments. Aware of our own mortality, we must avoid glib solutions and cheap answers. It is all too easy in the Christian Church to be dispensers of ready hope like an Alka-Seltzer which removes one from life's distresses. Those of us from the Judeo-Christian tradition have a lengthy heritage of thoughts and beliefs about the meaning of death and resurrection. And there is always the dimension of mystery. Saint Paul reminds us that "we see through a glass darkly with the hope that one day we shall know even as we are known."

Finally, a word of caution is needed. We must be careful that our interest and talk about the subject of death and dying do not lead us into neglect of the person who is dying. It is very easy to be caught up in ruminations about death and dying, to make a neat intellectual exercise of the subject, and to avoid spending time with people who are dying. Nothing other than being with dying patients can bring reality into our work. And there is nothing which helps one who is dying like the support and presence of another human being. If our theories and our ministries are to be relevant, they must be hammered out of the empirical realities of what it means to die. This work is demanding of our time and of our energy.

One day, I left the bedside of a man who was dying of stomach cancer. Since I was not part of his family and because he had come to trust me, we talked of things which he had shared with few others. Leaving his bedside and walking down the corridor of the private pavilion, I felt very deeply moved. I was close to tears and started to chide myself internally for losing professional distance. And then I corrected myself. *Why not feel deeply?* In this encounter with a dying man, the important issues of life became profoundly visible. The ideals which our mass-media culture tells us are important suddenly seemed to shift, and those values which bear eternal importance and lasting consequence came to the fore. As I continued down that corridor, I sensed in myself a new vitality. Working with the dying need not be depressing, for in sharing with the dying, the vitality of life is forced into perspective. We are then able to reach out with new vigor unto life.

## Notes

1. E. S. Shneidman, *Death and the College Student* (New York: Behavioral Publications, 1972).

2. H. Anderson, "The Teaching of Death" (Paper presented at the Annual Convention, American Psychological Association, Honolulu, Hawaii, September 1972).

3. E. A. Grollman, *Explaining Death to Children* (Boston: Beacon Press, 1967).

4. C. Saunders, "The Patient's Response to Treatment," in *Proceedings of the Fourth National Symposium: Catastrophic Illness in the Seventies* (New York: National Cancer Foundation, 1971; idem, "A Therapeutic Community: St. Christopher's Hospice," in *Psychological Aspects of Terminal Care* eds. B. Schoenberg, A. C. Carr, D. Peretz, and A. H. Kutscher, (New York: Columbia University Press, 1972).

5. C. M. Parkes, *Bereavement: Studies of Grief in Adult Life* (New York: Internation Universities Press, Inc., 1972).

6. Ibid.

7. J. W. Worden, "The Right to Die," *Journal of Pastoral Psychology* 23 (1972): 9.

# 28

## The Minister as Part of a Health Care Team

## — J. DONALD BANE and ELIZABETH DORSEY I. SMITH

Both clergy and health care personnel are professionals who minister to the dying. Both are seen, and often see themselves, as saviors—the health care professionals saving the body, the clergy saving the soul. Each group has traditionally acknowledged the role of the other without always recognizing its similarities to their own. The dying human being has sometimes been viewed as a collection of discrete parts, for which each group performed its separate task.

As all professionals have become more willing to confront their own feelings about death and their own roles in ministering to the dying and their families, they have become more aware of how many people make up the network of support for the dying and their families. They have also come to realize that care givers themselves need a support network to help them cope with their feelings of loss when someone whom they have cared for dies.

Interdisciplinary approaches to professional education, which introduce professionals to concepts about the stages the dying and those around them pass through, also provide settings for students to share their feelings. Such groups naturally deal with questions about who does what in caring for the dying. When different professionals begin to explore their personal feelings about death and dying, they move beyond stereotypes of each other's roles, to a clearer sense of the interdependence of all. They discover that no one group has a monopoly on feelings of helplessness, hopelessness, anger, and fear.

Students of pastoral counseling and medical students have expressed the same fears to one of the authors of this chapter. A pastoral-counseling student, in exploring his reluctance to touch a parishioner dying of cancer, came to realize that he was afraid of "catching" cancer. A medical student recognized the same fear in his discomfort in examining a cancer patient diagnosed as terminal, though he had not experienced fear when examining other patients who actually had diseases he might contract. Both students knew the fear was irrational, but it was very real. It was, of course, an expression of their own fear of death.

Once a realization of common feelings develops, a multiprofessional group can begin to think of itself as a team with interdependent functions. Role distinctions become less significant and less rigid.

## What a Multidisciplinary Team Can Do

Such a multidisciplinary team can serve four major functions: (1) mutual support among professional colleagues, (2) the coordination of total care of patients and their families, (3) relating the care given in the hospital to community resources, and (4) providing a forum for dealing with ethical issues. While the development of such a group could improve the care of the dying and the bereaved, the same benefits could also accrue to other patients. Bereavement is not confined to loss of life; patients facing amputations, mastectomies, colostemies, renal dialysis, and other therapies that irrevocably change their lives, experience many feelings similar to those of persons facing death.

The following description of ways clergy might participate in a team ministry with physicians, nurses, social workers, and other care givers in an institutional setting is, in one sense, a fantasy. It is a description of what we believe should happen, rather than what is happening. We know, from our own experience as well as reports from others, that all these things are possible within a multiprofessional team and that clergy can be valuable participants. But we do not know any place where there is consistent teamwork in all four functions. Traditions, stereotypes, logistics, and the sheer inertia of past practices would make it difficult for a minister to initiate such a program in most community hospitals. Chaplains in medical centers, however, who already have status as staff, are more likely to find colleagues who are receptive to this approach. We describe our dreams in the hope that readers will find ideas that they can implement, even though the full multidisciplinary-team approach to patient care may be more of a goal for the future than an immediate possibility. We hope that chaplains and community clergy will find ways to develop this kind of team ministry for total care.

## Mutual Support

The most supportive thing we can do for each other is to listen. Doctors and nurses may feel responsible for a patient's death. In some cases they may *be* responsible. Clergy can help most by listening with neither judgement nor reassurance, and by indicating openness in sharing candidly their own feelings about patients who die. Listening is the key to mutual support; there is often nothing that can be done, and reassurance sounds phony. Emphatic presence with one another is the only thing that helps.

Many clergy might be surprised at how readily busy nurses and physicians welcome opportunities to talk about their feelings when they are listened to. Doctors and nurses may see clergy as preachers who think they have all the answers or as priests who have a magic that cures—if not the body, at least the soul. To learn that clergy are interested listeners may be a revelation. Ministers and health care staff may learn from each other how it feels to have neither the answers nor magic—religious or medical—for someone who faces death.

Health care professionals can preoccupy themselves with the technical aspects of caring for the patient in order to avoid confronting the dying patient directly. Clergy can exercise the same avoidance by the automatic use of prayers and sacraments (sometimes going into their routines assuming health care professionals will participate whether they want to or not). Some doctors and nurses have seen patients seriously disturbed by insensitive clergy preaching a brand of morality that implies that their illnesses are punishment for their sins.

Clergy also have experiences that support their stereotypes of doctors. One of the authors was once sitting at the bedside of a retarded adult patient who had just undergone a second painful operation on a deformed foot, the first operation having failed to completely remedy the problem. The patient's foot was in a cast, elevated, and tubes connected it to a small electric drainage pump. The attending surgeon, followed by an entourage of residents, arrived without greeting or warning at the end of the bed and began examining the foot. He pointed out certain things to the residents; one of them checked the machinery; without a word and hardly a glance to the patient or his visitor, the seven doctors left the foot and proceeded to another piece of anatomy in the next bed. Connected to that foot was a frightened and bewildered human being who under any circumstances had difficulty expressing his concerns. Seven doctors had attended to his foot as if it were a discrete entity suspended in space. Had there been staff communication about the total needs of this patient, the surgeon might have been aware of the man connected to the foot he was treating and could have addressed a few words to his concerns.

## Coordination of Care

In the coordination of care for patients, clergy know the patient's history and family can offer information that bears directly on plans for future care—whether the patient should return home, enter a special-care facility, be encouraged to undertake a new endeavor, and so on.

The minister can also be a catalyst for viewing the patient as a whole person who has a past, other relationships beyond the institution, hopes and fears, strengths and weaknesses, and above all a need to be an active participant in determining the course of his own life. He or she can help others to think of "patients" as "clients" who are engaging professional assistance to do something for themselves, rather than as passive recipients or victims of what is done to them.

In the case of a terminal patient the question arises, "What is the patient and his family to be told about his condition?" In a hospital, where the primary care is directed by the physician, other care givers are often unsure about what the patient and family have been told and what they are not to be told. Each professional, in relating to the patient and family, is accountable to them first and to members of the staff second. This becomes important when there has been a decision to withhold information, especially if the decision has been made by the physician alone. A patient may ask a nurse or a minister questions such as, "Do I have cancer?" "Am I going to die?" "How long will it take?" Such direct questions can make the listener anxious if he or she is not prepared. Is the response to be, "You'll have to ask your doctor," or is the nurse or minister willing to hear the patient express feelings of anxiety, fear, helplessness, and anger? It is possible to respond to those questions with invitations to talk further, such as, "You sound worried about how serious your condition is. What have you been thinking about it?" or "It sounds like you are thinking some disturbing thoughts. Would you like to talk about them?" or "Can you tell me more about how you feel?" In this way the trust of the patient is not lost. The minister or nurse focuses on the patient and not on the relationship to professional colleagues. This does not mean that she or he gives information a physician has decided to withhold, but simply that he or she does not isolate the patient by implying, "This is too scary a subject for *me* to discuss with you," or "I'm too fragile to expose myself to your anxiety." The patient is not lied to and the contract with (or order from) colleagues is not broken. All members of the team should be informed about the conversation, both the questions asked and the responses given.

The anxiety that care givers feel when patients ask questions about their conditions would be alleviated if they all shared in the decisions about how patients' needs are to be treated, including their concerns about prognosis, rather than assuming that physicians must make all decisions for everyone else caring for the patients. If the professional team could share their own feelings about death and treating the dying, they are more likely to share such decisions. Facing their own feelings in an atmosphere of mutual support and understanding would make it likely that fewer decisions to withhold crucial information from patients will be made. Such withholding often serves more to protect the professional from his or her own anxieties than to serve the patient's need. In most cases, the question is not whether a patient should be told of his or her condition, but *how* the patient should be told.

Frequently we miss a patient's request for information because we assume the patient will ask for what he wants to know in plain, direct language. Instead, as Kübler-Ross and others have said, the questions may be in symbolic or nonverbal language. For example, one of the authors was told by a woman who knew her breast cancer had metastasized and what the probable outcome would be, "They took me down to the physical therapist today to work on my legs. It seemed to help." A plain statement of fact on the face of it, but it was delivered in a quizzical manner which was puzzling at first. What the woman was, in fact, asking was: "Does this attention to getting my legs working better [the muscles had weakened due to long confinement to bed rather than to direct involvement with the cancer] mean that the doctors now think I might be cured? Or is my condition still hopeless?" For this woman there were two important levels in this disguised questions: (1) "Am I really going to die of this disease?" and (2) "If I am going to die of this disease, is there any hope that I can still function, even in a limited way, and have whatever time is left to me mean something, or is everyone going to give up on me as a hopeless case?" For her, since the answer to the first level of the question was yes, exploring the second level was particularly important.

All who minister to the dying and their families need to be sensitive to these "coded" signals. This sensitivity is particularly important for both health care personnel and clergy at large medical centers where an impersonal atmosphere frequently develops and where the care givers are often unaware of how the client and family have reacted to stress in the past.

A complicating factor in the coordination of care is the handling of confidential information; guidelines of confidentiality are needed to protect both patients and care givers. Confidential information is often involved in the communications among doctors, nurses, and clergy. It should go without saying that information shared at conference should not be divulged outside without agreement of the persons affected. It is the responsibility of the doctors and the nurses to protect the confidentiality of the patient charts. Clergy should not presume that they automatically have access to charts without checking. In most cases, clergy best get the information they need not by reading charts, but through team conferences or conversations with physicians and charge nurses. Among the appropriate things for the minister to know are diagnosis, prognosis, patient's attitude and state of mind, summary of his treatment and progress, what he has wanted to know and what he has been told, and in general what has been happening with the patient on the ward. This information should be in the charts, but unless a minister is conversant in the language of medical and nursing records, he or she could find out a lot that is irrelevant and incompletely understood and still miss the pertinent information.

The importance of protecting confidential information is often balanced by the need to share information that will enable all concerned to provide realistic support. For example, a woman dying of cancer was visited regularly by her husband who on the surface appeared to provide support to his wife. Her pastor, who also visited her regularly, and the chaplain knew that the patient's marriage was a painfully destructive relationship that had worsened during her illness, a fact that she had withheld from the health care personnel who had surrounded her for months. When the clergy told the nursing staff about this "secret," the nurses and doctors were able to encourage the patient to get support she needed from hospital staff and her friends rather than assuming that her husband's visits met important needs, and they were more realistic in their expectations of the husband's responses to the final crises in his wife's dying. She did not need to know that the nurses and doctors knew about her marriage; the knowledge simply helped them help her. The key to the sharing of such sensitive information is the development of trust among all the people providing care.

In the professional education of health care personnel, including hospital chaplains, death and dying has always been a topic of lecture and some discussion, but sometimes only in an isolated way. In the past five years faculty and students at medical schools and medical centers have asked for more dialogue about how their feelings about damage, loss, and death affect them and their attitudes about their work. These seminars are most effective when they are interdisciplinary rather than isolated within one profession's training. It is helpful to have students share their feelings and reactions to stressful situations as close to the time of the clinical experience as possible; if too much time intervenes, the student's grief and possible sense of helplessness and guilt may become a burden to carry or it may be intellectualized and dismissed without examination of feelings that leads to deeper understanding and sensitivity.

## Relating to Community Resources

Clergy can serve as "brokers" or intermediaries connecting patient services of the hospital with individuals and groups in the community who can supplement service to patients and families, while patients are in the hospital and following discharge or death. Clergy and social workers can be helpful partners in this task, complementing one another's knowledge of patients' circumstances and of community resources. In hospitals where there is no social work staff or where it is too small to meet the needs, clergy can do much to bridge a gap. The minister should be careful in filling the gaps lest he let himself become a substitute for the trained social work staff the hospital needs for comprehensive care.

Clergy are most helpful when they do not overdo their helping role. Patients often ask ministers to do things for them—call relatives, take care of business matters, deal with housing problems, and so forth—and many clergy feel obligated to respond to all requests without question. Such responses may be motivated by a desire to be of service, but they sometimes are a defense against the minister's own sense of helplessness and lead him or her to take on unrealistic tasks and invest time and energy in pursuits more effectively handled by someone else. When a patient requests specific aid, a minister should ask himself:

First, is this primarily a practical need or an expression of anxiety that calls for empathetic listening to enable the patient to express his feelings more openly? For example, a request for some kind of assistance to the patient's family might have more to do with the patient's feelings than with realistic need; a response that invites expression of those feelings could be, "You are really worried about how your family is going to get along without your help."

Second, is what the patient asks something that he could be encouraged to do for himself? For example, a patient facing death who is able to put his business and financial affairs in order for himself—by phone, visits from colleagues, working in his room or even by brief periods of returning to his own office—can complete his life still feeling useful and in control of his own life rather than defeated and totally dependent. Such encouragement of patient activity and initiative sometimes conflicts with attitudes of doctors and nurses who see patients primarily as receivers of care and who want the patient to conserve all of his energy for getting well or living a little while longer. Open discussion of these differences is important to maintaining a trusting, working relationship. In fact, sometimes there is real risk involved, and the quality of life must be weighed against longevity—a decision that finally should be the patient's.

Third, are there other persons in the hospital or the community better equipped to respond to the request? It is important that the minister know the social work resources of the hospital and the community. He or she should also learn what is already being done for the patient; often out of anxiety a patient will repeat a request that is already being acted on by someone else.

## Ethical Issues

In the fourth function of the professional team, dealing with ethical issues, the minister's role might best be described as that of a consultant. Two essential characteristics of a consultant's role are: (1) he or she is a resource person who offers information and opinions for the use of others in the formation of their own decisions, but the consultant does not take responsibility for those decisions, and (2) the consultant does not require that his ideas be accepted for satisfaction of his own needs. In a multidisciplinary team ministry, each person would operate in a pluralistic society, no one would impose his or her values on others, though the values of each person, effectively expressed, might raise important questions for other members. Within an effective team there would be various value systems held by different individuals with equal integrity. On sensitive issues like abortion, euthanasia, the right to die, and decisions about who receives limited, extraordinary lifesaving resources, such as renal dialysis, these values might clash. The minister who could maintain and persuasively share his or her own convictions, without attacking the integrity of others on the team whose values differ could be a facilitator and contributor in urgently needed dialogue in a field where technological change has outmoded many of the ethical guidelines that seemed adequate in the past.

## Minister's Unique Role

Some clergy fail to recognize the common ground they share with other professional colleagues, but others fail to appreciate the unique contribution they can make and have only a vague sense of their own professional identity. The rationale for the minister's involvement in the professional team caring for persons facing illness and death goes beyond the roles that would be shared with other team members. It is based on the conviction that all persons are religious in that they have ultimate concerns about the meaning of their lives and about existence. In institutions where illness and death radically alter life patterns and change or end crucial relationships, questions of meaning are acute. The minister, trained to think in religious dimensions, has a unique professional role in the care of whole persons, whether or not they express their ultimate concerns in traditional religious language.

Ministers who can work only with people who are religious in their way, who share their vocabulary and affiliation, will not be effective in a team ministry to the dying and bereaved. A young parish clergyman described to one of the authors a funeral at which he had recently presided. He said that an actor could have met the needs of the survivors as well as he did because he did not know the deceased or any of the family, and they were not really religious or a part of his congregation. During the service two of the survivors had openly wept and loudly expressed their anguish. He said he felt like going over to them and telling them to get hold of themselves because their behavior was not doing anyone any good. The author responded to these complaints, "You sound as if you were very uncomfortable in that situation and angry at the people." The clergyman confirmed this and went on to say that he felt as if he were being used in a way that bothered him. Feeling manipulated is a typical experience of care-giving personnel when they find themselves unable to alter the behavior of others or the course of the dying process. The assurance that others often felt this way and that it is a frustrating part of one's professional life did not lead this young man to reexamine his own feelings. He might have exercised a valuable ministry to these people in their distress had he been able to meet them where they were and translate his own religion into symbols that would help them make sense out of their pain.

The minister who is clear about his or her own professional identity is able to use the language of faith and tradition when that has meaning for a client. He also knows that the meanings for which religious words are symbols can be symbolized in other words by persons who eschew religious language, and that, on the other hand, religious language can have meanings for some people quite contrary to the intended meanings. So the minister as a religious professional on the multidisciplinary team needs to be skilled at interpreting those meanings, no matter what the words.

A healthy religious perspective is one that reflects a basic sense of trust and relatedness to the universe, that promotes caring relationships with other people, that stimulates inner freedom and personal responsibility. Healthy religion helps people move from guilt to forgiveness, strengthens self-esteem and a sense of goodness and importance of life. By their presence and their words, ministers can assist those struggling with religious issues, even those who do not consider themselves religious. This is the minister's unique contribution to the care-giving team.

## Suggested Readings

Breim, O., et al., *The Dying Patient* (New York: Russell Sage Foundation, 1970).

Engel, George, "Grief and Grieving," in *The American Journal of Nursing* 64:9 (September 1964), pp. 93–98.

Glaser, B. T. and Strauss, A. L., *Awareness of Dying* (Chicago: Aldene Publishing Co., 1965).

Kübler-Ross, Elisabeth. *On Death and Dying* (New York: The Macmillan Company, 1969).

Reeves, Robert B., Jr., "Professionalism and Compassion in the Care of the Dying"; Wood, Barry G., M.D., "Suffering, Death, and Practical Theology"; Neale, Robert E., "Explorations in Death Education: Denial, Fear, Grief, Belief, Martyrdom"; and Bailey, Lloyd R., "Death as a Theological Problem in the Old Testament," in *Pastoral Psychology*, vol. 22, no. 218 (November 1971). (Special issue on Death and Education.)

Smith, Harmon L., "The Minister as Consultant to the Medical Team," *Journal of Religion and Health* 14, (January 1975).

# PART V

# WHAT DOES DEATH MEAN?

*This section addresses the theological and philosophical issues raised by the inescapable human experience of dying. These chapters are less clinical and more abstract than what has gone before. Earlier sections focused on the practical, because abstract concepts, no matter how sound, are not as important as the way an individual integrates those concepts into his own experience and meaning system. The following chapters are offered as material for reflection to clergy and other professionals struggling to integrate their own ideas, the teaching of their traditions, and the human experiences shared with those to whom they minister.*

*When a person is dying, what difference does it make if he or she is agnostic or religious? In Chapter 29, a pastoral counselor reviews research on this question and the implications of the findings for those who care for the dying. A physician with philosophical interests discusses the meaning of bereavement in Chapter 30. In Chapter 31, a professor of New Testament reviews the mixture of lamentation and hope which characterizes the New Testament view of bereavement.*

*When does death occur? How do you know that someone is dead? These questions are more complex than they appear, as Chapter 32 demonstrates. Chapter 33 reviews the cultural tradition about the meaning of death and offers direction for*

203

*further thought. Chapter 34 compares Biblical with clinical observations of the effect of religious convictions on persons facing death.*

*Chapter 35 offers ideas for developing a theology of death. The attempt to avoid the reality of death is equivalent to avoiding life and is an example of "excarnation," according to the author of Chapter 36, who links an understanding of incarnation with facing the reality of death.*

# 29

# *The Agnostic And The Religious: Their Coping With Death*
## — PAUL E. IRION

For the past several years I have been deeply concerned with the sources of men's understanding of death. Through the centuries most Western men have articulated the meanings they attached to death in terms of their religious faith: Judeo-Christian religious doctrines. Their ceremonial behavior at the time of death has sought to act out these religious meanings. But as more and more people find traditional religious meanings uncongenial, and as a secular viewpoint becomes more prevalent, many persons discover that their understanding of death or their capacity to cope with death is seriously affected by their shift in viewpoint.

It has been argued on the basis of a variety of studies that religious conviction enables a person to cope more adequately with death. The findings on this point are, as we shall see, far from unanimous. This chapter will make the effort to shift the problem slightly and to seek to demonstrate that the adequacy of coping is less dependent on whether the person's point of view is religious or agnostic than it is dependent upon whether or not the person can articulate an understanding of death that is meaningful for him.

## A Review of the Research

Numerous studies have been made of the aging, the terminally ill, the recently bereaved, and the general population in an effort to probe the correlation between one's religious belief and one's ability to face death with equanimity. The studies have not been conclusive in their findings.

The Jeffers, Nichols, and Eisdorfer study[1] which surveyed 260 volunteer adults, 94 percent of whom were persons with viable church affiliation in their North Carolina communities, found that those who read the Bible with some regularity, those who held a belief in an afterlife, those who referred to death with religious terminology, seemed to have no fear of death.

Wendell Swensen[2] also describes the religious person as manifesting less fear of death. He surveyed 210 older people who were members of various social and residential organizations for the elderly. All of his subjects were volunteers (and it is reported that 40 percent of the potential subjects were not willing to participate in the study). His sample was also predominantly (75 percent) female. His hypothesis was: "The more fundamental one's religion and the greater his religious activity, the more positively he will look forward to death." He found those who had little religious activity or interest either avoided dealing with death or were afraid of it. The religious were seen looking forward to death without a great deal of conscious fear.

Eissler in *The Psychiatrist and the Dying Patient* and Freud in *Inhibitions, Symptoms and Anxiety* both seem to be observing that the generalized trust and support which usually characterizes the religious viewpoint may alleviate much of the psychological suffering of the dying person. Neither is making reference to particular religious dogma but rather is thinking of a kind of feeling tone toward the universe or existence.

Cappon[3] studied 20 terminal patients and found that in this sample those who were religiously oriented tended to accept their physical fate more readily. But he also found that more often than not they refused religious ministration rather than actively seeking it out. In another more extensive survey he found that there was a slight tendency for those who believe in an afterlife to make fewer statements of fear of death than those who had no such belief. But on a strict statistical basis, statements regarding fear of death were independent of statements of faith in God or afterlife.

Other research reports that there is no significant correlation between religious belief and the ability to cope with death. Feifel[4] sees the diminishing of religious faith in a secular age as a contributing factor in the extensive evasion of death in Western culture. This would imply that a religious orientation enabled a person to cope with death. But in another research report he writes, "The hypothesis was also entertained that a correlation might exist between religious outlook and rankings of fear of death in old age, but no significant relationship was evident."[5]

Rosenthal in *Death: Interpretations* has several articles describing psychotherapy for the dying in which the clear implication is that she is much more confident of the ability of psychotherapy to help the dying to cope with their situation than she is of the potentiality of religious ministration.

Adolf Christ,[6] in a survey of over 700 patients admitted to a psychiatric ward, concluded that religion or religiosity did not seem to have any effect on the fear of death.

Kalish[7] analyzed a questionnaire from 210 advanced psychology students and indicated that he found very little difference in terms of fear of death in subjects whose religious orientation was characterized as Protestant, Catholic, Jew or atheist-agnostic.

Marris[8] reports a study of interviews with 72 young and middle-aged widows in England and concluded that religious beliefs entered as little into their bereavement as it had in their previous lives. For the religious there was some comfort because their faith in immortality made rational their refusal to accept the reality of death.

Gorer[9] states that there appears to be little significant difference between the attitudes toward death of the recently bereaved and the general population. He finds that recent loss neither reduced skepticism nor increased belief in an afterlife. Responding to growing secularization, he argues that mourning becomes dysfunctional for so many because only religious rituals, thought forms, and symbols are available to interpret death and bereavement. Thus he implies that for the religious their faith may help them to cope with loss, but for the nonreligious sufficient resources are not at present available.

*Psychology Today* published a questionnaire on death to which 30,000 of its readers responded. The results were published in an article by Shneidman[10] which sought to indicate correlation between religious background and attitudes toward death. He notes that comparison of respondents under 20 years old and older adults indicates that 57 percent of younger people tend to espouse belief in an afterlife, involving ideas of heaven and hell, while only 30 percent of older individuals still hold a belief in an afterlife. He also reported that 65 percent of respondents with Jewish background, 42 percent with Protestant background and 25 percent with Catholic background strongly doubt or do not believe in an afterlife. According to this survey, the older a person gets, the more likely he is to be convinced that there is no life after death. If belief in an afterlife is an aid to coping with death, it would seem that those who are closer to death would be more inclined toward holding that article of faith. Of the total sample, 19 percent were fearful in thinking of their own death, with the 25–29-year-old group indicating 30 percent of the respondents fearing death.

Feifel is correct when he asserts that research is inconclusive in demonstrating that a religious outlook is necessarily helpful in confronting personal death.[11] There are probably many explanations for this. In some instances special variables may skew the results. In other instances the disparity in results may arise from the particular way in which questions have been phrased, or it may be that terminally ill subjects were at different stages of the process of confronting death as recently described by Kübler-Ross, and so one person's response may fail to correlate with that of a fellow-patient who is at a different stage of coping. It may be that statistical surveys cannot, at least at present, provide us with a definitive answer to the question: Does religion necessarily help a person to cope with death?

The lack of conclusive data from nomothetic studies suggests that following the lead of Gordon Allport it may be fruitful to pursue an idiographic approach, describing individual instances and seeking to learn from each instance.

## Author's Research

As part of a research project examining the effect of secularization on the meanings people give to death, I interviewed seventy-three persons in England and the United States, inquiring into their understandings of death. Since the research was not intended as a statistical study, carefully balanced samples were not sought, although some effort was made to provide a variety of viewpoints by seeking out people of different age groups, socioeconomic classes, and educational levels. Almost all the subjects were people who see themselves as unorthodox, radically critical, secularized church members or those who are totally outside any organized religion. In describing in this chapter some of the statements from these interviews, the intent is not to prove prevailing majority views but to describe and illustrate a situation, a condition. Within the limits of this space it will be asserted that these people give evidence of coping with death by accepting it without great fear while attributing to death meanings expressed in terms other than traditional religious affirmations.

Each of these persons in his way describes the abandonment of a once acceptable and helpful myth, or metaphor, or dogma, which once functioned to give meaning to death. This abandonment is not regarded as a hostile, aggressive, "anti" position. No one is angry or hurt, cynical or disillusioned or despairing. Most of them are saying in their own words, "What once worked for people (or for me) as a key to understanding no longer works." This malfunction leaves some with a sense of emptiness and confusion. Others either tolerate the loss or struggle to articulate new understanding.

## Search for Meaning

The search for meaning is an effort to meet a number of needs man faces in his confrontation with death. The most important of these are: (1.) the need to make death significant, (2) the need to make death less fearful and more tolerable, (3) the need to seek knowledge of the unknowable, (4) the need to deal with the frustration death causes, and (5) the need to affirm the value of life.

The extent to which these needs are dealt with provides a basis for assessing the functional adequacy of a meaning system which the person has worked out. The needs are never fully satisfied in the sense that they cease to be needs. Rather there is a response to the need sufficient to enable the person to cope with the thought of death: to accept it without loss of self-esteem, without paralyzing anxiety or despair.

It is not difficult to understand the way in which traditional religious meanings have been attached to these various needs. Death has been made significant as an ultimate experience, a moment of crisis toward which all of life is directed as preparation. Its fearfulness has been mitigated by belief in an afterlife, which enables a definition of death as entry into new life rather than as annihilation. Death is made more tolerable by portraying the new life as superior to present existence. The search for knowledge is somewhat satisfied by the interpretation of the religious teaching about death as revealed truth. The frustrations caused by death are modified by assuming that after death all the incompleteness and imperfection of present life will be corrected in a state characterized by infinity, justice, timelessness, the absence of suffering, peace. The value of life is affirmed by seeing it as a foreshadowing and preparation for death and the new life to follow. Although through the centuries there may have been some slight variation in the formulation of Western religious teaching, these basic themes have persisted.

The religious mind has customarily conceived of the agnostic or the nonbeliever as facing death without hope. Too often it has been assumed that the secularist could find no significant meanings for interpreting death, that he confronted death only with terrible anxiety or shortsighted bravado.

In recent years there has been growing recognition of a viewpoint which secularizes death and which seeks its meaning in terms and symbols which do not have their rootage in the Judeo-Christian tradition of the West. These secular meaning systems are not well developed, largely because they do not have the support of continuing institutional structures. They tend, at this time, to be personal and sometimes idiosyncratic. They are, nevertheless, effective, if my interviews are at all indicative, in helping individuals to cope with death. Let me report as illustration some statements about death made by people who do not accept traditional religious formulations and reflect on their effectiveness in the confrontation with death, using fulfillment of the five needs described above as a criterion of their functional adequacy.

## Need To Make Death Significant

A considerable number of interviews stated that death is a natural process and thus shares fully all the significance we accord to any part of life. For example, "The death of every living thing is essentially the same. The physical happening is part of the ecological process. Death is seen as a natural necessity, where once it was understood in terms of moral necessity." Or, "I never really thought of man as apart from nature; he lives and dies as a part of nature. I can't buy any sort of dualism."

But at the same time it was necessary for most respondents to refer to the significance of death with meanings that have emptiness as their theme. Often in the interviews participants were asked to complete the similes: "To die is like . . ." "Death is like . . ." Frequently responses were, "Death is like nothing," "Death is like oblivion," "Death is like a sleep in which you never dream." Others described death as the irreversible end of life, the last experience, the termination of any form of consciousness, entry into nothingness.

The acceptance of death as natural and the definition in terms of nothingness do not cancel each other out. The theme of nothingness does not imply that death is of no consequence. There is implied no effort to avoid confrontation of death. This illustrates one of the difficulties in finding new meaings: In the past when men sought to confront death, they felt that they had to define it in substantive terms in order to make death significant. Too often it may have been assumed that to see death as leading to nothingness failed to signify the importance of death. But in its contemporary expression, particularly under the influence of Heideggerian existentialism, facing the nothingness of death enables man to live his remaining days with authenticity. Most of those interviewed affirmed this existentialist posture.


## Need To Make Death Less Fearful

Comments made in the interviews indicate that a variety of fears can be associated with death. A few of the subjects were describing their own fears; some remarked about anxiety which they observed in others.

It was interesting that the agnostic sometimes sees a good bit of fear of death existing in the religious person. A woman said, "I was brought up on the exclusive view of Christianity, and death was the final point for making a decision. People thought of someone going to be with Jesus. Death was rather frightening. When the musical chairs stopped, would you make it?" Another person said, "My mother was absolutely scared of death. When she was getting old, this sheer fear was always with her. It probably related to her early religious background as a Methodist—teachings of fire and brimstone."

A good many of those interviewed explicitly stated that they had no fear of death or dying. This statement was made at the initiative of the respondent because the direct question was never asked, "Are you afraid of death?"

These assertions of fearlessness could be interpreted negatively as the products of superficiality, bravado, or rationalization. In response to such interpretations it can be stated that all of those who participated took the interviews very seriously. No one was ever facetious or flippant. From the youngest to the oldest they were speaking thoughtfully and seriously about their own understandings of death. Those who expressed lack of fear of death very often also explicitly described death as oblivion or the end of consciousness or annihilation.

It has been easy to assume that religious meanings dispel these fears and that the absence of traditional meanings would keep the person quaking in terror. This is not borne out in the interviews.

It is difficult to assess the extent to which the profession of no fear results from rationalization. In a sense, intelligent man's response to threatening situations involves rationalization. Man uses his reason to cope with threat, so any meaning which dispels fear is a rationalization. Traditional religious meanings which reduce fear of death are as much rationalization as other meanings. The effectiveness of the rationalization can be judged pragmatically; does it satisfactorily, from the standpoint of the person, diminish his fear of death?

The kind of rationalization present in those who do not espouse traditional religious meanings is summed up in the words of one subject: "I suppose that the person who really believes in afterlife (and I don't know how you distinguish between those who do and those who say they do) does so out of fear. The person who doesn't believe either has to have the courage to accept the meaninglessness of his life and his annihilation and handle it, or he has never faced it at all." This theme of acceptance of death occurs regularly in the comments of those who say they have no fear of death.

The question then becomes: what meanings do these people give to death which enable them to make death less fearful? Two themes predominate: death is natural and death is inevitable. Death is part of life and is involved intrinsically in the life of every man. There is no recourse from dying. The secular man has only two options: face the fact and live in its light, or try to cover it up with unrealistically excessive vitalism and thus truncate life with denial.

One of the major ways to make death more tolerable is to see it in a context of purpose and design. Classical theology describes this design in terms of providence and theodicy. A less orthodox position intuits a purpose which is vague and undefinable.

Yet another understanding moves further toward a naturalistic position. To illustrate, "Science helps us to see the randomness in physical death, that in the biological and physical realms there is no perceptible order. For example, in conception there are millions of sperm cells present, but there is a kind of random selection in that only one fertilizes the ovum. What at times seems totally random and arbitrary is part of the natural order."

Thus, scientific understanding of the natural world provides a basis for explanation and interpretation. Everything that happens occurs in the world of nature and is thus seen as part of an order. But it is an open-ended order, because even the cause and effect system which man uses as explanatory principle is vague and obscure in many instances.

When death is seen as part of the natural order, this has bearing on the idea of acceptance. Death occurs whether man "accepts" it or not. Acceptance has to do with man's subjective reaction to approaching death: does man cope with this reality positively or negatively?

A candid intellectual description of this approach was stated: "It is true that men looked at death in a religious motif in order to cope. He still has that need, but is seeking new meanings . . . I would take the approach of Freud and Durkheim in explaining religious mythology. It is reassuring when men have emotional demands of existence which without some explanation, some understanding, some action which appears to cope with uncontrollable events, involves them. It may seem irrational or even ineffectual from any objective and detached point of view; nonetheless, the fact that one is busying oneself, one is involved with something in which one believes, is reassuring. Familiarity with the situations and the actions that go with them is a strong emotional prop for men. Even superstition can be helpful in this way."

## Need To Seek Knowledge of the Unknowable

All the people encountered in these interviews were rather explicit in acknowledging the impossibility of really knowing, in the sense that we ordinarily use the word, much about death. They were very reluctant to make any claims or explanations that went beyond personal impressions, intuitions, or feelings. The subjectivity demonstrated in their statements is both intellectual humility resisting the temptation to make dogmatic assertions, and at the same time it is an indication of the dearth of workable metaphors for dealing with unknowable death.

So man is faced with a dilemma. If Freud is correct that every man in his unconscious posits his immortality, man wants to think in terms of some "existence" which goes on after death, but he also faces an impenetrable screen because of the limits of his mind. He has the need to seek knowledge of the unknowable. Some will transcend the barrier by just going on with the process of "knowing," but this is easily exposed as facile pretension. Others struggle to find metaphors or mythological interpretations which are not regarded as fact or knowledge but as devices by which one can come to terms with the unknowable.

The search for knowledge about death often centers around three basic questions: What is the nature of death? What causes death? Is there any justice in death?

Statements about the nature of death indicated a much greater readiness to see death as entirely part of the natural process with no supernatural causal components. A major theme of this natural interpretation is inevitability. There were statements such as: "Death is going to happen anyway. So how can you see it as punishment," and "It's going to happen to everybody. We just don't know when."

In a way this sees death as no less inexorable than the old view of God calling individuals from this life, an interpretation thoroughly rejected in the interviews. But there is an important difference. Nature is not here regarded as intelligent; the cause and effect processes are not regarded in any personal or moral light. Death is a natural event that happens. It is determined only by the total process, not by any deliberate exercise of will or intelligence.

This is related to the rather general rejection of the notion of death as moral judgment. If death is a mark of participation in natural process, it is morally neutral. Death is regarded as evil only when viewed in the light of its tragic consequences. But in and of itself death is morally neutral in these naturalistic terms. Nor is death seen as the precipitating occasion for eternal judgment. Some of those interviewed saw death as an event which causes the living to make some assessment of their own values and meanings, human judgments about what has worth.

## Need To Deal with the Frustrations Death Causes

Those who were interviewed saw death as causing frustration but sought new modes of approaching the problem of nonfulfillment. To project completion, fulfillment, compensation into a life beyond death was not a workable solution for many of them. One person observed, "I don't think that people feel that afterlife is necessary to complete or fulfill life. They feel increasingly that your morality and activity in this world are self-justifying."

The physical model by which scientifically-oriented man thinks involves an expanding universe, surprising irregularities, acknowledgment that the "reality" of material objects is in part dependent on the perceiver. This kind of model has produced a greater tolerance for incompleteness and partiality. The this-worldly meanings articulated by many of the persons interviewed accept the partial and incomplete as the only matrix of existence we know. They do not anticipate some sublime denouement to bring all the disparate fragments of life into a synthesis. Rather they think in terms of relating the instance to the dimly perceived "totality," the individual to the "community."

Meanings of this kind are not extensions of time into eternity or of finitude into infinity. They are simply extensions beyond the person. They can be conceived in terms of the reconstitution of the atoms of the body of the deceased, the carrying of his genes in his offspring, the effect of his influence (for good or ill) on others, the contribution of his labors to the community. Such extensions are understood in terms of demonstrable rather than hypothetical features, related to the here and now.

Rather than assuming that frustration caused by death could be mitigated by the benefits in an afterlife, there was more commonly manifested a kind of poignant acceptance of the frustration of nonfulfillment, joined with a desire to make the most of remaining life.

## Need To Affirm the Value of Life

Most of those interviewed saw a close relationship between the way one accepts death and the way one values life. One stated: "I can't remember ever in my whole life having believed in eternal life; that my life would be eternal. I always thought of this life as all that I knew about or all that I can count on." "The old scheme of life being a preparation for death is in a way replaced with a scheme of death being a preparation for life in this world," was the way in which another expressed himself.

A key concept here is that death must be understood as a part of life and that it is possible to see their relationship supporting mutual meaning rather than negating it. This can take place in several ways.

Existentialism, or more correctly, a portion of that school of thought, indicates that by facing the reality of one's own approaching death, a person is moved to live with greater intensity, integrity, and authenticity. In the interviews, subjects were asked to respond to this viewpoint. It received support from all but very few.

The more positive side of the affirmation of the value of life is expressed, as this student did: "When one dies, the chain (of life) does not break. We are all part of one living thing. It is sort of like the way one cell replaces another in the organism. It's not that we're all that important, but each cell has its function—to live to its fullest—and we do that."

Many of the interviews brought out the importance of the contributions made in one's life. No one dealt with this attention to life in terms of a hope for reward in an afterlife or fear of judgment after death. The concern is for this world, for present existence, and for the contribution one hopes to make to a somewhat limited future. In this view, death is not understood as the negator of life's values. Rather there is the potentiality for affirming one's own value system in the interpretation one gives to life and death.

## Conclusions

The meanings used by people in these interviews are naturalistic, this-worldly, congruent with the contemporary scientific understanding of the universe. Their focus is on present existence almost exclusively. The future is understood in a very time-limited sense, rarely extended beyond the lives of a generation or two. There is no notion of any escape from death or its consequences and no mitigation of the ultimacy of death so far as the continued conscious existence of the person is concerned.

It appears from reading the transcripts of entire interviews that many of the participants are working with very tentative meanings which enable them to cope with thoughts of death. On the basis of their comments about their feelings toward death and dying, they seem to have functionally adequate meaning systems. They give evidence of being able to accept the fact of death and their own dying. While they do not desire death at present, they talk about it readily and matter-of-factly. Many of them voluntarily state explicitly that they have no great fear of death.

No attempt is being made on the basis of this limited research to state a firm conclusion regarding the relative adequacy of a religious as over against a secular understanding of death. However, it can be asserted that these interviews show that individuals with a decidedly secular stance can give evidence of coping effectively with the fact of death on the basis of a meaning system that uses none of the traditional religious doctrines or symbols. This would offer support for the hypothesis of this chapter: the adequacy of coping is less dependent on whether the person's point of view is religious or agnostic than it is dependent upon whether or not the person can articulate an understanding of death that is meaningful for him.

The persons involved in these interviews may be somewhat exceptional. Certainly not every secularized individual has been successful in working through his understanding of death or in articulating meanings. This provokes some questions worth further consideration. To which resources within the culture can secular man turn, as the religious man has turned to his church or synagogue, for support, guidance and stimulation in his search for the meanings of death? What part do the arts—literature, poetry, drama, music—play in this process? To what extent is science, including the behavioral sciences, a fruitful resource for models or metaphors?

The question any man must ask is not merely what does death mean, but what does death mean to him? Naturally, answers will be individual and idiosyncratic. But meaning always searches for community, for shared expression, for mutual enrichment. This at the present time is the major disadvantage of the secular man; he lacks an institution which is in touch with all socioeconomic classes, educational levels, age groups, to serve as a community within which meaning is stimulated and shared.

## Notes

1. Frances C. Jeffers, Claude R. Nichols, and Carl Eisdorfer, "Attitudes of Older Persons toward Death: A Preliminary Study," *Journal of Gerontology* 16 (1961): 53–56.

2. Wendell M. Swenson, "Attitudes toward Death among the Aged," *Minnesota Medicine* 42 (1959): 399–402.

3. Daniel Cappon, "The Psychology of Dying," *Pastoral Psychology* (February 1961), pp. 35–44.

4. Herman Feifel, "The Problem of Death," in *Death: Interpretations*, ed. H. M. Ruitenbeek (New York: Delta Books, Dell Publishing Co., Inc. 1969), pp. 125–129.

5. Herman Feifel, "Attitudes of Mentally Ill Patients toward Death," *Death and Identity*, ed. Robert Fulton, (New York: John Wiley & Sons, Inc., 1965), pp. 131–141.

6. Adolph E. Christ, "Attitudes toward Death among a Group of Acute Geriatric Psychiatric Patients," in *Death and Identity*, pp. 146–152.

7. Richard Kalish, "Some Variables in Death Attitudes," in *Death and Identity*, pp. 170–177.

8. Peter Marris, *Widows and Their Families* (London: Routledge & Kegan Paul, Ltd., 1958).

9. Geoffrey Gorer, *Death Grief and Mourning in Contemporary Britain* (London: The Cresset Press, 1965).

10. Edwin S. Schneidman, "You and Death," *Psychology Today* (June 1971), pp. 43ff.

11. Feifel, "Problem of Death," pp. 126f.

# 30

# *The Concept Of Bereavement*
## — H. TRISTRAM ENGELHARDT, JR.

One sketches concepts to understand the boundaries and geography of meaning. Concepts form the structure of what we can say and what can be made sense of. By the concept of bereavement, I mean to indicate a fabric of meaning in language (or thought) about the death of another person, significant in one's life. Or more precisely, I will focus on a core of the meaning of loss which is integral to that situation: bereavement. Though the approach is obviously an intellectual one, the emotions and their significance will not be overlooked. After all, sketching a concept properly involves a phenomenology of its type of significance, and the significance of bereavement is embodied in the full fabric of human life.

The focus is upon a unique category of loss, unique in terms of the quality of the object and the quality of the loss. Of the objects which furnish our world, those that are also subjects command an acknowledgment of value in terms of their co-enterprise with us of bestowing the world with meaning. Objects which are not also subjects have their value in themselves only because of us, the subjects of the world who value them. Subjects, though, reflexively apprehend themselves and have their value in and for themselves, not only for others. Yet, the role of others in valuing us remains central. As Hegel indicated, we come to know ourselves through our reflection in, and contrast with others." In being reflected into myself, I am immediately reflected into the other person, and, conversely, in relating myself to the other I am immediately *self*-related."[1] That is, the freedom and integrity of each individual is involved in a relationship to another. Individuals as Hegel put it "throw light upon each other."[2] Intersubjectivity, and its implied relatedness with others, is core to our own individuality. Intersubjectivity is essential to our coming to know ourselves and our own bodies as elements in an objective world. In a deep sense, the objective significance of the world is dependent upon an encounter with an other. "The other Ego," as Husserl indicated, "makes constitutionally possible a new infinite domain of what is 'other': an *Objective Nature* and a whole Objective world, to which all other Egos and I myself belong."[3] That is, the presence of an other has noticeable significance in the origin of the objective meaning of the world. The world as we experience it, as we live in it, our life-world, is a social fabric in which distances and time intervals are understood basically in terms of social parameters; face-to-face encounters and intimate contacts with fellow men grade into anonymous interactions with mere contemporaries or references to distant predecessors or possible successors. Personal identity itself develops within this social matrix, and, as Alfred Schutz has indicated, is structured and sustained by it.[4]

Given this social understanding of the human condition, the often-quoted phrase of John Donne's "Devotion,"—"never send to know for whom the bell tolls; It tolls for *thee*,"[5]—illuminates the significance of bereavement. In the loss of an other, one loses a part of oneself and one's reality. The fabric of human reality is sewn so tightly that the death of a human is never of isolated significance. As Donne put it, "No man is an *Iland*, intire of it selfe; every man is a peece of the *Continent*, a part of the *maine*; if a *Clod* bee washed away by the *Sea*, *Europe* is the lesse, as well as if a *Promontorie* were, as well as if a *Mannor* of thy *friends* or of *thine owne* were; any mans *death* diminishes *me*, because I am involved in *Mankinde*."[6] The loss of another human is always the loss of an object who is also a personal co-laborer in the human endeavor. This category of object loss is thus unique and singular. It is subject loss—the loss of that which endows objects in the world with meaning. Of course, the magnitude of the loss is dependent on the intimacy of prior relations—the more intimate the other, the more crucial is the loss for the significance of the world of the bereaved. Or put another way, the more intimate the relations, the more important the other was for the significance and meaning of the world of the bereaved. Since the value of the life-world of the bereaved is not dependent on or sustainable by the bereaved alone, the loss of the other changes the bereaved's surrounding world itself. The other is no longer there to give an expected perspective and value. The other no longer sustains a fabric of meaning, important and implicit in a way of life. Now, through the loss of the other, an area of meaning collapses where the other previously sustained it.

In short, bereavement involves an intimate loss because it concerns the loss of an other important for the significance and fabric of one's life. Lives have structures of meaning sustained not only by the ones who live it, but by those who live *in* it as well.

The quality of the loss is unique in that it is permanent and irretrievable. A possibility is closed forever. A separation of distance does not preclude a meeting again. Death closes possibilities. This closing of avenues to value is the force of bereavement. Values once possible become precluded. In respect of the quality of the object and the quality of the loss to the bereaved, bereavement touches intimately and deeply the being of the bereaved. It is not external to his life, but integral to his existence and the meaning of his world.

Being such a drastic affair, it is not unexpected that the death of a significant other should be viewed in overwhelming terms. We are contingent beings—we exist, but that could be otherwise. We have no claims to ourselves or to the structure of our lives which can prevail against our rank contingency. In this context of contingency, the death of a loved one is viewed as absurd—a meaningless loss of meaning or, at best, an unnatural affair. The reaction of Western man has been to place this contingency outside himself. Death has been considered an unnatural occurrence due to sin and error, not a part of the intrinsic nature of man. That is, the mortality of man has been viewed as peripheral and not essential to the human predicament. The story of the Fall and St. Paul's interpretation of it is classical in this respect. "By one man sin entered into this world, and death by sin" (Rom. 5:12). In this view, death is an external force which falls upon our lives. Man is passive, death an active external force. In *Everyman*, God sends Death to sinful man, to "cruelly out search both great and small."[7] The bereaved suffers the results of this onslaught.

The language of bereavement reflects the passive picture of the bereaved. The past participle, to be bereaved, is defined as being "deprived or robbed; taken away by force; *spec.* deprived by death of a near relative, or of one connected by some endearing tie."[8] This language of violence and deprivation suggests an external agency, yet the loss has significance because it is internal to the life-world of the bereaved. Bereavement has thus a counterpoint of meaning. It is an intimate state of loss, due to an external force: the loss is personal, the force causing the loss itself distant, almost impersonal. The emotions of loss and grief contrast helplessly with the inexorable force that despoiled the bereaved of the other who previously endowed the bereaved's life with meaning. The futility of finitude and contingency consequently invites both grief and rage. Albert Camus' reaction to death provocatively underlines the anger which is the other side of such lament; it is revolt. As Camus stated, "It is essential to die unreconciled and not of one's own free will."[9] Revolt, though, is ultimately futile and is, as Camus indicated, therefore absurd. It is a vain rebellion in the mode of Sisyphus. In this, bereavement goes beyond the loss of meaning due to the loss of the other; it indicates the possible absurdity of life itself, the possibility that enduring meaning is impossible. The single loss involved in bereavement thus indicates more global themes of loss. The suggestion here, of course, is the one most guarded against—that the destiny of loss is internal to our very being, that it is not an external onslaught, that we are passive not to an active external force but to our own contingency and finitude against which there is no hope of a successful reaction or countermove. Bereavement threatens ultimately.

In summary, bereavement as a unique category of loss indicates the intimate dependency of our life on others for meaning and significance. Further, it suggests more embracing themes of contingency, questions which challenge us to the core. They call us to consciousness of the contextual and finite themes of our lives.

## Notes

1. G. W. F. Hegel, *Philosophy of Mind*, trans. William Wallace, Rev. A. V. Miller (Oxford: Clarendon Press, 1971), no. 436, Zusatz, pp. 176–177.

2. Ibid., no. 437.

3. Edmund Husserl, *Cartesian Meditations*, trans. Dorion Cairns (The Hague: Martinus Nijhoff, 1960), no. 49, p. 107.

4. Alfred Schutz and Thomas Luckmann, *The Structures of the Life-World*, trans. Richard M. Zaner and H. Tristram Engelhardt, Jr. (Evanston, Ill.: Northwestern University Press, 1973), especially p. 245.

5. John Donne, "Devotion," XVII, in *The Complete Poetry and Selected Prose of John Donne* (New York: Modern Library, Inc., 1941), p. 332.

6. Ibid.

7. *Everyman*, in *An Anthology of English Drama Before Shakespeare*, ed. Robert B. Heilman (New York: Rinehart & Company, Inc., 1959), p. 76.

8. *The Oxford English Dictionary*, vol. 1, "A–B" (Oxford: Clarendon Press, 1961), p. 810.

9. Albert Camus, *The Myth of Sisyphus*, trans. Justin O'Brien (New York: Vintage Books, Inc., Alfred A. Knopf, Inc., 1960), p. 41.

# 31

# *Bereavement In New Testament Perspective*

## — SCHUYLER P. BROWN

What is the Christian response to bereavement? More specifically, is grief—the natural, human response—somehow un-Christian? It might seem that the answer to the latter question should be affirmative. One could argue that, according to Christian faith, death is the way to final and perfect happiness, and that consequently grief over the passing of a loved one suggests either selfishness or unbelief. The psychological importance of grief, as a necessary step in the acceptance of death, may be readily acknowledged, but its expression would still be regarded as, at best, an understandable, but nonetheless imperfect, concession to the weakness of human nature. The purpose of this chapter is to show that the answer is not that simple, because the Christian view of death is not that simplistic.

This question has a special relevance today, when liturgical reforms have made the uninhibited expression of grief more difficult for the bereaved. Gone is the Requiem mass with its black vestments and mournful chants. The death of the deceased is celebrated as the fulfillment of his mystical death with Christ in baptism. Amidst white vestments and Easter songs, what place is there for tears? The bereaved seems constrained to simulate a joy which he can scarcely feel. The Madonna of Michaelangelo's Pietà would probably feel out of place in the triumphant jubilation of a contemporary Mass of the Resurrection.

The Christian's attitude toward death may be expected to keep in mind the death of Christ, "the first fruits of those who have fallen asleep" (1 Cor. 15:20). But if we examine the Gospel accounts of Jesus' crucifixion, we find three quite different sayings attributed to him just before he breathes his last. Matthew and Mark have him pronounce the psalmist's cry of dereliction: "My God, my God, why hast thou forsaken me?" (Matt. 27:46, Mark 15:34; Ps. 22:1). Luke places upon his lips the prayer that every pious Jew recites at close of day: "Father, into thy hands I commit my spirit" (Luke 23:46). Finally, according to John, Jesus bursts forth with the triumphant cry: "It is finished" (John 19:30).

If such different sentiments can be attributed to him who is the model for Christian dying, we can scarcely expect a uniform response from either the dying or the bereaved Christian. The depiction of Jesus' death by the evangelists is governed by theological, not biographical, interests. Just what passed through Jesus' mind as he lay dying on the cross we will probably never know, but the freedom with which the Evangelists represent this scene indicates that they viewed this crucial event in salvation history in quite diverse ways. This is of importance for our topic, because it means that the New Testament writers present us with different responses to Christian death. Their portrayal of Jesus' death is the reflection of their understanding of death itself.

In the fourth Gospel Jesus' death is presented as his glorification: "When I am lifted up from the earth, I will draw all men to myself" (John 12:32). The Evangelist uses the words "lift up" with two meanings in mind. At one and the same time Jesus is "lifted up" on the cross and "exalted" to heavenly glory. Such a triumphalistic understanding of Jesus' death is in keeping with the Johannine word from the cross: "It is finished" (John 19:30).

But the schema of humiliation and exaltation which lies behind the Johannine presentation is not the only understanding of death in New Testament theology. In 1 Corinthians 15:3–4 the confession of Jesus' death is coupled with the confession of his resurrection: "Christ died for our sins in accordance with the scriptures; he was buried; he was raised on the third day in accordance with the scriptures." Quite apart from the enigmatic phrase "on the third day," this schema suggests that Christ's death is not identical with his resurrection. The latter, metaphorical expression, which means an awakening from the sleep of death, implies that the intervention of God in raising Jesus from the dead did not perfectly coincide with his death. Death is no longer the perfect fulfillment, as in John. It provokes a divine response which is somehow distinct from it.

Viewed together, Christ's death and resurrection represent a definite turning point in salvation history. Paul speaks of Christians as those "upon whom the end of the ages has come." Nevertheless, he does not regard the Christ-event as total fulfillment. On the contrary, in 1 Corinthians, chapter 15, he attacks this view. Certain Christians at Corinth so stressed the resurrection of Christ that they believed that there was nothing more to look forward to. Specifically, they denied the resurrection of the dead at the end of the world, believing, it would seem, that "the resurrection is past already" (2 Tim. 2:18). Paul rejects their exaggerated enthusiasm, which was based on a one-sided consideration of what had already been accomplished through the death and resurrection of Christ. Implicit in Paul's criticism of the views of his opponents is an insistence on the seriousness of death, which some of the Corinthians evidently regarded as merely the passage to a fuller enjoyment of the mystical delights which they already possessed through Christ's exaltation. Paul consistently opposes the notion that all has been accomplished, now that Christ has been raised from the dead. In Philippians 3:12 he writes: "Not that I have already obtained this [the resurrection from the dead] or am already perfect; but I press on to make it my own, because Christ Jesus has made me his own." In Romans 8:19–20 he says, "The creation waits with eager longing for the revealing of the sons of God . . . We know that the whole creation has been groaning in travail together until now." Finally, in a letter from the Pauline school we read: "In my flesh I complete what is lacking in Christ's afflictions for the sake of his body, that is, the church" (Col. 1:24). It is this notion of the Church as Christ's body which prevents the Christian from considering Christ's resurrection in isolation from the plight of the world, which is still awaiting final redemption.

Christ's resurrection, then, is not a total fulfillment, such as would make all expectation for the future illusory. This emerges with great clarity in the Gospel according to Mark, where the resurrection of Jesus is notably underplayed. The Evangelist recounts no resurrection appearances to the disciples, and in Jesus' farewell discourse (chapter 13) he does not even mention his resurrection. The climax of the discourse lies in the prediction of his return: "And they will see the Son of man coming in clouds with great power and glory" (Mark 13:26). It has been suggested that Jesus' exaltation, which is associated by John with his death, and in other traditions with his resurrection (Acts 2:34; Rom. 8:34), is considered in Mark's Gospel to be deferred until Jesus' return. The resurrection is simply a translation, resulting in Jesus' absence: "He is not here" (Mark 16:6).

The Christian attitude toward death, then, is complex, because it is related to *several* affirmations of Christian faith: the death and resurrection of Christ "on the third day"; Christ's return and the resurrection of the dead "on the last day"; Christ's exaltation, variously conceived as coinciding with his death, his resurrection, or his return. However much we may stress the symbolic character of these objects of Christian faith, we should not overlook their force or minimize their influence.

We have already noted the Christian understanding of the Church as Christ's body and the view that the fate of the material universe is connected with the destiny of Christ's body, that is, "the revelation of the sons of God." The doctrine of the body of Christ prevents Christ's resurrection from being understood in isolation from the rest of creation. Hence, Christ's triumph over death is still incomplete in a certain sense (cf. 1 Cor. 15:26).

Just as the concept of the body of Christ brings out the solidarity between the risen Lord and the nonresurrected, mortal universe, so too does the notion of the resurrection of the body. Crude, materialistic interpretations of this Christian tenet should be avoided. Above all, the body is not to be understood as a *part* of man but rather as man himself in his visible relationship to the rest of the universe. At death this visible relationship is interrupted; the doctrine of the resurrection of the body affirms that it will be restored. Furthermore, Christian belief in Christ's resurrection furnishes the basis for this confidence. After Christ's death God caused Jesus' association with his disciples to be resumed in visible fashion, that association which had been broken off not only by his death but also by the disciples' abandonment of him. This restoration is expressed in the table fellowship with the risen Lord which is a characteristic of several Gospel resurrection stories.

Death, therefore, is not adequately understood, from a New Testament perspective, if it is considered in exclusively individualistic terms. To be sure, it is the "perfection" or "fulfillment" of the individual existence (John 19:30; cf. Luke 13:32). But this "perfection" does not consist in liberation from the bonds of material creation, as in the Platonic view. On the contrary, the necessity of interrupting (temporarily!) the visible relationship with material creation is precisely what makes this individual "perfection" imperfect. Christ's death is his exodus (Luke 9:31), his departure from the company of those whom he came to save. As such, it has a negative component.

To be sure, the fourth Evangelist stresses the advantage of Christ's "departure": "It is to your advantage that I go away, for if I do not go away, the Counselor will not come to you; but if I go, I will send him to you" (John 16:7). But even here the "advantage" is not absolute. The divine plan requires that Jesus' place be taken (temporarily!) by the Counselor, that is, the holy spirit. This necessity is rooted not in some inherent superiority of the spirit to the fleshly Jesus but in the fact of Jesus' mortality, which prevents him from "abiding" with his followers, except in a spiritual manner. For all its emphasis on the life-giving power of the spirit and the uselessness of the flesh (John 6:63), the fourth Gospel, in its final version, retains both the resurrection of Jesus (chapters 20–21) and the resurrection of the dead "on the last day" (John 6:39–40,44,54).

The New Testament affirms the necessity of passing through physical death to obtain eternal life, but it does not abandon the Old Testament view of death as something unnatural, which is contrary to God's original intention (Genesis, chapter 3; Wis. 2:24: "Through the devil's envy death entered the world"). Consequently, the Christian's attitude toward death and his response to bereavement is inevitably ambivalent. On the one hand, the pagan centurion, symbolizing the Gentile Church, sees in the crucified Jesus the Son of God (Mark

15:39). But the same Evangelist regards Jesus' death as his "removal" from the community and, as such, the cause for visible expression of grief: "The days will come, when the bridegroom is taken away from them, and then they will fast in that day" (Mark 2:20). Following the death of the first Christian martyr, "devout men buried Stephen, and made great lamentation over him" (Acts 8:2), and after the death of Tabitha, "all the widows stood beside Peter weeping" (Acts 9:39).

The scandalous character of death was all the greater in the early Church because of the fervent hope of experiencing while still alive the Lord's return (Mark 9:1; 13:30). The apostle Paul expresses this hope when he includes himself in the phrase "we who are alive, who are left until the coming of the Lord" (1 Thess. 4:15). Because of this expectation, the death of individual members of the community caused dismay. Paul feels constrained to explain such occurrences as God's punishment for sin (1 Cor. 11:30). However mistaken this expectation of the first Christians may have been, it reveals a view of death which is basically sound. As long as the course of salvation history remains incomplete, death cannot be regarded as an unmitigated blessing. To be sure, a martyr's death is a special case. In the fourth Gospel the risen Jesus first predicts Peter's martyrdom: "When you are old, you will stretch out your hands, and another will gird you and carry you where you do not wish to go. [This he said to show by what death he was to glorify God]" (John 21:18–19). Peter's fate is then paired with that of the beloved disciple: "If it is my will that he remain until I come, what is that to you?" (John 21:22). The martyr is certainly not deprived of the blessings of those who live to see the Lord's return (cf. 1 Thess. 4:15). But to die in bed, as the beloved disciple evidently did, was a cause for some embarrassment to the Evangelist and his community.

Indeed, even a martyr's death is not the supreme good. Paul in prison, as he awaits his sentence and reflects on the alternatives of life and death, writes to the Philippians: "For me to live is Christ, and to die is gain. If it is to be life in the flesh, that means fruitful labor for me. Yet which I shall choose I cannot tell. I am hard pressed between the two. My desire is to depart and be with Christ, for that is far better. But to remain in the flesh is more necessary on your account" (Phil. 1:21–23). Here concern for the community outweighs the personal advantage of "being with Christ" through a martyr's death. The good of the individual is subordinated to the greater good of the community. Thus, sheerly individualistic considerations are shown once again to be inadequate for a fully Christian view of death. The glory of the martyr is not that he dies, but rather that he dies for the sake of Christ and the Gospel: "Whoever loses his life for my sake and the gospel's will save it" (Mark 8:35). Salvation is promised not to all who die but to those who endure to the end (Mark 13:13).

This chapter may seem to simply state the obvious, that grief, as the natural and psychologically necessary response to bereavement, is not un-Christian or sub-Christian. Yet it seems appropriate to give a *theological* justification for this position, since, as I remarked at the beginning, the current liturgical emphasis is on the notion of death as fulfillment. This understanding of death, though true, is not the whole truth. And to oblige the bereaved Christian to concentrate on this partial truth at a time when his emotions may be driving him in quite another direction seems ill-advised. The medieval ritual, which emphasized the somber aspect of death, was not without its scriptural justification. Christians should not be expected to suppress their grief over the loss of their loved ones. The consequence of their faith is that they "do not grieve *as others do who have no hope*" (1 Thess. 4:13). In other words, the Christian's response to bereavement includes both grief and hope.

# 32

## *The Trouble With the Concept "Death"* — GEORGE M. SCHURR

Though most of us seldom deal directly with death, unless we do so professionally—as soldiers or mobsters, clergymen or morticians—we do seem to know what the word *death* means. At least we have little trouble using it, beyond occasional psychological discomfort. Conventionally defined, death is a straightforward matter of fact, "the cessation of biological processes and the termination of social interaction." But are matters quite so clear? Is this literally all there is to death?

### Facts

If death is a simple and straightforward matter of fact, then it should be specifiable by clear and unequivocal criteria, for that is the way descriptive facts are identified. However, recent medicolegal attempts to define clinical death have failed to produce simple and unequivocal criteria for the first half of the conventional definition, "the cessation of biological processes." We have, for instance, long known that biological processes may continue within the tissues of an organism long after all conventional signs of continued viability of the organism are gone. This has led to a differentiation between the death of cells within the organism and the more global issues of death of the organism.

So far, so good. Now, what are the criteria for the cessation of biological processes in the organism? Traditionally, a person was considered biologically dead when no trace of a heartbeat remained. If his heart was not beating, then he was considered biologically, or clinically, dead. However, we now know that hearts can start again—often with stimulation, and sometimes spontaneously. An apparent lack of heartbeat alone, then, cannot be the criterion of death. At this point modern technology has provided an alternate criterion—the cessation of brain function, as measured by a "flat" electroencephalogram (EEG). The problem here, however, is that certain pathological condi-

227

tions can include a period during which there is a flat EEG, from which there can be almost total recovery. To make a long story short, the inability to find any single criterion for a clinical specification of the cessation of the viability of the organism has led to proposals to use multiple criteria, including a flat EEG, absence of spontaneous respiration, complete abolition of reflexes, and loss of response to the environment—each for a suitable time.[1]

In the summer of 1968 the Council for International Organizations of Medical Sciences and the World Medical Assembly each attempted to arrive at a satisfactory clinical definition of death using just such criteria. Very subtle sets of criteria were proposed, including considerations of artificial support for certain vital functions. However, to every combination of clinical criteria proposed, an exception could be cited from the clinical experience of at least one of the participants.[2] They concluded that *no* satisfactory objective definition of death could be established. So far as they could tell, death is not a simple and straightforward matter of fact which can be specified by clear and unequivocal criteria. The trained judgment of the physician still has to be the last word—and he could be mistaken. The formal statement of the World Medical Assembly, sometimes called the Declaration of Sidney, concludes, "No single technological criterion is entirely satisfactory in the present state of medicine nor can any one technological procedure be substituted for the overall judgment of the physician."[3]

As if this were not enough, an even more extreme challenge to using any biological criteria for death (short of chemical dissolution of the body) is posed by those who, with a faith in science fiction, support cryogenics.[4] They are freezing human bodies before decomposition becomes serious, in the confident expectation that medical science will one day be able to replace *any* damaged or worn-out organ, start the vital processes again, and generally restore all the biological processes of life. In their view, so-called biological death need be only temporary. At any rate, they pose for us a question. How long does one need to wait after biological processes have apparently stopped before one is certain that a person is unequivocally dead?

What, then, is one to say? "It is a fact that a man is dead when certain crucial biological processes have stopped for an indeterminate time?" But which ones? For how long? Having begun with the convention that the simple fact of death amounts to "the cessation of biological processes and the termination of social interaction," we have come to see that the specification of criteria for the final cessation of biological processes is ambiguous. Perhaps the second half of the conventional definition will prove to be more fruitful. Could the termination of social interaction be the key to specifying the fact of death?

Effective termination of social interaction certainly designates a good deal of the human significance of death. Current proposals for clinical definitions of death illustrate this concern by using as a reference point whether or not there is any hope for future social interaction. In spite of pet cemeteries, or perhaps even illustrated by them, people are concerned about death because it seems to mark the termination of relationships with those who are loved and hated. Could it be that the fact of death is primarily social? Can simple criteria be found to designate the termination of social relationships? If so, then it could be argued that, if biological processes are a precondition for social interaction, then the cessation of the relevant biological processes (say, effective brain function) is identified as death *because* the lack of these processes is tantamount to the termination of the possibility of social interaction. The fact of biological death would have its status as a derivative from the specifiable fact of social death.

The simplest criterion of social interaction would seem to be some form of symbolic communication, the most common being conversation. "Dead men tell no tales" is the old shibboleth we all learned from *Treasure Island* or gangster films. However, many eminently respectable investigators, such as those banded together in the British Society for Psychical Research, have become convinced that, in some sense, dead men do tell tales. They have documented something very like communication without the use of the normal physiological components of the ostensible communicator. Is an ostensible communicator dead when his physiological components, which we usually call the communicator's body, have so clearly ceased to function that there seems no doubt about saying, "He is biologically dead?" A mass of data has been gathered by, and debate over the interpretation of this data has taken place among, investigators of paranormal phenomena. The literature of parapsychology, from F. W. H. Myers' monumental study *Human Personality and Its Survival of Bodily Death*[5] to C. D. Broad's recent book *Lectures on Psychical Rearch*[6] makes it hard to escape the conclusion that at least some criteria for symbolic communication between a few of the ostensibly dead and the apparently living have been satisfied. But the question remains: Is this social interaction? Just what kinds of data would convince us that it is? Or, is not?

Now work it the other way around. Is a person dead if his biological processes are still functioning but he seems incapable of social interaction? We use the expression, "He's dead to the world," for deep sleep, suggesting that in some sense we think of the inability to communicate as signifying death. We all understand that a man who is called "politically dead" can no longer interact in the narrower social context known as politics. These are not mere metaphors, they designate social facts which can be given criteriological specification. Certain types of congenital idiots are incapable of symbolic communication. At the extreme they may be referred to as vegetables. Are complete idiots ever alive as human beings? How about the other end of the line, as encountered in such psychoses as senile dementia? Are the utterly senile dead socially, or psychologically, while still biologically alive?

How little responsiveness must be encountered before social interaction has terminated and death be a fact? What do biological processes have to do with this fact? Which are the primary facts? The biological? The social? Both? Neither? Can, in fact, the so-called facts be separated from the conceptual frameworks which enable us to specify them? Are facts impersonally objective, independent of systems of interpretation and our subjective involvement?

## Meanings

When deliberately pushed to their limits, conventional expectations about the facts of death seem to be in some sort of trouble. They don't seem to be able to provide as simple and clear-cut an understanding of death as simple facts should. We have come up against the problem of meaning. Facts do not interpret themselves, nor are they noticed by themselves. Biological facts are meaningful within a system of biological concepts, while social facts are meaningful within a system of social concepts. So long as one does not try to break down the normal boundaries of the languages in which these concepts are articulated, there is little trouble with the relationship of terms we use to the data they are taken to designate, and hence confusions do not arise over what the facts are or how words are meaningful. Within the normal boundaries of a way of talking, words are blithely taken to indicate certain sorts of facts, and those same facts are considered trustworthy support for the meaningfulness of words.[7]

Languages enable the identification of facts because a language is something like a game in which words are articulated to each other within the framework of rules of the game. In a particular situation one knows what words can be used, just as in a game one would know what cards can be played. But sometimes somebody plays a wild card, or a situation comes up which seems to be within the possibilities of the game, but lies outside the rules of the game. What, for instance, would a move "up" be called if one used the designations of conventional chess while attempting to play three-dimensional chess? What happened when the flying wedge, or the forward pass, were first introduced into football?

The game model is not altogether adequate, but it can provide some idea of the problem of understanding concepts like death. So long as somebody does not play a wild card, for which there are no rules, the language is understood, and facts are given a designation. By pushing to the limits of biological language and then treating social language as if it were of a biological order, I have called attention to the possibility of both biological and social data which seem to be within the possibilities of some sort of death language, but lie outside normal rules of use within biological or social language. Recent developments in biotechnology show that the issue is not merely verbal. These strange moves, when attempted in an established game, encourage one to think rather carefully about the rules of the game, or, it may be, games. Most of the time we do not talk *about* these rules, because we talk with or by these rules. They are a tacit component in our understanding. But they are not invariant, and they can be called into question.

The first trouble with the concept of death, then, seems to be that we have to deal with *both* facts and meanings. Data, and the rules of the languages (games) which enable us to signify data, cannot be separated. The picture is becoming more complicated. These conceptual complications are mirrored in the physician's problem of when to "turn off the taps."

Treating the biological and social routes to a concept of death separately led to an analogous problem of the relationship between fact and meaning. Perhaps the problem has been aggravated by attempting to separate the two avenues. We may play two language games, but they could both be to one purpose. After all, as human beings we may be both more, and less, than biological and/or social beings. Languages do intersect, and the intersections may be the places to check our directions in order to avoid dead ends and blind alleys. The following case from forensic medicine may illustrate something of what can happen at the intersection of ways of talking.

A certain man, upset over the marriage of his daughter to a fortune hunter, disowned her; however, he fancied the possibility of being a grandfather. He rewrote his will to provide a rather large bequest to any child born of his daughter before his death. Some months later he had a heart attack, became comatose, and was rushed to the hospital. In the emergency room it was determined that his heart had stopped beating. A physician immediately opened his chest and began heart massage. Under stimulation his heart began to beat again. It continued to beat without artificial support for half an hour, during which time he did not regain consciousness. Then the heart stopped. Further efforts proved futile, and the man was declared dead. Meanwhile, in the same hospital, a child was born to his daughter during this half hour.

The legal issue, which had to be settled in court, was: When was the man legally dead? When his heart stopped the *first* time, or the *second* time? Remember, he did *not* regain consciousness in between. So far as anyone could tell, he never knew he was a grandfather, which is clearly what he had looked forward to when inserting the clause in his will. When was he "in fact" dead? When was he "legally" dead? Do we use biological criteria? Social criteria? Both? Neither? Without traffic controls, one can get into traffic jams. Without signposts, one can go in circles.

The second trouble with understanding the concept of death is now in the open. Not only must one deal with the relationship between facts and meanings, there is the further complication of the relationship between different meaningful articulations. There are different systematic ways of using the term *death*, and while they often support each other, they sometimes conflict. One could say that the grammar of death is not always grammatical![8]

## Values

The crossing of biological and social languages, which generated the legal issue in the case of the "death-clause will," shows how systems of meaning can have ambiguous relationships to each other. The rationalist tradition in Western thought opposes permitting significance to fundamental ambiguity. We try, at least at first, to sort ambiguities out into some consistent system of meaning. Relating ambiguous meaning claims to each other either requires a decision as to which one is primary, or leads to an attempt to reconcile them through a more general system of meaning. In the first case, a decision is made as to which way of talking is fundamental, or "literal." In the second case, a search is instituted for an integration of alternative meanings at a higher level of abstraction or generalization.

Should one attempt to choose among systems of meaning, opting for a primary meaning to which other possible meanings can be reduced, he will have to decide which one is better, preferable, or obligatory. Whether this judgment applies to all situations and makes universal claims or is limited to a specific situation, it is still a value judgment. Such a reduction would amount to claiming that the "proper" or "good" meaning of death is, for instance, social. Or one might say that death "ought" to be thought of as primarily biological.

It could be said that the heart-attack victim in the case of the death-clause will clearly intended to be aware of his grandchild; therefore, if one ought to carry out the intent of the will, it would be better to use social criteria to decide when the testator was legally dead. Under this interpretation he could be argued to be dead from the time he first became comatose. On the other hand, we might think it better to consider the financial welfare of the child and allow his sometime grandfather a last, somewhat uncharacteristic, act of generosity. Under this interpretation one could argue that he ought to be dead at the last possible moment, hence minimal biological criteria should be used to decide when he was legally dead. Either way, some form of valuation would have been used. Hence, how the concept of death is to be understood seems to require a consideration of the relationship between value and meaning along with the question of the relationship between meaning and fact. It may even be the case that the relationships are not strictly linear; there may be some direct ties between value and fact lying behind the scenes. We are not yet in a position to decide whether or not there are such relationships; we have only discovered that it makes sense to ask *if* there are such relationships.

However, we have not yet found out what happens when one tries the second route to an ajudication of apparent differences in meanings. Can different ways of understanding death be reconciled at a higher level through a general system of meaning, or language of all languages, about death? Those who favor this way of getting out of claimed conflicts between meanings would argue that to select among meanings which are of the same logical level is trivial or purely arbitrary. Such a decision, they would say, has nothing to do with the *true* meaning of death. What is wanted, in this view, is the "real" meaning of death. Instead of reducing one way of talking about death to another, the question which is asked is, "When is a person really dead?" If this question is answered, so goes this line of reasoning, then it will become easy to solve derivative issues. Traditionally, this question has been taken to be a metaphysical issue, dealing with "reality" or "being as such." The one who asks it is attempting to reconcile the apparent conflict of meanings by resolving the conflict at a higher level. The difference between the level of meaning found in the various language types we have been using and this language of all languages is frequently claimed to be the difference between the appearance of death and the reality of death.

The traditional metaphysical answer has been, "A person is really dead when his soul leaves his body, otherwise he only appears to be dead." But is that "really" a very good answer or even helpful? If we go back to the Greek terms which lie behind this answer we find that we have said, "A person is really dead when his psyche leaves his soma." But what is his psyche, or his soma for that matter? What if psyche is merely a term for life, and soma the term for organism? Those are intelligible translations. Might saying, "A person is dead when his soul leaves his body," just be a fancy way of saying, "A person is dead when his organic processes cease"? Perhaps *psyche* should be taken to mean a locus of social interaction and *soma* to be the organic vehicle of that interaction. Again, possible translations. If so, how have we improved on the problem of discovering if a man is socially dead before or after biological processes stop in the organism which is the mediator of social interaction? How *ought* we to decide among these possibilities?

Of course, this kind of quibbling would irritate the traditional metaphysician. He would claim that it misses the whole issue. If he is a

Platonist, he would urge us to notice that there are certain universal, enduring truths which are there, undergirding (or overgirding) our knowledge, apart from any particular claims about, or uses of, language. These eternal ideas, he would say, determine the possibility of meaningful facts and allow us to discover which meanings are closer to the unchanging truth about death. This timeless concept would conform to "death itself," the recognition of which would show biological and social judgments about death to be possible only as feeble shadows of the true basis of all judgment about death. But he is also saying that certain ways of understanding death are *better* than others. Simply pointing out that Plato places the form of the *Good* in, or close to, a supreme position among the eternal bases of true judgments would serve to remind him that he has not escaped the problem of the relationship between values and meanings, not to mention facts. Granted, there are other kinds of metaphysicians than Platonists, but in every case it is still possible to ask if a particular metaphysics is the *best* way to understand the reality of death. *Ought* one to accept any particular way of sorting out meanings and deciding which facts are really real?

The third trouble with the concept of death is now out in the open. Whether one way of designating death is reduced to another, by opting for a primary linguistic context, or differences in ways of talking about death are resolved by subordinating them to a universal standard, value judgments are involved. Should someone claim that neither move should be made, that ambiguity ought to be tolerated and alternate ways of understanding death be maintained, that is still a value judgment, though it may be nothing more than an expression of preference. We have now found that a complete articulation of the concept of death involves not only questions about the relationship between facts and meanings, but also the issue of the ties between both of these and our valuations. And our valuations include our valuation of death.

## Ultimates

The introduction of metaphysical considerations also leads to traditionally religious issues. Once the relevancy of values to meanings has been admitted, we cannot get around the question of the ultimate basis of valuation and the ultimate justification of a search for meaning. This is a version of the "god question." Of course, this question can be formulated in various ways, such as asking about our ultimate concern, searching for a sacred order, or demanding a response from a transcendent personal agent. Regardless of how we articulate the question, it is still there. I suspect that the issue of the ultimate basis of conceptualization is not a conscious question for most people, most of the time. It is even possible to confuse it with the "fact question," for, as with facts, an ultimate basis of conceptualization marks one of the points at which discussion stops. Hence, *both* facts and ultimates are often designated by the adjective *obvious* in discussions of death. In terms of each other, though, facts and ultimate sanctions for our ways of talking are not obvious; rather they are counter poles in the process of understanding. We are controlled by that which we take to be ultimate when we look for facts, and it is on the basis of recognized facts that we support or question whatever is accepted as being ultimate. This occurs whenever a religious person relates the love of God to the death of a child. It also happens when a scientific-minded scholar relates the death of a child to a general theory of evolution.

In moving from facts to meanings to values, the question of how death is *ultimately* to be understood has surfaced. Is one way of understanding death *ultimately* better than another? Or are there several, ultimately independent, ways of understanding death? For that matter, why not ask if death (perhaps enunciated "DEATH") is itself ultimate. People have certainly been known to say, "Death has the last word." Are they assuming that death explains life? If so, in what way? Could one find out by going back to the value question to ask, in turn, if death is good or bad, desirable or undesirable, obligatory or optional? But then, what is the ultimate, or controlling, value? For instance, could it be death that sanctions living, so that mortality is the justification of life?

The link between ultimates and values has been the focus of much traditional reflection on death. However, contemporary thinkers find it hard to agree about the specification and function of ultimates. As a result there is no established method for legislating the meanings and facts of death. It is difficult for us to specify the ultimate consideration which ought to control our understanding of death not because such specification is impossible, but because it is so easy to find views which would take exception to the validity of almost any claim for ultimacy.

Precisely because the considerations which ultimately control our understanding are tacitly communicated in our education, or culturation in its widest sense, claims to ultimacy are hard to explicate. Further, the plurality of traditions behind our contemporary civilization provides alternative, and even mutually exclusive, bases for comprehending death. This is one of the phenomena noted when people observe that we no longer live in a universe, but rather a multiverse— that we no longer find ourselves established in a sacred cosmos, but adrift a secular chaos.

The fourth trouble with death, then, could be formulated as a theological issue. The seriousness of this problem may even indicate why death is often thought of as a theological, rather than scientific or philosophical, problem. From Aristotle to Tillich, theology has been concerned with first (or ultimate) principles, which, if they are not claimed to be the ground of being, are at least thought to be the basis of understanding. Whether or not there are, ultimately, any such principles is itself one of these theological-type issues. Such issues are not decided simply by fact, meaning, or value claims. However, they certainly involve such questions as adequacy to facts and legislating the possibility of facts. They must deal with the meaningfulness of languages and the ultimate basis of meaning. They must take account of valuations expressed in commitments, or preferences, and the status of the ultimate sanction of valuation.

## Conclusions

Considerations of facts, meanings, values, and ultimates, individually and severally, have a bearing on how death is understood. Any attempt to make a beginning at investigating the concept of death will have to take into account questions raised by interrelationships among facts, meanings, values, and ultimates. Most discussions of death move rather carelessly through these intersections, assuming or proclaiming interconnections without carefully examining them. Maybe that is all that can be done, but at least in having noticed the questions which arise in the different dimensions of a discussion of death, we may be ready to recognize the complexities which are, willy-nilly, going to be present in any actual concept of death. To have recognized that much is already a first step.

I have tried to show that there is no simple way to nail "death" into a box, drop it into a slot, and set up a marker. Such a realization may be frustrating, but it is also therapeutic. It can save us from simplistic claims and trivial conclusions. On the other hand, I hope we have also begun to see that there is more involved in reflecting on death than concern with the physician's clinical data, the sociologist's identification of cultural expectations, and the metaphysician's prescriptions of truth and reality.

## Notes

1. F. W. Camps, "Defining Death," *Science Journal*, vol. 3, no. 6 (1967), pp. 81–84, is an example of such an attempt to define death within the criteria-which-define-the-fact tradition. There are many others. Camps' article has the virtue of recognizing some of the complexities and ambiguities which turn up along the way when death is taken to be specifiable in terms of a simple summation of clinical criteria.

2. For instance, *The New York Times* reports Sir Edward Mallen, presiding officer of the World Medical Assembly, as saying that "even rigor mortis was not a complete indication in view of new methods of resuscitation that are constantly being developed" (Aug. 10, 1968, p. 25).

3. As reported by Stanley S. B. Gilder, "Twenty-second World Medical Assembly," *British Medical Journal*, vol. 3, no. 5616 (Aug. 24, 1968), p. 493. The "Declaration" of the CIOMS Round Table is more explicit about listing specific considerations to be used in deciding the choice of a heart donor, but avoids calling these indications of "death" and includes the following explicit reservation: "These criteria are not valid for young children or for subjects in hypothermic states or with acute toxic conditions" (Council for International Organizations of Medical Sciences, Document CIOMS/RT2/ VR, p. 48). For a good discussion of the problems involved in clinical identification of death, see A. Kieth Mant, "The Medical Definition of Death," in Arnold Toynbee et al., *Man's Concern With Death* (London: Hodder and Stoughton, Ltd., 1968), pp. 13–24.

4. Robert C. W. Ettinger's *The Prospect of Immortality* (Garden City, N. Y.: Doubleday & Company, Inc., 1964) provided the first big push for these dreamers.

5. F. W. H. Myers, *Human Personality and Its Survival of Bodily Death* (London: Longmans, Green, & Co., Ltd., 1903).

6. C. D. Broad, *Lectures on Psychical Research* (London: Routledge & Kegan Paul, Ltd., 1962).

7. W. E. Hocking expresses a more traditional way of getting at the same problem by observing that meaning is not a simple sort of thing, it must be looked for in two directions: the particular intended and a general frame of reference. See William Ernest Hocking, *The Meaning of Immortality in Human Experience* (New York: Harper & Brothers, 1957), p. 110.

8. The following imaginary problem may illustrate how confusing things could get if we took the fact-meaning problem on a science-fiction holiday:

A team of lawyers, physicians, and social scientists has been brought together in order to arrive at a decision as to whether or not they ought to declare me to be dead. The physicians report that they can find no heartbeat or respiration, but for some reason they get a normal EEG reading, and my body shows no signs of decay. The social scientists report that they hear voices answering questions addressed to me, though the voices do not seem to come from my body and say different things to different listeners. The lawyers report that my family is destitute because my paychecks have stopped coming and the insurance (not to mention social security) people will not start payment until and unless I am pronounced dead.

If you were called in as philosophical consultant, what considerations would you suggest to the team to guide them as they attempt to decide whether or not I am dead?

# 33

# Perspectives on Death: Philosophical and Theological
## — JAMES M. DEMSKE

A terrible scene in the film *Zorba the Greek*[1] shows the townspeople of a small island village condemn a young widow to death because she has spurned the attentions of a young man of the island in favor of a handsome visiting Englishman, thus contributing to the suicide of the disappointed native. The father of the spurned young man murders the woman in cold blood, in the sight of all, thus wasting a beautiful life in the name of the ancient law, "an eye for an eye and a tooth for a tooth." After this horror, Zorba asks his friend, the young Englishman who has loved the murdered girl: "Why do young people die? Why does anybody die? Don't your books and all your study tell you that?" After a long pause the Englishman replies: "My books only tell about the agony of not being able to answer questions like yours." To which Zorba passionately replies: "I spit on your agony."

Zorba's expostulation certainly throws down the gauntlet to anyone who would presume to philosophize about death. He poses the problem in the most striking, dramatic, existential way imaginable. Why death? Why this destruction of all that is good and joyous and beautiful? Why this utter contradiction of life, this obscene frustration of the will to live?

But men have always gone further and asked: Is that all there is? Is death sheer horror, pure tragedy? If so, it would indeed be better not even to think about it, because even the healthiest of us ought to get neurotic thinking about something which is pure disaster. What is death? Is there more to it than catastrophe? Can our thinking, can all our books and studying really tell us anything significant about it?

As an object of human speculation, death is something like time. You will recall St. Augustine's famous words: "Time—what is it? If you don't ask me, I know; but if you ask me what it is, I don't."[2] To be sure, philosophers have given definitions of death, but none of us has ever experienced it—not yet anyway. We have seen it from the outside, but have never known it from the inside, from having undergone it ourselves.

Let us see what, if anything, we can discover about death by our own philosophizing. To be sure, we have some experience of death, even though it be of the death of others. We also have certain human experiences during life which bear some resemblance to, or contain intimations of, death. And we also have the whole history of human thought on the subject, which ought to shed some light on our path. We shall first study the classical view of death in Western philosophy, stemming from Socrates and Plato, then present a contemporary view based on modern phenomenology, especially Martin Heidegger's version of it, and finally discuss a direction in which this modern thought might lead, approaching the threshold of religion and theology.

## Classical View of Death

The traditional view of death in Western philosophy can be gleaned from Plato's famous dialogue *Phaedo*, the last of the four dialogues which tell the story of the trial, imprisonment, and death of Socrates.

*Phaedo* is a record of Socrates' farewell speech in prison, as he awaits the hour of execution. True to character right to the end, he does not regard death as a terror to be avoided or an unpleasantness to be ignored. He speaks of it explicitly and at length, even describing it as the fulfillment of his greatest yearning. He has always claimed to be nothing more than a philosopher, a lover of wisdom, and the philosopher is practicing death all during his life. For the philosopher is in constant pursuit of truth, and truth is perceived only by the soul, not the body. The body with its senses, its emotions and feelings, its passionate involvement in the here and now, can do nothing but obscure the pure truth, which is susceptible only to penetration by the soul. "[The soul] reasons best when none of the senses disturbs it, hearing or sight, or pain or pleasure; . . . when it is completely by itself and says goodbye to the body, and so far as possible has no dealings with it, [then] it reaches out and grasps that which really is" (65c, Rouse 468).[3]

Death is thus highly desirable to the philosopher, because it is "a freeing and separation of the soul from the body" (67d, Rouse 470; cf. 64c, Rouse 467). Only in death is the soul "pure and rid of the body's foolishness" (67a, Rouse 470). Thus "one who is really in love with wisdom . . . holds firm to this same hope, that he will find it in the grave, and nowhere else worth speaking of" (68b, Rouse 471).

Socrates thus looks with calm and composure upon the lethal hemlock he is about to drink. His last recorded words echo not despair or resentment but an ironic kind of reverence. After admonishing his friend, Criton, not to forget to pay his debt of sacrificing a cock to Asclepios, the god of healing, he says: "But at least, I suppose it is allowed to offer a prayer to the gods and that must be done, for good luck in the migration from here to there. Then that is my prayer, and so may it be!" (117b–c, Rouse 520–21). Having said this, the dialogue reports, Socrates put the cup to his lips and drank it up quite easy and content.

What do we learn about death from this scene? What do Socrates and Plato, the founders of Western philosophy, think of death?

1. Death is not the greatest of all evils, but something to be desired, because it leads to a better kind of life. (In the *Apology*, Socrates has made it abundantly clear that dishonor is a much greater evil than death.)

2. Death is the separation of the soul from the body, the dissolving of man into his two component parts, body and soul.

3. The death of a man is simply another example of the general phenomenon of passing away which we find in all living things. The cycle of life includes *generatio* and *corruptio*, *genesis* and *phthora*, coming-to-be and ceasing-to-be.

4. Death is the last event of a man's life, the final moment of the time allotted to him, the outer limit of his own individual time-line or life history.

5. For each living person, death lies in the future, as something which is not yet with us, but which we must look forward to.

6. The soul lives on after leaving the body, and since it is unencumbered by the senses, it can perceive absolute truth; it can "grasp that which really is."

It is easy to see why Christianity could so readily adopt this Platonic and Socratic view of death. If we conceive of God as the source and fullness of all being and truth, if we substitute the words "Supreme Being" for "that which really is," we have a perfect philosophical underpinning for the Christian doctrine of immortality, heaven, and the beatific vision. The idea of man's being composed of two basic parts, body and soul, fits in well with such New Testament sayings as "What does it profit a man to gain the whole world and suffer the loss of his soul?" (Matt. 16, 26) and even with the original Genesis account of the creation of man: "The Lord God formed man of dust from the ground, and breathed into his nostrils the breath of life." (Gen. 2, 7).

Thus, the classical view of death gives a plausible definition of death, provides a basis for facing death with hope and courage, affords the assurance of personal immortality, and gives a consistent view of the value and meaning of life. On the other hand, there are certain questions left unanswered, which have provoked further thought in modern times. For instance, what happens to man's body? Does it enjoy a share of his immortality? The Greek doctrine stresses

the immorality of the *soul;* how does this fit in with the Biblical doctrine of the resurrection of the flesh? Moreover, the dualism of man's
composition is not always immediately evident. Our experience tells
us that we operate as unified beings. I am me; I am not conscious of
being two things welded together. The dualism, however necessary it
may be for any complete and balanced philosophical explanation of
reality, still must leave room for the unity and integrity of the human
person. We are not just body and soul; we are individuals striving for
the perfection and completion of our unified personhood.

Thus it was perhaps inevitable that, in the long history of philosophy and theology, new perspectives would have to arise on the subject of death. We shall now look into some of these, centered about the
thought of one of the most influential of contemporary philosophers,
Martin Heidegger.[4] Let us see whether Heidegger can illuminate the
dark area surrounding the mystery of death.

## Heidegger's Contemporary View of Death

How does Heidegger approach the problem of death? First of all, he
sees death as a determining factor of man's existence; since he is a
thinker in the existential era, Heidegger is not at all interested in the
passing away of plants or animals, but only that of man. Secondly,
Heidegger approaches death, as he approaches everything else, as a
phenomenologist. This means that his method is phenomenology, not
the metaphysical analysis of philosophers in the Platonic-Aristotelian
tradition.

Phenomenology studies phenomena, that is, things as they appear
to man. The question therefore is not: What is death in its essence?
Why does death occur? What are the ultimate causes of death? The
question is rather: How does death appear to man? How does it manifest itself in human consciousness? What does death mean to me?[5]

How can we find out something about death through the phenome-
nological method? Not by dissecting a cadaver in a laboratory, not by
measuring heartbeat, or checking skin color, or determining other biological aspects of death, as a medical scientist might. And not just by
thinking of death in the abstract, of death as a common occurrence in
all of nature, as a Greek philosopher or a metaphysician might.
Rather, the phenomenologist approaches the subject of death as he
finds it in his own consciousness, not in a purely subjectivistic or
solipsistic way, but rather taking into account the whole range of his
experience with other people, with things and events as they present
themselves to his reflection.

And how does death manifest itself in human consciousness? At
first glance, it seems to be something outside of man, a distant event

awaiting him in the far-off future—this is why paintings often represent death as the grim reaper, an old man or a skeleton with a sickle in his hand, waiting to cut down the ripened crop of human lives.

But it takes just a moment's reflection to realize that death does not just lie in wait in the distant future. The grim reaper can do his work at any age, at any time, even right now. As the old saying has it: As soon as a man is born, he is old enough to die. So death is not just something or someone way out there; it's here right now, confronting me as a possibility of my existence. In fact, because it's an ever-present possibility of my being, it is one of the very *structures* of my existence.

Looked at in this way, death is actually part of life. Death determines my existence continually, as it were hovering over me, always present in everything I do. To borrow another familiar image, death is the sword of Damocles suspended over my head. The important point is that it is always *here,* always with me, a concomitant and a determinant of my existence. Death is thus a built-in structure of existence, what Heidegger calls an "existential."

To fully grasp this "existential-ontological" concept of death, we must contrast it with death as it is more generally understood by ordinary "common sense." Ordinarily we think of man's life as a series of events stretched out on a time-line. The totality of existence embraces all aspects of life, from beginning to end, from birth to death. At any point of the line there is a certain incompleteness. As long as man lives, there remains something which he can be, but is not yet. Man's life is like a painting which is never finished; he always has further possibilities not yet realized, aspects, events, accomplishments which are not yet a part of his actuality. In fact, the picture will never be completed until death. Death is the final stroke on the painting, the final arc in the circle of existence. Seen thus, the death of man is his completion. Death belongs to the totality; in fact, it completes the totality of man's existence.

This death—death seen as the last stroke of the brush, or the final moment of a person's life—is death in the ontic sense, death as a single, external event occurring at the end-point of a man's life-line. Death in the ontological or existential sense, however, is not just a point or a moment or an event; it is an ever-abiding and built-in structure of existence.

What kind of a structure? It is a possibility of man's being, something which he can do. Here is another unfamiliar notion. The totality of a man's existence includes not only what he is at any given moment, but also whatever he can be. Man is not only what he is right now, not only all that he has been, has done, and has produced, but also all that he can be, can do, and can produce. His possibilities are part of his actuality, part of the total reality of his existence. Man in

Heidegger's view is a three-dimensional being, corresponding to the three dimensions of time; his existence includes being-ahead-of-one-self, already-being-in (the world), and being-with (the beings encountered within the world).[6]

Now death is one of the possibilities of man's existence; in fact it is the most definitive of his possibilities. Death as an existential is a way in which man *can be*; it is a power-to-be, not just the power to cease being. In Heidegger's words, "death is a way to be, which Dasein [man] takes over as soon as it is" (BT 289).

As a mode of existence, death is an ever-present potentiality which belongs necessarily to the being of man, determining it not just at the moment of dying, but always and already, even prior to our noticing it: "(Man) is dying as long as he exists" (BT 295). In this sense, death is the structure by which man exists as being-unto-death, his structure of being-mortal. Death (or, in more ordinary terminology, *dying*) is a way to be, in fact *the* way in which man exists.

Death is one of man's possibilities; in fact, it is the possibility of all possibilities, because it stands before man in a unique way, forming the most ultimate possibility of his being. Moreover, it is ultimate not just in a temporal sense; it is the extreme possibility not just because it is the last point on a man's time-line, but in a much more profound way, because it has an aspect of totality which no other possibility has. Man can run, he can walk, he can sleep, he can eat, he can love, he can hate, but all of these engage him only partially and temporarily. When we say man can *die*, we immediately recognize the difference; death engages him totally and definitively. Thus, the possibility of death enfolds, includes, and engulfs all his other possibilities, just as it enwraps man's total being-in-the-world, completely and entirely. What is at issue in death, says Heidegger is "nothing less than Dasein's being-in-the-world. Its death is the possibility of no-longer-being-able-to-be-there" (BT 294).

Death involves the totality of man's own irreplaceable and incommunicable being. What follows from this? First of all, death affects all that is most distinctive, proper, and personal to man; it is the most proper and individual of all his possibilities. Secondly, death throws man completely on his own, dissolving all his relations to other beings; it is a nonrelational possibility. Thirdly, since death is the extreme and total possibility, man has no means of avoiding it or recovering from it; death is an insuperable or unsurpassable possibility. Fourthly, death is not something which man can opt out of; he is rather "thrown" into it; it is given with his very existence.

But death is also something against which he protects himself by habitually trying to ignore it. Man tends to live inauthentically with regard to death, because he tends to follow the crowd and its own escapist thinking on the matter. He tends to accept the evasive and pacifying general attitude that death is really not relevant to life, indeed it is not even to be mentioned in polite, enlightened conversation. If at times one becomes aware that he too must face death, he generally sidesteps the problem with the comforting cliché: "Everybody dies someday, but as for me . . . not yet." We tend to think of "everybody" dying, but not of ourselves. We also blind ourselves to the existential reality of death by pushing it off to the distant future. Man flees from his own death, death as a determination written into his own basic structure; man usually exists in the mode of inauthentic flight, thus concealing the existential reality of death.

This brief analysis reveals death as man's possibility-to-be, which is most distinctively his own, which is utterly individualizing and nonrelational, which is unsurpassable, into which he is thrown, and from which he usually inauthentically flees by concealing its true nature as a determinant of his existence.[7]

We must add one further note to this description. We have said that death is the ultimate possibility of man's life, not simply as the last in time, but also and more importantly in the sense of the most universal and all-embracing. As a consequence of this, not only is man's existence touched by death, but so are all his other day-to-day possibilities. His power to love, to hate, to eat, to sleep, to run, to think—all these are touched at their core by the possibility of death. Moreover, death is normative for the proper understanding of all the other possibilities of man, since these can only be authentically understood and properly brought to realization if they are seen in the light of the preeminent possibility of death. All these other possibilities are repeatable, retrievable, intermediate, and thus secondary. Since man is a unity, all these must be subordinated to and understood in terms of the primary, unrepeatable, and irretrievable possibility of death. Thus death is not merely one of the possibilities of Dasein, but it is rather the overarching, all-embracing possibility, what we might call the *transcendental* possibility of man's existence, towering over all others in such a way as to include them and to enter into them as part of their very structure. Death is thus structurally constitutive of all other possibilities of man, as well as being normative for their proper understanding and authentic realization. All of this is contained in the phrase "man exists as being-unto-end or being-unto-death."

Doesn't this all sound rather pessimistic? Doesn't it remind us of the flippant statement of the village atheist type who is said to have proclaimed: "I am like my dog Rover; when I die, I die all over"? Doesn't existential analysis lead to the conclusion that death is a total annihilation of the human personality, the end of all possible forms of existence? It may sound that way at first, but there is another side to it. Let us explore more fully what it means to say that death is the existential of totality, the transcendental possibility of human existence.

We have said that death is not just the ultimate possibility of man in the sense that it is the last thing he can do, but rather in the sense that it embraces all possibilities of this existence. In the philosopher's attempt to understand man, death is not just one existential structure alongside several others; it embraces the totality of the structure; everything about man is enveloped in the term "being-unto-death." Because of this feature of completeness, man cannot fully understand himself unless he fully understands death. But he cannot fully understand death while he is alive, because he has not experienced it personally. Thus death is the one feature of man's existence which remains ˙mpervious to his intellectual quest for understanding. It is also the one aspect in which man is powerless over his own structure. Death refuses to fit neatly into the list of existential structures, because it is broader than all these combined. It remains the one unknown factor, the indissoluble remainder in every question of human existence.

This is extremely important. Because there is death, man cannot be a neatly solved puzzle or a tidy package of intelligibility closed within himself. This is where all purely naturalistic humanisms break down. Despite all attempts to understand man in purely naturalistic or secularistic terms, there has to remain an element of the unknown, an element of mystery. Death leaves man open, it is the "open wound" which leaves the problematic of existence susceptible to further development. Because of death, human experience does not offer sufficient evidence to answer man's own questions, and in this case, his own *deepest* question. Death means that man's existence necessarily points to something beyond itself, ultimately to the entire mystery of being itself, and in the context of religion, to the question of some superhuman "other," some Supreme Being who controls not only all existence, but also all intelligibility.[8]

We must dwell a moment on this *mysterious* aspect of death. Since death shows that man needs more than his own structure to explain his existence, death is the key to the fact that man must transcend himself in order to fully understand himself, or even in order to fully be himself. Death confronts man with a kind of nothingness, with the prospect of the disappearance of all that is familiar to him, of all that makes up existence as he knows it. But this "nothingness" which is the first face that death presents to man is not the absolute non-being which would be the denial of all reality. (In fact, we can't even think absolute non-being; try it some time.) The nothingness revealed by death is rather a screen behind which being itself hides.

Man's questioning about death leads him beyond himself; but this cannot mean that it leads him into absolute zero. It leads man beyond himself into some other kind of being. To be sure, the fact of death reveals a deep negativity in man's existence, and in being itself as being reveals itself to man. This negativity affects every aspect of man's life and experience, no matter how exalted they may be. Man's existence is deeply penetrated by a "not," in fact, his whole life is a series of positive actions, accomplishments, etc., all of which are penetrated by limitations, by negative aspects. Poets have remarked that there is an unseen guest at every banquet, an invisible interloper at every celebration, an angel of death at every Mardi Gras. The German theologian Karl Rahner has written similarly: "Because we die our death in this life, because we are continually taking leave, continually parting, looking towards the end, continually disappointed, ceaselessly piercing through realities into their nothingness, continually narrowing the possibilities of free choice through our actual decisions and actual life, . . . we die throughout life, and what we call death is really the end of death, the death of death."[9]

Death thus reveals most strikingly that our entire existence is a combination of positive and negative elements, of actions circumscribed by limitations, of exultation sobered by the realization of transience, of joy tempered by sorrow, of beauty marred by the rusting of time. Death is the feature which reveals most thoroughly the negativity inherent in human existence and in all of being as man sees and knows it. But being reveals itself in death precisely by concealing itself, by showing only its negative face. Heidegger compares death to a mountain fastness or hidden fortress, in which being reveals itself precisely by concealing itself. Being reveals itself in death as mystery, as a combination of positive and negative elements, as something impenetrable which is best known when it is acknowledged to be impenetrable. This is one good working definition of mystery: that which we know best when we know how little we know of it.

All of this is, in my view, what Heidegger is hinting at when he says in one of his later writings: "Death is the shrine of non-being, that is, of that which is never and in no way a mere being, but which nevertheless is present, indeed as the mystery of being itself. As the shrine of non-being, death conceals within itself the presencing of being. As the shrine of non-being, death is the redoubt (or mountain retreat) of being."[10]

How is death "the shrine of non-being"? In death all the things which made up man's world dissolve and fade away, so that the totality of beings seems to disappear. Death exposes the totality of beings as frail and perishable. Thus it is "a shrine of non-being," the place in which the seeming ultimate nothingness of all things appears.

But further thought moves quickly beyond the element of negativity to something positive. In spite of the fragile negativity of all things, still they have being, they are real, they are, and have constituted an undeniable and incontrovertible part of my human existence. Thus all the beings of my world are not nothing in the absolute sense. We are faced with the question of what it means to say that something is, and yet is at the same time touched by non-being. What does it mean "to be"?

In this way death forces upon us the question of the meaning of being. The negativity revealed by death points out the questionableness of beings, compelling us to ask about being itself. Thus, the non-being involved in death is really a pointer toward being, a "veil" of being. In fact, non-being could be said to be the mode of appearance by which being shows itself in death. Thus death, as the "shrine of non-being," is, in a deeper sense, "the redoubt or hidden retreat of being."

Death is the self-withdrawing communication of being, the supreme point of the double movement by which being both manifests and enshrouds itself. It is the outstanding example of the hiddenness of being. By showing being as essentially withdrawing itself as soon as it reveals itself, or rather by showing that being reveals itself precisely by concealing itself, death leads man to the threshold of mystery. It is not something he can completely ignore, and yet it is not something whose meaning he can ever fully fathom. Before such mystery, man learns something about himself and about all being, possibly the most important lesson of his life, namely that he cannot dominate, master, and manipulate the whole of reality. Before such mystery, man's only proper attitude is a kind of puzzled acquiescence, akin to the wonder which the Greeks called the beginning of philosophy, perhaps even a kind of wondrous awe and reverence.

But awe and reverence reveal the presence of mystery, of what Rudolf Otto called the numinous or "the holy."[11] Is death holy because it brings man into his completion or wholeness, because it lets man be whole? Is death the completion, the crown of life, the final peak of self-fulfillment? If so, is not death something to be desired with fondest yearning, although for reasons quite different from those of Socrates?

But what does fulfillment or completion mean here? What is the definitiveness wrought by death? What is man's ultimate mode of being? Is it a kind of being or non-being, or a combination of both? What kind of being can man have in death? And what is the non-being involved here? What is it that is both concealed and revealed in the redoubt of death? What is it that is both feared and revered in this shrine?

Heidegger's thought, and perhaps philosophy of its very nature, provides us with no final answers to these questions, but makes us aware of their profundity and leads to the threshold of mystery. It encourages us to assume a posture of reverent questioning and submissive awe. Our proper attitude before death is not an inauthentic fleeing from it, nor is it bitter resentment or haughty pride, but rather the same enlightened reverence that Socrates exhibited before he drank the hemlock.

In the case of death, as in the case of all profound problems of human existence, philosophy points beyond itself. It leads us to a locked door, the key to which must be provided by something other than human reason alone. For Heidegger, the answers are subject to the pleasure of being, which reveals and conceals itself as it will. Man can only wait, hold himself ready and open, dwelling serenely in his reverence before the mystery of his own existence and of being. Heidegger says this poetically:

> Could perhaps wonderment open the locked door?
> In the manner of waiting . . .
> If this is relaxed . . .
> And man's being stays pointed there . . .
> From where we are called.[12]

## Death in the Religious Context

We have spoken of death as leading into the realm of mystery, of death as "holy." But these are ideas proper to the context of religion. What about death in modern Christian thought? Can phenomenology give us any leads to a new religious interpretation of death?

We have seen that death is a part of man's existential structure. It determines his existence right from the beginning, as one of his powers or possibilities, one of his modes of being. Death is not merely something which man submits to, which he must suffer passively to happen to him, but rather one of the things he *can* do, in fact the most important, all-enveloping thing he can do. When the final event of death occurs, it will be something that man will be actually performing, not just suffering.

Obviously, man does not have a choice as to whether or not he will perform this action, but he can choose *how* to perform it. He can live his life with acceptance and even reverence toward death, he can even practice dying every day, both in the sense of Socrates who thought the philosophic vocation was to pursue truth which could only be attained when the soul was separated from the body, and also he can practice dying in the sense of the medieval spiritual writers who often recalled to themselves the fact of their mortality, so that they would always be ready to stand in the presence of God.

What we said before about the existential nature of death as the transcendental possibility of man has great importance here. If death is the existential of totality, that is, the aspect of man's life which affects every other aspect and indeed includes them all, then the act of dying is not just the last in the series of acts that man performs throughout his lifetime, but it is the most important, because it is the one act by which he can sum up his whole life. This possibility is perhaps reflected in the popular conviction that a person's whole life passes before his eyes at the moment of death. The act of dying is the one act in which a person takes his whole life and either presents it to God in open, humble submission or clutches it to himself in eternal rejection of the profferred love of an other.

A gifted contemporary thinker and writer, Ladislaus Boros, has advanced the fascinating thesis that death is the first completely personal act of man, by which he makes the ultimate decision about his eternal destiny. He writes:

> In death the individual existence takes its place on the confines of all being, suddenly awake, in full knowledge and liberty . . . Being flows towards him like a boundless stream of things, meanings, persons and happenings, ready to convey him right into the Godhead. Yes; God himself stretches out his hand for him; God who, in every stirring of his existence, had been in him as his deepest mystery, from the stuff of which he had always been forming himself; God who had ever been driving him on towards an eternal destiny. There now man stands, free to accept or reject this splendor. In a last, final decision he either allows this flood of realities to flow past him, while he stands there eternally turned to stone, like a rock past which the life-giving stream flows on, noble enough in himself no doubt but abandoned and eternally alone; or he allows himself to be carried along by this flood, becomes part of it and flows on into eternal fulfillment . . . death gives man the opportunity of posing his first completely personal act; death is, therefore, by reason of its very being, the moment above all others for the awakening of consciousness, for freedom, for the encounter with God, for the final decision about [one's] eternal destiny.[13]

This theory of death as the act of man's final decision is indeed a striking one. It means that man's existence, from the very beginning and even up to the act of dying itself, is pointed toward an ultimate acceptance or rejection of God. Death is the supreme moment of decision, when we can place our whole selves in God's hands, even along with the distasteful and painful aspects of our existence which are summed up in the ultimate pain and frustration of death. Death is the end of our state of pilgrimage, the ending of all the temporariness of life, and the adoption of our definitive, ultimate state, the end of all our leave-taking, all our disappointments, all our saying good-bye which marked life on earth. As Rahner says, death is really the end of dying, it is the beginning of definitive life. As Christ won life for the whole world by dying himself, so, in the Christian tradition, we can appropriate Christ's death and win life for ourselves by dying positively, by making our last decision a resounding yes to the God who awaits us in eternity.

André Malraux represents a strong current of naturalistic humanism which has characterized much of twentieth-century writing. In *La condition humaine* he records a pessimistic conversation between husband and wife: "Listen, May: it does not take nine months to make a man, it takes fifty years—fifty years of sacrifice, of determination, of—so many things! And when that man has been achieved, when there is no childishness left in him, or any adolescence, when he is truly, utterly, a man —the only thing he is good for is to die."[14]

This bitter remark sounds like an expression of the futility of life. For if human death has no meaning, then the whole of life has no meaning either. But if, on the other hand, death offers the possibility of man's placing himself confidently into the hands of his Creator, if there is in death a fullness of being which life does not possess, then life itself acquires a whole new rich meaning. The Christian view of death transforms the expression of futility noted in Malraux's words into a completely affirmative, optimistic statement. To say that a man at the end of life is good for nothing but to die really means that it takes a whole lifetime to get ready to die. All the smaller acts of love, kindness, courage, patience, faith, and hope, etc. are nothing more than a preparation for the final great act of decision performed in the act of death.

Zorba the Greek was right. If all our books and all our thinking and all our human labor can't tell us anything about death, what good are they? We have to know death to know life. He who hates death will hate life. He who despises death will hold life cheaply. As you understand death, so you will understand life. As you live, so shall you die; and as you die, so shall you live.

# Notes

1. Based on the novel of the same name by Nikos Kazantzakis, New York: Simon and Schuster, 1952.

2. St. Augustine, *Confessions*, Book XI, chap. XIV.

3. The *Phaedo* is cited according to the standard Greek text of Plato by Henricus Stephanus (Geneva: excudebat, Henr. Stephanus, 1578) and also the English translation by W. H. D. Rouse, in *Great Dialogues of Plato* (New York: New American Library, Inc., Mentor Books, 1956).

4. Martin Heidegger has a lot to say about death, because he started his philosophical career as an existentialist, according to the majority of the critics. Perhaps it is better to say that, although his starting point was the problematic of human existence, he always had the broader problems of the whole range of being in mind, and his later works show a greater

preoccupation with being than with human existence. For a fuller discussion of the importance of death in Heidegger's thought, see my book, *Being, Man, and Death: A Key to Heidegger* (Lexington, Ky: University of Kentucky Press, 1970).

5. Another example might be helpful. Phenomenology does not ask what is a tree in itself, striving to give some absolutely objective definition, but rather: What does the presence of trees mean for man, how do trees appear to man? What do they mean for his perception of the world and himself? How do they fit into the scheme of his consciousness and his existence? For example, they might appear as serving man, by providing wood for his shelter, or beauty and quiet for his appreciation and recreation, shade or even food for him, etc. Or looked at another way, trees make up forests, and forests create the atmosphere in which man works out a civilization, forests provide inspiration for man in his reflective or poetic or artistic moods, etc.

6. See the analysis of man's existence as "care" or "concern" in Heidegger's *Being and Time*, (trans. John Macquarrie and Edward Robinson (New York and Evanston, Ill.: Harper and Row, Publishers, Inc., 1962), pp. 235–241. This English translation contains easily locatable references to the corresponding passages in the German original, *Sein und Zeit*, first published in 1927. In subsequent references in the present article, *Being and Time* will be identified as BT.

7. See the elaboration of the existential concept of death in BT, pp. 293–303.

8. For a forceful literary presentation of the problems involved in naturalistic humanism, see the masterful fantasy-for-adults by C. S. Lewis, *That Hideous Strength* (New York: The Macmillan Company, 1946).

9. Karl Rahner, *On the Theology of Death* (New York: Herder and Herder, Inc., 1965), p. 85.

10. Author's translation of a passage from *Vorträge und Aufsätze* (Pfullingen: Neske, 1954), p. 177.

11. See Rudolf Otto, *The Idea of the Holy*, trans. John W. Harvey (New York: Oxford University Press, 1958).

12. Author's translation of a passage from *Gelassenheit* (Pfullingen: Neske, 1959), p. 73.

13. Ladislaus Boros, *The Mystery of Death* (New York: Herder and Herder, Inc., 1965), pp. viii–ix.

14. André Malraux, *La condition humaine* (Paris: Gallimard, 1946), p. 403; English version, *Man's Fate*, trans. Haakon M. Chevalier (New York: Random House, Inc., 1961), p.282.

# 34

## Mortality and the Fear of Death
## — LLOYD R. BAILEY

I live, but know not how long;
I die, but know not when;
I travel on, but know not where.
'Tis strange that I should be so happy.

—German folk rhyme

In recent years a number of social scientists have investigated the relationship between asserted religious belief and ability to face death.[1] Thus far the results have been inconclusive or contradictory. Herman Feifel, for example, surveying eighty-four persons of middle age, concluded that "the religious person, when compared with the nonreligious individual, is personally more afraid of death."[2] Irving Alexander and Arthur Adlerstein, testing fifty undergraduate males at Princeton, decided that both "religious and non-religious" subjects have comparable negative feelings about death.[3] In another report on the same investigation, they suggested that each group had reduced anxiety in its own way and with about equal success (the former by stressing afterlife, the latter by repression of thoughts about dying).[4] David Martin and Lawrence Wrightsman, studying fifty-eight adults of all ages who attended three small churches in Tennessee, found that religious *attitude* had no effect upon one's concern over death, but that religious *practice* reduced fear in this regard.[5]

Because of the smallness and homogeneity of the groups thus far investigated, no generalizations can be drawn about the effectiveness of religious belief or practice for the population as a whole. Even more serious is the absence of a well thought out methodology in some of the research.[6] In most cases there has been a failure to define and measure the various *kinds* of anxiety associated with death: fear of what happens after death, of the process of dying, of the loss of control over events in the world, or of destruction of the "self."[7] Is there a difference between what the person being tested says and what he actually believes?[8] Specifically, what are the elements of faith or practice which are relatively effective or ineffective in reducing anxiety?

Can any accurate determination be made apart from conversation with and observation of the dying person, as opposed to word games at an earlier time when death is at most a theoretical possibility? In sum: serious investigation in this area is yet to be undertaken.

## Life after Death

Past researchers have generally assumed that, among various aspects of religious belief, it is life after death which should be most effective in reducing anxiety about dying. Indeed, Alexander and Adlerstein structured their entire project around this concept: "The belief in an afterlife concept was employed as an absolute point of differentiation between the groups."[9] While the expectation that such a belief will reduce anxiety is logical, and although Alexander and Adlerstein's division is understandable given the centrality of this belief in Judeo-Christianity for the past two thousand years,[10] the examination cannot proceed in so simplistic a fashion. *Why* do some Jews and Christians approach death with great calmness, even joy,[11] while others, despite a firm faith and unfailing practice, react to it with terror?[12] Weariness with life may make the "believer" and the agnostic alike view death as a liberating experience. The words, "It is easy for me to end my life. A brief moment and I'm freed of everything, liberated from this painful existence," might well have been spoken by a saint, but in actuality are those of Adolf Hitler.[13] Does the person being tested affirm that man as man is immortal (which is, from the point of view of the foundation documents of the tradition, a non-Christian view[14]), or does he hope for an act of God's grace, the resurrection of the "body"—and what effect does the latter (religious) view have upon anxiety as opposed to the former (humanistic) one?

By defining the "religious" person in terms of this belief, all possibility of discovering other resources within the tradition for coping with death have been foreclosed. Does the modern Christian's increasing inability to accept the idea of an afterlife need necessarily engender an inability to face death?[15] It must be remembered that, prior to the second century B.C.,[16] Israel had no expectation of a meaningful afterlife, nor did the view arise at that time in response to personal anxiety about human mortality.[17]

## Fear of Death

Ancient Near Eastern literature outside of Israel is much concerned with the phenomenon of death. Fear was occasioned by belief in the death-demon, usually an inhabitant of the Underworld whose task it was to seize the living and carry them away.[18] When the Sumerian

fertility goddess Inanna was allowed to leave the Underworld temporarily (to assure the cyclical fecundity of nature), she was accompanied
by demons whose task it was to secure a substitute. The chosen victim
was her husband Dumuzi, whose terrifying experience is described
thus: "The lad: put his feet into fetters [?] . . . throw a noose [?] over
him . . . they gash him with large axes . . . they cover his face with a
'garment of fear.' "[19] Such a fate might be delayed through amulets,
prayers, or incantations,[20] but finally not even the great gods were
able to save their worshipers from being snatched away. The terror at
death is seen in the description of the demons as devouring dragons,
serpents, raging bulls, or circling vultures. "No door can shut them
out; no bolt can turn them back; through the door like a snake they
glide; through the hinge like a wind they blow."[21]

The most sustained record of revolt against death which has come
down to us from the ancient Near East is the Epic of Gilgamesh.[22]
When the story opens, the hero is young, strong, and contemptuous of
death. Should he fall in combat, his fame would be memorialized by
poets for generations to come. "Gilgamesh fell," they will say, "in
combat with terrible Huwawa."[23] So self-sufficient is he that he
spurns the advances of a goddess. Acknowledgment of deity is irrelevant to his existence. When his heroic companion dies, he is so unable
to accept the fact that he keeps the body, hoping it will revive, until
it is filled with maggots. The unreflecting innocence of youth now
ended, he wanders, alienated from everything which formerly gave
him an identity, driven by fear to search for immortality. He finally
gives up in despair, his turmoil unresolved.

## Mortality

When we turn to the literature of ancient Israel, on the other hand,
we are immediately struck by the contract with the rest of the ancient
Near East. Human mortality is stated and accepted calmly.[24] Although
there are individual protests that impending death is unjust or premature, the ultimate fate of all mankind is accepted as part of the definition of being human. Man is a creature, to be bracketed with beasts,
birds, and fish (Gen. 1:24–27).[25] He is made only of dust, and to dust
he returns (Gen. 2:7; 3:19). The very idea of such a creature believing
that he should be immortal, to say nothing of proclaiming that the
world is meaningless if he is not, might strike one as humorous were
it not so pathetic. Such a demand, commonly heard in the modern
period, may spring more from megalomania and immaturity[26] than
philosophical profundity. And that it need not arise is adequately
demonstrated by the literature of ancient Israel.

By what logic does man arrive at the conclusion that his existence is more important than that of any other species? That his death is of more consequence than that of the lowliest creature? Is his survival worth the more than one hundred species he may have brought to extinction in North America alone since his migration here some ten thousand years ago?[27] Is he the most beautiful creature? The most benign to his fellows? The best adjusted to the world of nature in which he finds himself? The strongest? The most efficient?[28] It may be debated, given the nuclear and ecological brink to which he has brought the entire world, whether he is the most intelligent . . . provided that is a worthy criterion for evaluation.

The idea of human immortality, given man's perverse nature and willingness to justify even his most monstrous atrocities rather than admit error,[29] caused the Biblical writer to recoil in horror: God removes the "tree of life" after man has refused to accept any boundaries upon his activity (he has seized the "tree of the knowledge of good and evil") (Gen. 2–3). As a further limitation upon the mischief which a given individual or generation may inflict, the human lifespan was diminished (Gen. 6:1–3).

This acute perception of human limitation and pride led the Biblical writer to suggest that death was not only justifiable for man, but even desirable. It is hoped that such a realization and admission is not beyond the ability of modern man as well. Death is the ultimate and thus far inescapable judgment upon those who would preserve the status quo (which, without radical change, tends to become progressively more oppressive), the one sure hope for a different future. Rather than a source of anxiety and a negation of all meaning in life,[30] it may, upon sober reflection, be a basis for rejoicing and that which makes hope and meaning possible.

Moreover, in Israel's monotheistic faith, the origins of which are still obscure,[31] the death- and disease-demons of the neighboring cults are either derided as nonexistent or are reduced to mere messengers at God's bidding. It is the one God, benign toward man, just in his activity in history although radically free and sometimes mysterious, and he alone, who summons a man to his death.[32] No longer was there a fear of capricious deities or demons with an intrinsic power of their own. Death was not an irrational, intruding enemy of man, but part of an ordered, controlled, harmonious creation.[33] Mortality may not be part of the script humans would have written for themselves; they may lament the separation from life, even fear death as an unknown experience, but for those able to acknowledge the sovereignty of God, sovereign even of death, it is acceptable.

Such faith is stated in unparalleled fashion in Psalm 90, whose author looks at the transience of human existence with unflinching candor:

You return man to dust; "Back, O Mortal!" you say.

. . . . . . . . . . . . . . . . . . . . . . . . . . . . . . . . . . . . . . . . . . . . . . . . . . . .

They fade like grass which springs up in the morning
but when evening comes it is parched and withered.

. . . . . . . . . . . . . . . . . . . . . . . . . . . . . . . . . . . . . . . . . . . . . . . . . . . .

The years of our life are threescore and ten, . . .
they are soon gone, and we fly away.     (vss. 3,6,10)

This state of affairs, so lamentable to modern writers, does not engender either anger or pessimism, for the writer has interspersed his
observations with praises of God's eternal being. Human mortality is
noteworthy in that it enhances man's awe of the deity!

Before the mountains were born,
or the earth and world came to birth:
From eternity to eternity you are!

. . . . . . . . . . . . . . . . . . . . . . . . . . . . . . . . . . . . . . . . . . . . . . . . . .

In your sight a thousand years are as yesterday,
like an hour passing in the night.     (vss. 2,4)

Transitory man is sustained by the realization that his life is an
unmerited gift from the One who alone has unending life. And an
inseparable part of that gift is death. To be grateful for the former is to
accept, even be grateful for the latter; to despise death is to have no
appreciation for life.[34]

It is often pointed out that the individual in ancient Israel did not
feel the threat of death acutely, in part because his predominant concern was with the group and its future destiny.[35] Since the group had
already succeeded in a fashion that defied chance,[36] and since its
societal structure was widely admired by its neighbors,[37] it was logical
to suppose that God had chosen them to be his "realm of priests and
holy nation" (Exod. 19:6), that through them all the peoples of the
earth would find blessing (Gen. 12:3). Thus, if that age did not come
in one's lifetime, the supreme goal was to raise up offspring and pass
on the traditions and hopes to them. There can be little doubt that this
orientation gave satisfaction to the dying and preserved the identity of
the whole, despite the reverses of history, while their neighbors per-
ished without a trace.

Other societies, of course, have *their* transcendental values to which
the individual may dedicate himself and achieve a measure of immortality: heroic deeds, public monuments, academic or artistic accom-
plishment, dedication to political ideology or structures, progeny,
even participation in the unending process of evolution.[38] But, as
Hans Morgenthau has acutely observed, there is no longer any comfort
in exchanging a shallow belief in human immortality for hope of the

immortality of the world one leaves behind. The possibility of "nuclear death" is at hand: the destruction of *all* life, and with it *all* value.[39]

While the Biblical writers could not have imagined the total destructive power now within human hands and hence the crisis of meaning we now face, some of them do suggest that the "religious" individual's identity lies in something more basic than Israel's historical destiny.[40] The Book of Habakkuk closes (3:17–19), for example, with the articulation of a hypothetical collapse of nature. What might one's response be, when the world is on the verge of reverting to the chaos of creation?

> Although the fig-tree may not blossom,
> though no fruit is on the vine,
> though the olive crop has failed,
> though the fields give us no food,
> though the folds have lost their flocks,
> and in the stalls no cattle lie:
> yet, in the Lord we will find our joy.

Although acknowledging the possibility of the annihilation of the world, one rejoices! "Are you not from everlasting, O Lord my God, my Holy One? *You* will not die"(Hab. 1:12).[41]

# Notes

1. For brief surveys and summaries, see David Martin and Lawrence Wrightsman, "Religion and Fears about Death: A Critical Review of Research," in *Religious Education* 59 (1964): 174–176; "The Relationship between Religious Behavior and Concern about Death," in *The Journal of Social Psychology* 65 (1965): 317–323.

2. Herman Feifel, ed. "Attitudes toward Death in Some Normal and Mentally Ill Populations," in *Meaning of Death* (New York: McGraw-Hill Book Company, 1965), pp. 114–129, at p. 121.

3. Irving Alexander and Arthur Alderstein, "Studies in the Psychology of Death," in *Perspectives in Personality Research*, eds. Henry David and J. C. Brengelmann (New York: Springer Publishing Co., Inc., 1960), pp. 65–92.

4. Irving Alexander and Arthur Alderstein, "Death and Religion," in *Meaning of Death*, pp. 271–283.

5. Martin and Wrightsman, *Journal of Social Psychology*.

6. Ibid., for a brief review of some of the past inadequacies.

7. For a brief clarification and some procedural suggestions, see Robert

Neale, "Explorations in Death Education," in *Pastoral Psychology* 22 (November 1971): 33–74, at pp. 41–49.

8. Will Herberg's *Protestant, Catholic, Jew* (Garden City, New York: Doubleday & Company, Inc., Anchor Books, 1960) makes this dichotomy in the religious sphere frightfully obvious.

9. Alexander and Alderstein, *Meaning of Death*, p. 277.

10. For a nonesoteric treatment of the development of the doctrine, see Milton Gatch, *Death: Meaning and Mortality in Christian Thought and Contemporary Culture* (New York: Seabury Press, Inc., 1969). For a more detailed treatment of the Biblical period, see S. G. F. Brandon, *The Judgment of the Dead* (New York: Charles Scribner's Sons, 1967), chaps. 3 and 5.

11. Acts 7:54–60 (the death of Stephen by stoning); Babylonian Talmud, Berakot 61b (the death of Akiba by torture); and an endless number of others. On martyrdom in general, see Karl Rahner, *On the Theology of Death* (New York: Herder and Herder, Inc., 1965) pp. 81–119; Neale "Explorations in Death Education," pp. 65–71.

12. For an illustration, see Arnold Toynbee's description of his great-uncle in "Changing Attitudes toward Death in the Modern Western World," in *Man's Concern with Death* (New York: McGraw-Hill Book Company, 1968), pp. 93–94, 130.

13. Quoted in an interview with Albert Speer, *Playboy* 18 (June 1971), p. 198.

14. Oscar Cullmann, "Immortality of the Soul or Resurrection of the Dead?" in *Immortality and Resurrection*, ed. Krister Stendahl (New York: The Macmillan Company, 1965), pp. 9–53.

15. Toynbee, "Changing Attitudes," p. 130, makes this connection, tracing its beginnings back to the seventeenth century.

16. It is generally agreed that the earliest explicit reference is in the Book of Daniel (12:1–3), although the idea had been considered and rejected as early as the sixth century (Job 14:7–22). Recently Mitchell Dahood has suggested that the belief is attested throughout Israel's literature, but his following has been slight (*Psalms III* [Garden City, N. Y.: Doubleday & Company, Inc.], 1970, pp. xli–lii.)

17. See Gatch, *Death*, and Brandon, *Judgement of the Dead*, chaps. 3 and 5.

18. "Demons and Spirits (Assyr.-Bab.)," by R. Campbell Thompson, in *Hastings Encyclopedia of Religion and Ethics* 4:568–571; Miriam Seligson, *The Meaning of nep ĕs mēt in the Old Testament* (*Studia Orientalia*, 16 [1951]); Henry Sigerist, *Primitive and Archaic Medicine* (New York: Oxford Galaxie), pp. 125–141, 442–453.

19. Samuel Noah Kramer, "Cuneiform Studies and the History of Literature: the Sumerian Sacred Marriage Texts," in *Proceedings of the American Philosophical Society* 107 (1963): 485–527, at p. 493, ll. 14–21.

20. Sigerist, *Primitive and Archaic Medicine*, pp. 141–153, 191–213, 453–477.

21. Text quoted by Sigerist, *Primitive and Archaic Medicine.*, p. 449.

22. For a translation, see James Pritchard, ed., *Ancient Near Eastern Texts*, 2d ed. (Princeton, N.J.: Princeton University Press, 1955), pp. 72–99; for text and discussion, see Alexander Heidel, *The Gilgamesh Epic and Old Testament Parallels* (Chicago: Phoenix Books, The University of Chicago Press, 1963). The date of the composition of the Epic is generally put at the beginning of the second millennium, *B.C.*

23. Old Babylonian Version, III. iv. 13–15 (*Ancient Near Eastern Texts*, p. 79).

24. For the statement of this somewhat unorthodox position, see Lloyd Bailey, "Death as a Theological Problem in the Old Testament," in *Pastoral Psychology* 22 (November 1971): 20–32.

25. The term used to describe man at his creation (nepeš hayyāh, "living creature" in Gen. 2:7) is likewise applied to the other land animals (Gen. 1:24). More recent interpreters, bloated on Christian orthodoxy and egotism, translated the former as "living soul."

26. For a discussion of the lag between man's physiological development and his psychological one, see C. G. Jung, "The Soul and Death," in *Meaning of Death*, pp. 3–15.

27. Paul Martin, "Pleistocene Overkill," *Natural History* (December 1967), pp. 32–38.

28. For biting sarcasm in this regard, see Bertrand Russell, *Religion and Science* (New York: Oxford paperback, 1961), pp. 221ff.

29. As a modern example of the magnitude of pride, consider the case of President Nixon, who, rather than become the first president to lose a foreign war, is willing to send thousands of his fellow human beings to their death.

30. So Jean-Paul Sartre, *Being and Nothingness* (New York: Philosophical Library, Inc., 1956), p. 539: "Thus death is . . . that which on principle removes all meaning from life."

31. The idea of earlier scholars that a development from animism to polytheism to monolatry to monotheism (in the eighth-century prophets) can be detected in the Biblical materials is now largely abandoned and attributed to the "evolutionary" world view of the late nineteenth century, A.D.

32. For the verb *to take*, with God as the subject, meaning "to die," see, e.g., Gen. 5:24; 1 Kings 19:4; and 2 Kings 2:3, 5, and 9.

33. This position was modified by some later writers, and in particular under the influence of the limited dualism of the New Testament period. "The Devil . . . was thrown into the lake of fire and brimstone. . . . Then Death and Hades were thrown into the lake of fire" (Rev. 20:10 and 14).

34. For a similar conclusion arrived at upon different grounds, see Robert Neale "Explorations in Death Education," pp. 43–46.

35. Gatch, *Death*, pp. 36-39.

36. The escape from the power of Pharoah; the survival in the wilderness; the triumph over the superior civilization of Canaan.

37. For the idea that Israel's view of man and society spoke to the slave class in the land of Canaan, precipitating a "peasant's revolt" which later generations would call the "conquest," see George Mendenhall, "The Hebrew Conquest of Palestine," in *The Biblical Archaeologist* 25 (1962): 66–87.

38. For the last of these, in view of the inadequacy of the others, see Sidney Mead, "History and Identity," *Journal of Religion* 51 (1971): 1–14. For a general survey, see Helmut Thielicke, *Death and Life* (Philadelphia, Pa.: Fortress Press, 1970), pp. 7–95.

39. "Death in the Nuclear Age," in *The Modern Vision of Death*, ed. Nathan Scott, Jr. (Richmond, Va.: John Knox Press, 1967), pp. 69–77.

40. This is true regardless of how "Israel" is to be defined. The subsequent issue of "religious community" (people) versus "nation" is a central struggle in the Old Testament.

41. Most English translations read, "We will not die," following an ancient custom. Even to raise the hypothetical question of God's death was considered offensive, and hence the change of reading.

# 35

# Developing a Theology of Death
## — PETER H. BEISHEIM

We theologize within and upon the human condition. And the human condition, Peter Berger writes, "fraught as it is with suffering and with the finality of death, demands interpretations that not only satisfy theoretically but give inner sustenance in meeting the crisis of suffering and death."[1]

## Role of Theology

In the past, however, Catholic Theology has been in dialogue mainly with philosophy—scholastic philosophy at that. This has tended to narrow the view of theology. Today in the context of a multidisciplinary university and a pluralistic world, it has become clearer that the sustained and systematic dialogue of the theologian with any branch of knowledge dealing with human life gives rise to a special and clearly definable theological inquiry into the conceptual language of this very dialogue.[2] In short, a specific contextual framework may well be a luxury we can ill afford in an age of constant change.

This direction is shared by some Protestant theology and in fact was anticipated among Protestant theologians; theology is becoming "secular." This gives forceful expression to the widespread conviction of theologians that divine revelation has to do not only with the religious dimension of human life, but with the entire process, personal and social, by which men enter into their humanity. Thus the situation is such that the theologian reflecting on the Word is not restricted to religious or ecclesiastical concerns. He will join the secular conversation going on in his own generation about man and society, and he will do this, not in specifically religious terms or by offering a set of moral norms derived from religion, but in secular terms, in the terms of the conversation itself, because it is in this coming-to-be of the human world that God's Word is present. This significant change in the process of theologizing and understanding the nature of theology signals the gap that increasingly grows wider between theology and popular religion.[3] The Churches are bound to rather conservative formulations of belief, and traditional attitudes are built heavily into hymns and other liturgical expressions. This causes one to wonder if radical change in theologizing about death really changes anything or anyone. We can't theologize about death in the abstract, yet the "existential situation" gives every indication that we have, and are.

Among the changes taking place in theology, there appears a tendency today to reject or ignore a belief in immortality. Why? First, there exists a skepticism about Biblical mythology resulting in a need to reinterpret the faith in contemporary terms involving a general uneasiness about the possibility of life after death.[4] In a recent religious studies class, the question was asked of eighty students, "What does Death mean to you?" At least half of the students responded, "Death means the end; the final process of life." Two possible reasons for this are: one, a demand for certainty about death which is not demanded in one's lifetime with the arising of a general attitude of mild malaise; and two, the thorough inculcation of an empirical methodology which leads one to conclude that death is the end. With a few individual exceptions the students answered that the meaning of death is termination of this life but with survival of the spirit. Yet most of those who held this position indicated that the weight of this fell upon religious education and tradition, not necessarily on a firm conviction that they have somehow embraced themselves.

Another motive for not taking the immortality of the soul very seriously derives from the Biblical concepts themselves.

## The Old Testament

In the Old Testament,[5] death was regarded as the termination of human existence, or in other words, the predominant concern was with the People and its historical destiny. The question of the significance of death for the individual rarely arose and was essentially meaningless. Thus death ends all bodily and religious activity, so that "Sheol" appears as a vague abode of suspended spirits—existing but not living. Both one's life and death assume significance in relation to the continual history of the People. The thrust, however, is within one's lifetime: birth to death.

## New Testament

In the New Testament,[6] no discourses attributed to Jesus explicitly on the subject of death appear in the Synoptic Gospels (Matthew, Mark, and Luke). What exactly Jesus conceived to be the nature of the life of resurrection is unclear, and it is unlikely that He ever considered the problem. His preoccupation was with the urgency of life in the present time, with the signs in his own ministry and in general historical phenomena which proclaimed or would soon proclaim that God is about to do something new, to inaugurate his kingship in a decisive way.

Jesus, in other words, was unconcerned with speculations either about death or about the meaning of resurrection. At the time of his crucifixion, there is abundant evidence in the Synoptic Gospels that Jesus showed both fear and terror in the face of suffering. Unlike Socrates, who faced death with triumphant composure, he took death as a terrible and serious thing. This face is either disregarded by design or overlooked in works dealing with Christian spirituality. Jesus was concerned with the quality of life expected by God of his people, because he believed that the new age was about to begin. Death is the end of historical existence, except insofar as one conceives of the dead as being with the fathers or a part of the living heritage of the People. To say that the dead shall be raised is to say that they will, as a part of the living heritage, participate in the life of the restored People which is about to begin.

Equating life after death as one of the essential constituents of revelation is a later development arising from historical philosophical systems. When the concept of individualism grew there arose the question of the individual surviving as individual rather than simply as a member of the People!

My approach in this chapter shall be one which accepts life after death as an unknown; its objective reality is not necessary for understanding human nature, the human condition, or Christian revelation. It can't be ignored either.

## Meaning in Life

If individuals fear dying without meaning, rather than nonexistence after death, then Christian revelation can and should be interpreted in this light instead of merely proving there is a life after death. This in no way devalues the meaning of Jesus and the redemptive function of his dying. Death is the culmination of my life, not in the sense of looking to the future, but that, in the fact of death, the meaning of all the decisions of my life leave me accepting them or despairing of them; this is the judgment. To live is to lose oneself. The development of the individual leads from the consciousness of "I" to Personhood; yet for the Christian, this development finds its complete fulfillment in the giving of the "I" for another (process of kenosis). Isn't this the search for the genuine community today? Genuine community may mean the total integration of individuals, all losing self for others, instead of keeping barriers and inhibitions intact so as not to lose individuality, which may be the source of alienation (original sin?) and isolation in today's society. The meaning of life, then, is realized in the process of humanization, which can be seen as "becoming Christlike". In the process of kenosis by which one "becomes like Christ", the fear of dying and death is overcome. The individual is reborn, is capable of truly living.

## Death of Jesus

Jesus died. I am going to die. What does this mean? Accepting the fact that I am going to die can liberate me in such a way that I can really be free to live, to enjoy each moment, to see each moment as a possibility for concern, care, and love. The imperative of the message is the *now*. I love my brother *now*, not later, for there may not be a later. Thus the freedom really becomes a burden because now the risk of lost opportunities makes despair a real possibility. It is possible that Jesus died because only in dying can one love passionately; one can risk being rejected, even hated, all the while losing oneself in love. Thus, in dying, my true creative capabilities and powers are realized; I am what I have become, or I am not what I truly could have been. This is the risk of living, of loving and of losing self. That is the paradox of Jesus.

## Resurrection and Ascension

Christ did not die. The resurrection can be interpreted as the symbolic assurance of man's transcendence over the fear of death; that death is truly conquered when one lives his life to the fullest. When one loses his life for another, he does not die. Because in the losing or giving, communion with one another is achieved and cannot be severed by death. Christ's dying for man establishes communion with His followers which is symbolized by the resurrection. Christ becomes one with the community, so that in dying, one really lives and in the giving of ourselves, we *really* live. Only in dying and in death is new life created, and "the death of death" through faith and trust in Jesus frees one to be alive, to be raised from the human condition.

The Ascension would appear to symbolize the ratification of the Resurrection. Ascension myths have been interpreted by historians of religion as indicators of man's desire to transcend his human condition.[7] Therefore, the Ascension emphasizes the fact that Jesus did transcend the human condition—that is, the fear of death; and that death is not the final or ultimate moment, but merely the last moment in a continuum which has, or does not have, meaning.

## Ecclesiastical Dimension

If these problems appear to be somewhat individualized, how does the ecclesiastical community react to the fact of dying, the reality of death? If the ecclesiastical community has traditionally pointed to life after death, must it continually do so?

The psychological needs of persons confronting death imply that beyond preaching the message of Christ, the community must somehow, in practice, overcome the growing isolation of the dying person who is left to face this human event alone.

Changes in the form of the rites of anointing which would allow each to share in the others' moments of suffering and joys of life could be initiated, thereby strengthening the communal aspect. Instead of the sacrament of anointing being administered as a routine action which one receives because of a particular condition, much like administering a pill, it may, rather than reassuring a member of his communal existence, alienate him all the more because the communal aspect may be entirely lost.

Possibly other types of activity would allow people to come to terms with this "fact of life," such as emphasizing the Christian obligation (not solely relegated to clergy) of visiting the sick as service to and by the community.

Hospitals which are controlled by ecclesiastical communities should allow all who are ill to be housed under one roof in order not to hide the reality (death) which for us is continually present. In this way, all can and should see that each is able to care for the other in order to fulfill Christ's mandate to love one another—even in the presence of death. Thus the ministry to the sick and dying can be participated in by the sick, dying, and healthy, thereby building a community which is truly a community of love.

There is no conclusion, because there can only be an evolving standpoint regarding this phenomenon. As I progress in dying toward the moment of death, my posture will either be one of liberation or despair. The questions and problems confronted will depend upon where I am in the continuum of maturity. The Christian attitude, to be achieved in a fearful society, is one which does not fear death, but sees it as the last human act to be participated in by me—as a human being, as a person, as a Christian.

## Notes

1. Peter L. Berger, *A Rumor of Angels* (New York: Doubleday & Company, Inc., 1969) p. 25.

2. Gregory Baum, "Where is Theology Going?" *The Ecumenist* 7 (March–April 1969):33–36.

3. Ninian Smart, "Some Inadequacies of Recent Christian Thought about Death" in *Man's Concern with Death*, ed. Arnold Toynbee, (St. Louis, Mo.: McGraw-Hill Book Company, 1969), pp. 133–137.

4. Ibid.

5. Milton McC. Gatch, *Death: Meaning and Mortality in Christian Thought and Contemporary Culture* (New York: Seabury Press, Inc., 1969), pp. 35–42; and John L. McKenzie, *Dictionary of the Bible* (New York: The Macmillan Company, 1965), pp. 183–184.

6. Gatch, *Death*, pp. 42–50; McKenzie, *Dictionary of the Bible*, pp. 184–185.

7. Mircea Eliade, *Myths, Dreams and Mysteries* (New York: Harper & Row, Publishers, Inc., 1967), pp. 99–115.

# 36

# *Death and Incarnation*
## — WILLIAM B. FRAZIER

Death is incarnate. It happens where man happens—in the flesh. It is there because death is native to man. It is tied to his very existence, and this from the very beginning. Innocent of its own genius, Christianity has always been somewhat uncomfortable with the incarnation of death. The burden of this chapter is to confront and contend with this curious inconsistency.

## Alienation

Man is alien. Chronically estranged from himself, his fellow men, his world, he has yet to discover and appropriate the true center of his existence. For more than a century and a half, sensitive minds and hearts have been announcing variations of this message with a special sense of urgency. The list is headed, of course, by Feuerbach, Marx, and Freud. Despite differing viewpoints and emphases, alienation as a contemporary estimate of the human condition is a product of their combined genius. But is Nietzsche who says it best: "This is [our] true predicament: together with the fear of man we have lost the love of man, the affirmation of man, the *will to man*." While the origin of this phenomenon is widely disputed,[1] Eliot's simple insight can hardly be ignored: we are alienated because "human kind cannot bear very much reality."[2] Hence, "our lives are mostly a constant evasion of ourselves, and an evasion of the visible and sensible world."[3]

If Christian theology has to be reminded that alienation touches the real predicament of man, it is only by way of reclaiming a genuine Christian insight. No tradition, humanistic or religious, is more affirmative than Judeo-Christianity in its estimate of human existence. No tradition attests more emphatically that man's vocation to be man can be compromised only at the price of separation from God. Old and New Testament Scriptures mount a vigorous attack on any and all attempts to detour around the human mystery. The traditions center-

ing around Israel and Jesus are extended commentaries on God's participation in man's search for himself. Not by way of replacing God as
the ultimate destiny of man, but to affirm that it is man *as man* who,
from the very beginning, is caught up in the mystery and life that is
God. Only by finding himself can he find the God whose image he
bears. "In biblical thought, perfection means letting God be God and
conversely that man must assume his finite condition. . . . For the
weight of finitude, not the exhibition of world-denying perfectionism,
is the true measure of authentic existence."[4]

The illusion some Christians have yet to escape is that man finds his
worldly existence far more attractive than the promise of an other-
worldly paradise. The point is illusory because it contradicts the testimony of history and experience. In a variety of sick and distorted
ways men have always had a greater flair for Project God than for
Project Man. Project Heaven has always been more popular than
Project Human.[5] The phenomenon is as easy to appreciate as Rieux
suggests in *The Plague*: "It's harder to remain human than to leap
beyond humanity." This is the critical tension, and this is what Judeo-
Christianity is really all about.

Meeting with God does not come to man in order that he may
concern himself with God, but in order that he may confirm that there
is meaning in the world. All revelation is summons and sending. But
again and again man brings about, instead of realization, a reflection to
Him who reveals: he wishes to concern himself with God instead of
with the world.

## Excarnation

While Christianity and secular humanism can agree that alienation
is what is wrong with man, they may differ in estimating its cause.
For the Christian, the practice of religion, ownership of the means of
production, and sexual repression, while capable of significant influence, do not touch the real depths of the problem. The only thing
that does is the ambiguity of man's bodily existence, the troublesome
territory of the flesh. The basic notion is alienation, but the term is a
little too sophisticated to capture the earthiness of the Christian insight. A better choice is *excarnation*. This word points directly to the
dynamic operative in man's refusal to be man. Carnal existence is
punctuated with limitation, weakness, and pain. To be in the flesh is
to be challenged to personhood and responsibility, always near cousins of loneliness. Flesh tires, ages, disintegrates. In a word, flesh is
the dwelling place of death. More radically than anything else, the
incarnation of death explains the excarnation of man. Or, to use the

words of Norman Brown, "the obstacle to incarnation is our horror of the void."[7] Excarnation comes as close as any one word can to capturing the Christian view of sin.

## Idolatry

Within the Judeo-Christian tradition, idolatry is the best example of sin as excarnation. This will not become clear, however, until we have taken a careful look at idolatry itself and disposed of some popular misconceptions.

As a Christian datum, idolatry is not just one sin among others, but, as Schoonenberg observes, "sin finds its most complete form in idolatry," which, in turn, is "the root of all sin."[8] The story of the Fall of man in Genesis is an account of submission to an idolatrous hope: "you will be like gods" (Gen. 3, 5). The remaining precepts of the Decalogue are rooted in that which heads the list: "You shall have no gods except me" (Exod. 20, 3). Such is the assumption at work in the Book of Wisdom: "For the source of wantonness is preoccupation with idols; and their invention was a corruption of life . . . the worship of infamous idols is the reason and source and extremity of all evil" (Wisd. 14, 12, 27). The New Testament witness is much the same. So convinced is Paul of the radical evil of idolatry that he is able to summarize the whole process of conversion to Christianity as a "turning to God from idols" (1 Thess. 1, 9). A similar theme is operative in Romans, where, much like the author of Wisdom, Paul develops the manifold consequences of idolatrous behavior (Rom. 1, 21–28).

Let this suffice to establish idolatry as the most important concretization of sin in the Bible. By comparison, other sins are symptomatic. But why? What is it that makes idolatry so odious in the sight of God? Much depends on the answer to this question. To maintain consistency with what has already been said, the evil of idolatry must be conceived in terms of alienation or excarnation, man's balking before the human mystery, his refusal to be man. But idolatry does not seem to be this kind of sin. For the worship of idols seems far less man's refusal to accept himself and his world than his refusal to accept the one true God. In his severe proscription of idol worship the God of the Bible seems far more intent on defending his own prerogatives than on preventing any dehumanization the idolater might suffer in the process.

Despite impressions of this kind, Biblical faith condemns idolatry first and foremost because it militates seriously against the human and worldly vocation of man. Nothing is more characteristic of the Bible than its defense of man and the world against the debilitating inroads

of religious abuse. Here is the secret behind the Old Testament's vigorous affirmation of the unicity and transcendence of God. There is no
question of defending Yahweh against the threat of rival deities.
Rather, it is man who is threatened when he absolutizes anything
short of God himself. The deep truth of monotheism uncovers the
relativity and provisionality of all that is not God. For in a world
peopled with gods, controlled by myths, and manipulated through
ritual magic the adulthood of man is impossible. One reason for this,
of course, is that human responsibility and initiative are not vital
commodities in such a world. But there is a more important reason,
and it has to do with the connection between idolatry and death.

According to the Book of Wisdom, idolatry originated in the
seedbed of tragedy: "men enslaved to either grief or tyranny conferred
the incommunicable Name on sticks and stones" (Wisd. 14, 21). Israel
is not alone. The desert places in human lives have given rise to more
than one golden calf. Idols offer an illusory exit from the land of death.
For they are gods-within-our-power, pretending to give us control
over the chaos which haunts the horizons of our lives. All this would
be more tolerable if the mystery of the tragic did not figure as promi-
nently as it does in the very definition of man. As it is, at least for the
Christian, the desert can be avoided only at the price of authentic
manhood. For only in the desert is man confronted with the elusive
and terrifying truth that his existence is not circumscribed by his own
power, that finding himself always entails losing himself. As Rahner
says, "radical self-abandonment is without doubt the very essence of
man . . . ."[9] A remark of Ebeling is similar:

> Man's true freedom consists in his receiving himself from elsewhere,
> that he does not owe it to himself that he is, that he is not his own
> creator and thus cannot free himself from himself . . . . For it is the
> mystery of human personal being that it is summoned from elsewhere,
> that it exists in response and as response, and that therefore man is
> wholly himself when he is not caught up in himself, but has the real
> ground of his life outside himself.[10]

Accordingly, it is in and through the mystery of death that man has
access to his true identity, for it is precisely here that he is challenged
to receive himself from beyond himself. The service of false gods is
evil because it provides a dehumanizing sedative for this painfully
paradoxical aspect of man. Excarnate man is the one thing idols have
power to create. This and this alone is why idolatry heads the Biblical
sin-parade.

## Iconoclasm

If excarnation is the fundamental human predicament, and if idolatry got us into it, then iconoclasm is the obvious way out. If sin is

basically idol building, salvation must be just as basically idol breaking, and this in the name of human emancipation and growth.

In its origins Christianity is thoroughly iconoclastic. The Old Testament tradition is not a religious answer to an irreligious world, but a
human and worldly answer to an excessively religious world. One
thing the ancient Semites did not need was more religion. What was
new and distinctive about Israel's faith was precisely its hard line
toward the established religious values of the day. "This and this
alone," says von Rad, "her insight into idolatry and myth, furnished
the key to her loneliness in the company of the religions of the
world."[11] Behind this was not merely a desire to defend the true God
and establish a new approach to religion. The fresh and revolutionary
truth of Israel's way was that it affirmed and supported the emergence
of man. What was wrong with many of the older theologies and rituals
was that they had proven themselves antagonistic to the unfolding of
authentic human and worldly values. Israel was different because Yahweh was great enough to allow and even encourage man to be man.
Other deities, whose security seems to have been threatened by the
emergence of man, were at once susceptible and deserving of death.
Here, then, are the real taproots of Biblical faith, the real foundations
of Judeo-Christian identity. According to Vahanian, "the Christian
faith is radical only if it is iconoclastic."[12] This makes the monotheism
of Israel clearly subservient to the task of idol breaking. "Iconoclasm
is, for all practical purposes, the essential ingredient of monotheism as
understood in the biblical tradition."[13]

To be faithful to the task of idol breaking, Christianity must learn to
minister more and more to the context of idol building. Prevention is
always preferable to cure. Christian energies must be addressed to the
mysterious interplay of life and death which occasions the search for
idolatrous alternatives to authentic manhood. To the extent that death
and absurdity can be understood and embraced as essential to the
mystery of man, so will the market for idols begin to decline. Radical
iconoclasm, then, is each and every attempt to assist man in the appro-
priation of his mortal flesh. To put idols to flight is to reject excarnate
existence. In a word, "incarnation is iconoclasm."[14]

## Incarnation of Death

The soteriological bond between death and incarnation is seriously
compromised by the margination of death which occurs in classical
Christian anthropology. Two theological doctrines are involved: the
natural immortality of the soul and the gifted immortality of the
body. Each in its own way excludes death from the original situation
of man. The immortality of the soul simply means that death never
happens where death really counts, that is, in the subjective center of

consciousness. Since bodily demise is not total demise, the genuine incarnation of death becomes an impossibility. One solution to this problem is already under way. In current Biblical anthropology the shift is clearly from immortality to resurrection, from survival of death to salvation through death.[15] Hence, to die in the flesh is to die totally, for death in this perspective is totally incarnate. Mortal flesh is survived solely by the regenerating promise of God.

The remaining theological roadblock to the incarnation of death is the doctrine of bodily immortality, or the exclusion of biological death from the original condition of man. The impact of this teaching on the margination of death as a human mystery would be difficult to exaggerate. It has given rise to a conceptual landscape thoroughly antagonistic to the wedding of mortality and maturity in man. In such a landscape, death is simply incompatible with man as he ought to be. Ideal man was never meant to know the company of chaos. And it was God who made him that way. God himself deprived the body of its dying. Only through the agency of sin could death reclaim its flesh. When sin happened, death happened by way of punishment and continued to make its presence felt under the rubric of something that should not have been. Death was made flesh, but dwelt among us as an alien, an intruder, having nothing at all to do with the proper dignity and destiny of man. As such, dying never had to be taken seriously as a genuine human task. Nor was there any need to question the cultural games of death denial which men so easily learn to play, for these could be looked upon as healthy distractions from an unfortunate and debilitating cosmic accident. In a word, death and tragedy were made to reside at the periphery of authentic manhood.

Here too, however, the theological tide is turning. A tradition nearly as old as Christianity itself is suffering the erosion of its Biblical and theological foundations. The Christian scholars responsible for this development are simply finding less and less reason to deny that death was there at the very beginning of human history.[16] The result, of course, is a new conceptual landscape which accommodates the integration of human life and death developed earlier in this chapter. If mortality precedes the emergence of sin, the whole tragic dimension of existence acquires genuine human status. Death is no longer a way of being punished, but a way of being man. Not a very attractive way, to be sure, but one that explains the phenomenon of excarnation. If the original call to be human was not just a call to life, but to life through death, the ambivalence of man's response makes better sense. This, in turn, recalls and confirms the point made earlier regarding the contribution of death to the genesis of excarnate man. Death is prior to sin not merely as a neutral context, but as the primal occasion or soil in which it comes to birth.[17]

## Incarnation of Man

The final answer to excarnation can only be incarnation. If sin is marginal manhood, then salvation is manhood revisited and reclaimed. In a word, salvation *is* incarnation. In light of what has preceded, the point is obvious enough. But there are complications when it comes to coordinating this view with classical Christian soteriology. In general, the older theories stop short of the bond between salvation and incarnation which this chapter is building toward. This applies even to Eastern Christianity, where, since the days of Irenaeus (c. 140– c. 202), incarnation has been accorded direct saving efficacy.[18] The basic difference concerns the way incarnation is thought to accomplish the divinization of man. According to the Eastern tradition, it occurs directly through the union of divinity and humanity in the person of the Word. This is clearly at variance with the present proposal. For, in this case, man is divinized, not simply by sharing human nature with the Word, but by patient fidelity to the journey which is man. Divinization happens on the way to manhood.

In the theological tradition of the West, on the other hand, salvation and incarnation are not equated. Incarnation is simply the mystery of union between the nature of God and the nature of man which happened in the conception-birth of Jesus and is celebrated liturgically at Christmas. Being incarnate, the Son of God was able to save the world through his passion, death, and resurrection. At best, incarnation attends the saving process as a kind of prerequisite or preliminary; it merely sets the stage. Conceived, and impoverished, in this way, incarnation is likely to remain what it once seemed to Eliot, "the hint half guessed, the gift half understood."[19]

A major obstacle to the convergence of salvation and incarnation in these earlier theories is what has already been described as the excarnation of death in the classical Christian view of man. As long as a humanly marginated concept of death is operative in the background, there is no stimulus to question the marginal status of incarnation in soteriology. For if death has little, if anything, to do with man as man, if death is merely a court sentence, an anthropological afterthought, then the saving death of Jesus can hardly be interpreted as an incarnational journey. This problem, as we have seen, is in the process of solution.

In the final analysis, the bond between salvation and incarnation depends on the underlying view of sin. Only when sin is taken seriously as excarnation is there sound basis for bringing incarnation into the center of the soteriological picture. For if man can refuse God only by refusing to be man, by refusing the challenge and the threat of authentic existence in the flesh, then incarnation is no longer a preliminary to salvation but the main event. This, in turn, means that the incarnation of the Word and the incarnation of man are inseparable components of one and the same mystery. The Word was made flesh that man might be made flesh in the Word. By assuming the flesh of death and contending with death in the midst of life, Jesus becomes man enough for glory—and this is resurrection.

The incarnation of the Word, therefore, is neither accomplished in the instant of his conception, nor adequately celebrated on the feast day of his birth. For taking flesh can only be the project of a lifetime. Accordingly, the Christian celebration of this mystery should have as much to do with Easter as with Christmas. The whole life of Jesus was a faithful probing of the flesh which sinful man rejected. Adam's desire "to be like God" was counterbalanced and redeemed by Jesus' readiness to be like man. For man is not merely on the way to God. Man *is* the way. And Jesus is the man. *Ecce homo!*

## Notes

1. Cf. Richard Schacht, *Alienation* (New York: Doubleday & Company, Inc., Anchor Books, 1971).

2. T. S. Eliot, "Burnt Norton," in *Four Quartets* (New York: Harcourt, Brace &, World, Inc., Harvest Books, 1943), I, p. 14.

3. T. S. Eliot, *The Use of Poetry and the Use of Criticism.* (New York: Barnes & Noble, 1970).

4. Gabriel Vahanian, *Wait Without Idols* (New York: George Braziller, Inc., 1964), pp. 65–66.

5. "A growing body of opinion and evidence suggests that most people harbor illusions of immortality and omnipotence. Sartre argues convincingly that the whole project of human consciousness is directed toward becoming God. Karen Horney makes a similar point in psychological terms. She shows that the key to neurosis lies in an effort to actualize an idealized, godlike image of the self rather than devoting the energies to realization of a realistic set of goals." Sam Keen, "Hope in a Post-Human Era," *The Christian Century* 84 (1967): 107.

6. Martin Buber, *I and Thou* (Edinburgh: T. & T. Clark, 1937), p. 115.

7. Norman O. Brown, *Love's Body* (New York: Random House, Inc., Vintage Books, Inc., 1966), p. 262.

8. Piet Schoonenberg, *Man and Sin* (Notre Dame, Ind.: University of Notre Dame Press, 1965), pp. 9–10.

9. Karl Rahner, "The Theology of Hope,' *Theology Digest* Sesquicentennial Issue (1968), p. 81.

10. Gerhard Ebeling, *The Nature of Faith* (Philadelphia: Fortress Press, 1962), p. 115.

11. Gerhard von Rad, *Old Testament Theology* (New York: Harper and Row, Publishers, Inc., 1965), II, p. 340.

12. Gabriel Vahanian, *No Other God* (New York: George Braziller, Inc., 1966), p. 5.

13. Vahanian, *Wait Without Idols*, p. 26.

14. Brown, *Love's Body*, p. 222.

15. Cf. Oscar Cullmann, "Immortality of the Soul or Resurrection of the Dead," in *Immortality and Ressurrection*, ed. Krister Stendahl (New York: The Macmillan Company, 1965), pp. 9–53; Pierre Benoit and Roland Murphy, eds., *Immortality and Resurrection, vol. 60, The New Concilium* (New York: Herder & Herder, Inc., 1970).

16. Cf. H. Wheeler Robinson, *Inspiration and Revelation in the Old Testament* (Oxford: Clarendon Press, 1946), pp. 93–94; L. L. Morris, "Death," in *The New Bible Dictionary* (Grand Rapids, Mich.: Wm. B. Eerdmans Publishing Co., 1962), p. 301; Roger Troisfontaines, *I Do Not Die* (New York: Desclee, 1963), pp. 194–195; Karl Rahner, *On the Theology of Death* (New York: Herder & Herder, Inc., 1964), p. 42; André-Marie Dubarle, *The Biblical Concept of Original Sin* (New York: Herder & Herder, Inc., 1964); pp. 235–237; Gerhard von Rad, "Life and Death in the Old Testament," in *Theological Dictionary of the New Testament*, ed. G. Kittel (Grand Rapids, Mich.: Wm. B. Eerdmans Publishing Co., 1964), II, pp. 844–846; Pierre Smulders, "Evolution and Original Sin," *Theology Digest* 13 (1965): 176; Robert T. Francoeur, *Perspectives in Evolution* (Baltimore: Helicon Press, Inc., 1965), pp. 281–288; William J. Rewak, "Adam, Immortality and Human Death," *Sciences Ecclesiastiques* 19 (1967): 67–79; Herbert Haag, *Is Original Sin in Scripture?* (New York: Sheed & Ward, Inc., 1969); J. H. Marks, "The Book of Genesis," in *The Interpreters One-Volume Commentary on the Bible* (Nashville, TN: Abingdon Press, 1971), p. 6.

17. Cf. Joseph Haroutunian, "Atonement," in M. Halverson and A. A. Cohen, eds. *A Handbook of Christian Theology* (New York: World Pub. Co., 1958), p. 21; Reinhold Niebuhr, *The Nature and Destiny of Man* (New York: Charles Scribner's Sons, 1941), I, pp. 167–186; "Intellectual Autobiography," in *Reinhold Niebuhr: His Religious, Social, and Political Thought*, eds. C. W. Kegley and R. W. Bretall (New York: The Macmillan Company, 1956), pp. 6–7; Alan Harrington, *The Immortalist* (New York: Avon/Discus, 1965).

18. Cf. J. N. D. Kelly, *Early Christian Doctrines* (New York: Harper and Row Publishers, Inc., 1959), pp. 170–174; 375–386; 395–399.

19. Eliot, "Dry Salvages," in *Four Quartets*, V, p. 44.

# List of Contributors

LLOYD R. BAILEY is Associate Professor of Old Testament at the Divinity School, Duke University in Durham, North Carolina.

J. DONALD BANE is a fellow of the American Association of Pastoral Counselors, director of a counseling center for the Foundation for Religion and Mental Health, and Assistant Chaplain at the Westchester County Medical Center, Valhalla, New York.

PETER H. BEISHEIM is an Assistant Professor in the Department of Religious Studies, Stonehill College, North Easton, Massachusetts.

JUDITH BEST is a Registered Nurse at Mt. Sinai Hospital in New York City.

SCHUYLER P. BROWN is Associate Professor of New Testament at the General Theological Seminary in New York City.

RICHARD G. BRUEHL is an Assistant Professor of Pastoral Theology and Counseling at Vanderbilt Divinity School and Assistant Professor of Clinical Psychiatry at Vanderbilt Medical School.

KENNETH A. CHANDLER is Professor of Psychology at Vassar College, Poughkeepsie, New York.

GLEN W. DAVIDSON is Associate Professor of Culture and Medicine and also Chief of Thanatology, Southern Illinois University School of Medicine, in Springfield, Illinois.

DANIEL C. DEARMENT is Chaplain at the Hospital of the University of Pennsylvania in Philadelphia, Pennsylvania.

WALTER DEBOLD is an instructor in the Department of Religious Studies at Seton Hall University, South Orange, New Jersey.

JAMES M. DEMSKE, S.J., is President of Canisius College, Buffalo, New York.

EDWARD F. DOBIHAL, JR., is President of Hospice, Inc., in New Haven, Connecticut.

EDGAR DRAPER is Professor of Psychiatry and Director of Residency Education at the University Hospital, University of Michigan Medical Center in Ann Arbor, Michigan.

H. TRISTRAM ENGLEHARDT, JR. is Assistant Professor of the Philosophy of Medicine at the Institute for Medical Humanities, University of Texas Medical Branch in Galveston, Texas.

ZELDA FOSTER is Mental Health Director for the Children's Aid Society in New York City.

WILLIAM B. FRAZIER is Professor of Theology at Maryknoll Seminary, in Maryknoll, New York.

JOHN FREUND is Director of Pastoral Education at St. John's University in Jamaica, New York.

ARNOLDUS GOUDSMIT is Research Associate in Cancer Chemotherapy at the Veterans Administration Hospital in Minneapolis, Minnesota.

JOHN M. HUMPHREYS is Chaplain at the Pacific Medical Center in San Francisco, California.

PAUL E. IRION is Professor of Pastoral Theology at the Lancaster Theological Seminary of the United Church of Christ in Lancaster, Pennsylvania.

JAMES A. KNIGHT has been Associate Dean and Professor of Psychiatry at Tulane University School of Medicine in New Orleans, Louisiana.

AUSTIN H. KUTSCHER is Associate Professor in the School of Dental and Oral Surgery at Columbia University and Director of Dental Services for the New York State Psychiatric Institute in New York. He is the organizer and President of the Foundation for Thanatology.

STEVEN MOSS is Chaplain at the Memorial Hospital for Cancer and Allied Diseases, New York City.

ROBERT E. NEALE is Professor of Psychiatry and Religion at Union Theological Seminary in New York City.

CARL NIGHSWONGER (before his death) was Chaplain at the University of Chicago Hospital and Clinics in Chicago, Illinois.

WILLIAM L. NUTE, JR., is a District Health Officer in New York City.

GRACE B. AND HARRY S. OLIN are from Boston, Massachusetts, where he is Clinical Instructor in Psychiatry at Harvard Medical School, Cambridge, Massachusetts.

RALPH EDWARD PETERSON is the Pastor of St. Peter's Lutheran Church in New York City.

JOSEPH R. PROULX is Assistant Professor in the School of Nursing at the University of Maryland in Baltimore, Maryland.

DAVID H. C. READ is the Pastor of Madison Avenue Presbyterian Church in New York City.

ROBERT B. REEVES, JR., is Chaplain at the Presbyterian Hospital, Columbia Presbyterian Medical Center, in New York City.

GEORGE M. SCHURR is Dean of Humanities at Sangamon State University in Springfield, Illinois.

ELIZABETH DORSEY I. SMITH is Assistant Professor of Nursing, at the Cornell University School of Nursing in New York City.

CIMA STAR is a free-lance writer who lives in New York City.

CARLTON J. SWEETSER is a Chaplain at St. Luke's Hospital and Medical Center in New York City.

RUDOLPH TOCH is Clinical Instructor in Pediatrics at Harvard Medical School, Cambridge, Massachusetts.

ROBERT M. VEACH is Associate for Medical Ethics and Director of the Research Group on Death and Dying at the Institute of Society, Ethics and the Life Sciences at Hastings-on-Hudson, New York.

CARROLL A. WISE is Professor of Pastoral Psychology and Counseling and Director of Student Counseling at the Garrett Theological Seminary in Evanston, Illinois.

J. WILLIAM WORDEN is Assistant Professor of Psychology at Harvard Medical School and Research Director of the Omega Project at Massachusetts General Hospital, Boston, Massachusetts.